BECOMING A PERSON
THROUGH PSYCHOANALYSIS

BECOMING A PERSON THROUGH PSYCHOANALYSIS

Neville Symington

KARNAC

First published in 2007 by
Karnac Books Ltd
118 Finchley Road
London NW3 5HT

British Library Cataloguing in Publication Data

A C.I.P. for this book is available from the British Library

   ISBN 978 1 85575 540 6

Edited, designed and produced by The Studio Publishing Services Ltd
www.studiopublishingservicesuk.co.uk
e-mail: studio@publishingservicesuk.co.uk

10 9 8 7 6 5 4 3 2 1

www.karnacbooks.com

ACKNOWLEDGEMENT   xi

ABOUT THE AUTHOR   xiii

INTRODUCTION   xv

PART I: JOHN KLAUBER: PSYCHOANALYST OF THE PERSON 1

CHAPTER ONE
John Klauber, Independent clinician   3

PART II: EMOTIONAL FREEDOM IN THE ANALYST   23

Introduction   25

CHAPTER TWO
The patient makes the analyst   27

CHAPTER THREE
The analyst's act of freedom as agent of therapeutic change   51

CHAPTER FOUR
Phantasy effects that which it represents   69

CHAPTER FIVE
Maturity and interpretation as joint therapeutic agents   87

PART III: THE INFLUENCE FROM TREATING   93
PSYCHOPATHS AND THE MENTALLY HANDICAPPED

Introduction   95

CHAPTER SIX
The response aroused by the psychopath   99

CHAPTER SEVEN
The origins of rage and aggression   115

CHAPTER EIGHT
The psychotherapy of a mentally handicapped patient   123

CHAPTER NINE
Countertransference with mentally handicapped patients   147

PART IV: PILGRIMAGE   155

Introduction   157

CHAPTER TEN
Independence of mind: attachment and the British Society   161

CHAPTER ELEVEN
Migration from the Tavistock: impetus for mental change   171

CHAPTER TWELVE
The struggle to achieve independence of mind in the
British Psychoanalytical Society   185

PART V: PAPERS ON NARCISSISM   199

Introduction   201

CHAPTER THIRTEEN
Narcissism: a reconstructed theory   207

CHAPTER FOURTEEN
Narcissism as trauma preserved   215

CHAPTER FIFTEEN
Corruption of interpretation through narcissism   227

CHAPTER SIXTEEN
The core of narcissism   239

PART VI: THE INFLUENCE OF WILFRED BION   251

Introduction   253

CHAPTER SEVENTEEN
The influence of Wilfred Bion on my clinical work   255

CHAPTER EIGHTEEN
Bion and trauma transformed   269

PART VII: PSYCHOLOGICAL UNDERSTANDING OF
PSYCHOANALYTIC CONCEPTS   281

Introduction   283

CHAPTER NINETEEN
Envy: a psychological analysis   285

CHAPTER TWENTY
The structure of paranoia   297

CHAPTER TWENTY-ONE
A theory of communication for psychoanalysis   313

PART VIII: EPILOGUE   327

Introduction   329

CHAPTER TWENTY-TWO
Self-analysis in flight   331

CHAPTER TWENTY-THREE
The way forward   345

REFERENCES   349

INDEX   355

In memory of John Klauber
For whose generosity of heart and depth of understanding
I shall be grateful until the day of my death

ACKNOWLEDGEMENT

I would like to express my gratitude to Cary Dilernia for his invaluable assistance with the preparation of the manuscript.

ABOUT THE AUTHOR

Neville Symington is a psychoanalyst in private practice with his wife (who is also a psychoanalyst) in Sydney, Australia.

As a young man he took a diploma in Philosophy and then in Theology. He later did a degree in Psychology and took a diploma in Clinical Psychology. He did his psychoanalytic training in London and is a Fellow of the British Psychoanalytical Society. He held a senior staff position in the Adult Department of the Tavistock Clinic from 1977 to 1985. He was also Chairman of the Psychology Discipline for the Adult and Adolescent Departments at the Tavistock Clinic in London.

In 1986 he migrated to Sydney, where he was Chairman of the Sydney Institute for Psycho-Analysis from 1987 to 1993. He was President of the Australian Psycho-Analytic Society from 1999 to 2002.

He is the author of *The Analytic Experience* (Free Association Press and St Martins Press); *Emotion and Spirit* (Cassel, republished by Karnac), *Narcissism: A New Theory; The Making of a Psychotherapist, The Spirit of Sanity; A Pattern of Madness; How to Choose a Psychotherapist; The Blind Man Sees;* and *A Healing Conversation* (all published by Karnac). He is joint-author with Joan Symington of

The Clinical Thinking of Wilfred Bion (Routledge). He has lectured in Britain, Norway, Denmark, Poland, Germany, the United States, Brazil, Israel, India, New Zealand and Australia. He has a website at: www.nevillesymington.com

Introduction

Up vistaed hopes I sped;
And shot, precipitated,
Adown Titanic glooms of chasmèd fears,
From those strong Feet that followed, followed after.

(Thompson, 1913, Volume 1, p. 107,
"The Hound of Heaven")

A patient once said to me *"It is terrifying if you exist."*[1] At the time she said it I had a half-formed sense that this was an utterance of immense significance. It struck a chord and I have spent thirty-five years attempting to elaborate its meaning. If I existed then the whole structure around which her life had been built would collapse. It would mean that she would have to rebuild her life around a core built of her own substance rather than hiding it within an imago that was alien to it. Narcissism is precisely that condition of mind that shuts out the existence both of myself and of the other. My exploration into narcissism many years later was part of the quest to solve this problem.

What terrified her, terrified me. It terrified me, yet I was drawn to it. It was in the very terror that I would find myself. This journey of self-discovery started long before I came to psychoanalysis—it was precisely in that from which I fled that I was to find who was me. Psychoanalysis was germane to this pursuit because in it one seeks the treasure precisely in the place of terror. That feeble word "resistance" is no good for me—"*titanic glooms of chasmèd fears*" is closer to the mark.

The goal of psychoanalysis is to come to knowledge of who I am. Who is this person whose name I hear called every day? The achievement of this comes through harmonizing three psychological axes: emotional experience, personal communication, and self-reflection. I divide these into three sections, but they cannot be thought of in isolation. Emotional experience is intimately linked with personal communication and this is gives substance for self-reflection. This book, therefore, is my own personal expression of these three psychological axes. Accomplishing this goal is thwarted if any of these three are curtailed. In my own development as a psychoanalyst there were five experiences that were crucial in this regard: my own experience of being analysed by John Klauber, the treatment early in my development of a psychotic patient, the treatment of a mentally handicapped man, the treatment of criminals and psychopaths, and learning to fly a light aircraft. There have been other experiences that are either too intimate or that involve others too closely to be recorded here. The deepest of these have been the most influential, but a veil must be drawn over them. Only an emotional autobiography of a somewhat confessional nature could encompass these experiences. I believe, though, that unless we are shaken up by intense emotional experiences we never reach the deepest levels of our being. I think that the training committees in psychoanalytic institutes are too controlling and too cautious. Again and again I have heard of supervisors preventing a candidate from taking on a disturbed patient. They deprive the candidate thereby of the chance of having their deeper layers of being shaken into consciousness.

The second axis is personal communication. One grows and develops through communication. This is only true, however, if the individual attempts with all the power of her imagination and concentrated thought to throw herself over the abyss that separates her from the other, and from what lies most deeply within.

The third axis is self-reflection. Socrates said that the unexamined life is not worth living. Understanding one's experiences and realizing one's own separate self has, since ancient times, been seen as the source of wisdom. What differentiates psychoanalysis from other means of achieving this is its focus on communication with another. Slowly, over the years, I have become convinced that it is this communication rather than interpretation that brings me, patient or analyst, to knowledge of this person who is me. It is, as Martin Buber (1987) emphasizes, the relation of *I* to *Thou* that both creates the person and at the same time gives me self-knowledge. The *I* to *Thou* is articulated in psychoanalysis as the *transference*. However, I need to turn to Buber if I am to be sure of understanding this relation properly and not be seduced by the false coinage that often masquerades as *transference*. The *transference* lies in those deep beliefs about the other which are false. Guessing about the anonymous analyst rarely touches the deep illusions that can sustain a psychosis in being for years or for a whole lifetime.

I have been a qualified psychoanalyst for thirty years. I have changed enormously during that time, yet my deepest intuitions have remained the same. My development has been a slow process of believing my own intuitions. That act of belief in the intuitions of the heart is what has made a given life my own life. "The current which I dare to call *my* life", wrote Teilhard de Chardin (1960, p. 55). My psychoanalytical development has been subservient to that and dependent upon it.

What I am attempting to do in this book is to trace the pathway along which I have travelled to become a person. This has run side by side with trying to become an analyst. The former is a deeper task, and one which requires me to stretch beyond the official reaches of psychoanalysis. Psychoanalysis is an essential ingredient, but not the only one. Ontological reflection has also been indispensable. I have made landmark discoveries when reading philosophy, sociology, history, and literature. Learning to paint, learning to fly a plane, and also the study of art and of aviation theory have opened up new vistas. So, while trying to discover who I am, I am also trying to become an analyst. I know I never shall be. I am permanently in a state of becoming. This account therefore is only a sketch. The completed picture will never materialize. It is, therefore, autobiographical, but only in a partial sense. I say nothing about the very formative experiences that occurred before I started analytic training, but instead I attempt to chart the way in which my theoretical position has changed from when I started with my first patient until today.

To become a psychoanalyst it is first necessary to be psycho-analysed oneself. I started my analysis with a view to training as an analyst in April 1970. Prior to that I had had three years of psycho-analysis with a different analyst. When I applied to train as an ana-lyst I soon realized that I had a decision to make. There are three schools within the British Psychoanalytic Society: the Freudian Group, members of which follow the teaching and method of Anna Freud; the Kleinians, who follow the teaching and method of Melanie Klein, and the Group of Independent Psychoanalysts, to which I refer simply as the Independent Group, the members of which wished to commit themselves to neither camp. I had been a priest in the Roman Catholic Church and I sniffed fanaticism in both the Anna Freud and Melanie Klein disciples. I had had enough of that, so I opted for the Independent Group. Although I have been very critical of some particular attitudes within this group, I am glad that I decided as I did.

This meant that I had to select an analyst from the Independent Group. Enid Balint, who had interviewed me when I first applied for training, recommended that I go to see John Klauber. I followed her advice and went to an assessment interview with him. After a little while he said to me: "Do you mind if I be very frank with you? I think you are very ill you know."

It was a great relief when he said that. I had been interviewed by three different psychoanalysts, all of some renown, who had not seen past the impressive façade to the sick man behind it.

So I started my analysis and continued it for three and a half years before I entered the training programme. Klauber insisted that I be in better emotional health before I started training. I was annoyed with him at the time, but knew also that he was right and have been grateful to him since.

I entered the training programme in September 1973. My first year was devoted to infant observation. I was in a seminar with three others (Patrick Casement, Paul O'Farrell, and Daniel Ivan-Zadeh) with Barbara Woodhead as our tutor. She had her consulting room on the top floor of 100 Harley Street and we travelled up to her flat in an old Heath Robinson lift; each time as we walked out on to the top landing we believed Freud's ghost must have been looking after us, because it always seemed a miracle that we stepped out of that cranky old lift alive. I only observed one thing that seemed to me significant in the behaviour of the infant I watched each week. When the baby had reached the stage of just beginning to walk he could toddle between the mother and me without falling, but when he tried to toddle between two inanimate objects he always fell. It reminded me of St Peter walking on the water of Galilee. He was able to do so while looking confidently at Jesus, but as soon as his eyes strayed to the churning sea he began to sink. I thought that per-haps that story was recording an early psychological truth; that the source of confidence lies in an act of trust directed towards another person. I had one other experience many years later, which tends to confirm this viewpoint.

I had learned to fly a light aircraft and had obtained my private pilot's licence, but I did not have confidence. Then I found a new flying school run by a married couple whose knowledge of aviation was in their bones. I trusted them. I found then that way up in the sky I still had this couple in my mind's eye and I had a confidence that I had not had before. I think that trust goes to something far deeper in the personality than any surface features. I can trust someone if what they do or say comes from the heart. If the func-tion of analysing a patient or piloting a plane has been assimilated into the being of the person, then I can trust, and it is this inner act that is the source of confidence. I suspect that this little baby that I observed had confidence to walk and so not fall when his trustful eye was directed to his mother or to me. I used to think that I had not derived very much from my infant observation when I listened to the many insights that other observers recorded, but over time I have come to think that this one phenomenon that I did observe was very important and has stood me in good stead.

While doing my psychoanalytic training I was engaged in two other activities. I was doing an undergraduate degree in psychol-ogy and I had a post as a psychotherapist at Grendon Prison. So, by the time I had finished my first year of infant observation and started my second, I had spent a lot of time reading Freud and I had made extensive notes on what I read; hence, when I started the academic seminars on Freud I already had quite a good grounding in the subject. I had, long before I came to psychoanalysis, come to the conclusion that one way to be educated in a subject is to have a thorough grasp of the mind of a genius. I had already done this while studying theology. I read with concentrated attention the whole of Thomas Aquinas's *Summa Theologica*. So, entering the portals of psychoanalysis, I applied the same principle and spent my time trying to understand and digest Freud. I must confess that I found grasping Freud more difficult than Aquinas. I have subsequently come to think that the reason for this was that Aquinas had an underlying principle that governed all that he wrote whereas Freud had two principles that did not harmonize with each other. In fact, they were incompatible with each other. The system of Aquinas had a coherence that was lacking in Freud. It was not that Freud did not attempt coherence; in fact, I believe he took great efforts to achieve it, but because he refused to go to the highest level of abstraction he never achieved it. It took me many years to reach this conclusion, whereas while I was training I just had a disjointed sense that something was not quite right. Wilfred Bion did, I believe, go to that higher level of abstraction.

The other principle that I had learned for myself in my previous studies was to read what really was personally significant for me and to leave aside the rest, however much people praised it. I stuck to this rigorously while doing my academic training at the Institute of Psychoanalysis. If I was deriving a lot from a particular book then I would stick with it even if the curriculum demanded that I should be reading something else.

It is always emphasized that one's own personal experience of being psychoanalysed is by far the most significant part of a psychoanalyst's education. For this reason I start this book with a paper that I wrote and presented to the British Psychoanalytical Society in 1985, four years after John Klauber had died and the year before I left England on our pathway to Australia.

So, this book starts with this paper, but my theoretical development had, to a considerable extent, already been forged by this time. In 1977 I was asked to give a series of thirty lectures to mental health professionals at the Tavistock Clinic. I gave these lectures each year until the end of 1984. I altered them considerably every year. Then I was asked to collect them together and they were published as a book called *The Analytic Experience* in 1986. The contents of that book constitutes my first theoretical position. This book was an exposition of the theories of Freud, his early followers, and then Fairbairn, Melanie Klein, Bion, Winnicott, and Balint. It was a personal exposition and therefore an interpretation of these seminal clinicians, but I was still in reverential awe of these founders and, although I was critical of some of their viewpoints, I had not yet discovered a theoretical framework of my own. I was still split between two incompatible theories. I have come to think that this split exists throughout the psychoanalytic world and this book will, I hope, make this clear.

I have left the papers as they were written except I have cut out some repetition and occasionally added something for clarification. I have also included additional comments in the endnotes where my thoughts have developed or diverged from those I expressed earlier.

Notes

1. This patient is referred to in the two chapters entitled "The patient makes the analyst" and "The analyst's act of freedom as agent of therapeutic change".

PART I

JOHN KLAUBER:
PSYCHOANALYST OF THE PERSON

CHAPTER ONE

John Klauber, Independent clinician

"Though force may coerce the body, it also has the effect of embittering the mind. He who uses it, though in the defence of the right, may, in the hour of victory, shut his heart to pity, and in doing so render himself or his children liable to the terrible penalties which the gods sooner or later inflict on the arrogant"

(Bryant, 1969, p. 68)

John Klauber died on 11 August 1981, while on holiday with his wife in France. I believe that he made a very distinct contribution to psychoanalysis, and yet I believe that it is underestimated and in danger of disappearing unnoticed. He may be partly responsible for this because he was a modest man and did not see himself as breaking new ground in the way that Balint and Winnicott did. Yet his contribution was in that area of psychoanalysis that, to every clinician, is the most important: in the clinical practice. He was, however, a deeply thoughtful man, so his technical innovations were backed with a theoretical structure (see pp. 19–22, 'Thoughts thirty years after', for a statement about this).

I was analysed by John Klauber. I came to him very definitely ill and in a state of inner and outer disarray, and I emerged from analysis some seven and a half years later a changed person. Although I contributed to this result, I know that his mediation of the analytic process was crucial. Over the years I have, in idle moments, tried to pinpoint those elements which seemed to be decisive in bringing about a successful therapeutic outcome. I want to start by looking at his clinical practice, before moving on to its theoretical underpinning and showing how the two are closely interwoven.

It may seem superfluous to enumerate the orthodox or traditional aspects of Klauber's clinical practice, and yet, in recent years, I have come to believe that sometimes the matters most talked about are by no means those that are practised in reality. So, from the beginning of the analysis until its end, he interpreted the transference. He very rarely spoke about what I was *doing* to him but instead looked for the deep underlying assumptions that I had about him, and in the early part of the analysis he put into words how I felt about him. I think technically it was extremely important that by tone or words he did not repudiate my assumptions about him. Quite simply he interpreted the transference phantasies. He did not imply that this was an incorrect way of viewing him. For a long time I thought that this was what every analyst did; that this was what was meant by interpreting the transference, yet I came to realize that it is not what is meant by many analysts. I have heard many presentations where the analyst points out what the patient is doing to the analyst, the way the patient is treating the analyst, or if, to use shorthand, a Klauber interpretation is made, the analyst soon points out to the patient the error of his ways and how he is misperceiving the situation. I will give a very simple example of what I mean. In a clinical presentation I listened to a colleague who reported how his patient said that he (the analyst) was a rigid Freudian. He repudiated this uncalled-for accusation and pointed out how bending and flexible he was. The Klauber version of that would be to notice that the patient felt this way about him and make an interpretation that would free the patient to say that he was a rigid Freudian. He would not suggest to the patient that he was misperceiving the situation.

Klauber believed, I think, that if the analyst bore these misperceptions for a reasonable period then the impulses of which they were the derivatives slowly became modified. In this way I think one could conceptualize Klauber's method by saying that he acted the role of container for the patient's projections in the early phase of the analysis, rather in the way that Bion said the good mother would do for her baby. After a reasonable time he would favour disillusioning the patient, rather in the way that Winnicott said the mother needs to disillusion her baby. Just in case I am misunderstood when I use the phrase "reasonable period", then I should perhaps say that in my case, especially with deeper phantasies, he would interpret them regularly but only start disillusioning after some five or six years. I believe that this capacity of his to contain a transference over several years was deeply therapeutic. I believe that this was the case for me; I would not want to argue that it would be for everyone. In my time as an analyst, supervising, being supervised, hearing papers, and listening to clinical presentations, I have neither heard of an analyst containing the transference as Klauber did with me, nor have I heard a presentation where an analyst interpreted the transference so consistently in this way as Klauber did.

In the interpretation of the transference he gave special attention to the negative transference. Again, he did not point out my negative attitudes to him, but consistently interpreted negative images as being directed at him. What is frequently described as interpreting the negative transference is a veiled condemnation of the patient's hostile or aggressive impulses towards the analyst. There is a big difference between the analyst who says, after a patient has spoken deprecatingly of someone called John Smith, "You are in a veiled way mocking me" and the analyst who says, "I think the feelings you are expressing towards John Smith really refer to me." The first statement can so easily be felt by the patient to mean, "You should not be mocking me" or "It is unfair of you to be mocking me", whereas in the second case the patient can feel that these hostile impulses can be received by the analyst. My overall feeling about Klauber was that I was received by him totally. I think it is probably significant in this connection that I do not remember him ever making a "There is part of you" interpretation. There was a definite sense of the whole of me being received by the whole of him. I never had the sense of being pushed away. I only once remember him being momentarily defensive. Interpreting the negative transference means, in the Klauber sense, that the analyst accepts the mispercep-tion of the patient. This is different from it being pointed out in such a way that it is clear that the analyst is not receiving it. This is the main point that I would want to stress about Klauber's orthodoxy. (I should also mention here that Klauber always kept to a fifty-minute session time and I do not think he ever ran over time. He occasionally changed a session time and only rarely cancelled one. There was always a sense of reliability in him.)

I will now turn to those aspects of Klauber's personal style of analysis that, although unconventional, were important to a thera-peutic outcome. After what I have said about the enormous empha-sis that he put on transference interpretations and the containment of transference phantasies, it may seem contradictory when I say that he stressed the non-transference elements in the analytic set-up. He believed that the patient was able to scrutinize with consid-erable accuracy real personality factors in the analyst. In his paper "The psychoanalyst as person", he says,

> When the patient visits the psychoanalyst for a consultation, it is not only the psychoanalyst who makes an assessment of the patient—the patient also attempts to make an assessment of the analyst. Though the transference, which begins to be formed before the consultation, has an important share in the patient's subsequent reaction, the capacity of the patient's ego to evaluate it is not para-lysed, as later analysis tends to reveal. Just as a psychoanalyst starts his report on a patient by describing what he looks like, how he moves and how he is dressed, so equally a fund of information about the psychoanalyst reaches the patient—about his capacity to respond, about his tastes and personal attitudes, as displayed, for instance, by the pictures on his walls. Some psychoanalysts seem to regard this as unfortunate and attempt to limit its effec-tiveness by establishing a so-called "neutral" setting. I believe that the second attitude fails to give adequate credit to human intelli-gence and the human unconscious. A woman, undoubtedly suffer-ing from paranoid tendencies, gave as her grounds for refusing treatment with a particular psychoanalyst that she could never be analysed by someone who decorated his consulting room with such bad art. The patient herself had a considerable sensitivity for the visual arts, which had been demonstrated by discerning purchases. One psychoanalyst reported this decision as the arch evidence for the unreasonableness of the patient. A second thought that the

perceptiveness which marked her character, perhaps in some respects sharpened by her paranoid tendencies, had made her quickly understand that a psychoanalyst with such taste in pictures would only with great difficulty acquire sufficient affinity with her own personality to understand it. [Klauber, 1968, pp. 129–130]

In this connection he thought that it was sometimes right for an analyst to acknowledge the accuracy of a patient's perception. I said once to him that I had the idea that he had been to a public school, but somehow could not place him as someone who had been to a boarding school. He answered good-humouredly that I did not think he looked ascetic enough to have been through the rigours of a boarding school, and then he said that he had been to St Paul's, which is a public school, but one of the few that is a day school and not a boarding school. Because he believed that there was a non-transference element to the psychoanalytic relationship he did not think that every communication had to be met with an interpretation. In his paper "Elements of the psychoanalytic relationship and their therapeutic implications", he says, "Do we sometimes pay too high a price for the sophistication of our techniques, for instance, if we reply only with an interpretation?" (Klauber, 1981, p. 59).

He quite frequently responded to a communication of mine with an answer other than an interpretation, and these fell into three classes. In the first class it did not immediately look like an interpretation but in fact was one. The second was an emotionally affirming response when I made some developmental step, and the last was a straightforward discussion about something. I will give an example of the first class and then refer to an example of my own before tackling the next two.

During a phase of the analysis I was working part-time at Grendon Prison, out beyond Aylesbury, and I used to spend one or two nights a week at the hostel there. So, for instance, I would have analysis on a Wednesday morning after seeing my training cases and then drive out to Grendon, stay there the night, and then return on the Thursday in time to see my two training cases and have analysis. On one occasion Klauber was giving a paper at the Society on the Wednesday evening, of which I had made no mention, and he drew my attention to my silence about it. I justified my silence by saying that I stayed the night away on Wednesday nights and it was anyway a long drive in to hear a paper. He simply said, '"Some analysands would drive further than that to hear their analyst give a paper", and laughed good-humouredly. It was, of course, an interpretation, though I think it only sank in sometime later. I think the ritualized style of interpretation was something he avoided as much as he could. In this I feel in complete sympathy. Again I have the feeling that it is so obvious a point and yet, listening to presentations, I am struck by the formal style of interpretations and I think this signifies a lack of emotional contact. I would just like to mention an example that occurred in the summer with a patient who was finishing his analysis at the end of July. He had opted not to continue with me until a later date when I was finishing with all my patients in preparation for emigration. A factor in his finishing before I went was that he felt that it would be a difficult time for me, saying goodbye to all my patients, and he had moments of panic when he thought he would have to support me and cheer up the sad and depressed analyst. Towards the end of the session I said, "But in fact I *don't* need your support." From previous experience I thought this would have an effect, which it did. When he returned the next day he said that he realized that all along he must have been thinking deep down that I did need him to cheer me up in my depression. He went on to say that all this had been set in train when I had said the previous day that I did not need him. My statement was an interpretation. I am also sure that if I had said to him, "You feel that I need your support", it would not have penetrated. With that patient there were two reasons for that. If I had put it in the stylized form he would have felt that I was indulging in "analytic talk". He would have felt that I was more concerned to be obedient to an authority than to be concerned about him. I think, too, that the phantasy that I needed his support for my depression was so deeply rooted that had I said, "You feel that I need your support", I think he would only have heard the confirming words, "I need your support", and only by countering the phantasy with a definite "No" did it become available to reach consciousness. In my own case, Klauber's laugh clearly communicates the sense that here he was rubbing shoulders with nasty old human nature but feeling reasonably at home with that, and that he shared the same blemished humanity. Klauber had great integrity, but also enjoyed finding corruption in high places, and this was very congenial for me, having been brought up as a Catholic.

The second kind of communication was that of emotional affir-mation. If I had come out of a passageway to a new emotional sense of things he would invariably be affirming and I believe that this was therapeutic. It was the equivalent of the mother smiling encouragingly at her baby as the child is beginning to succeed in a new endeavour. It would always take the form of him adding his own affirming comments, quite often relating to social attitudes. I realize that affirmations of this kind can make one dependent upon the positive smile, but I do not think this happened. I have been able to hold a view or a principle in the face of opposition. I think perhaps "affirmation" is the wrong word—"agreement" would be more accurate. I want now to turn to the third type of response, which was him speaking to me directly, and I want to spend some time on this as I think it was the most controversial aspect of his technique.

Klauber often spoke about aspects of life, whether it be discus-sion of a book, a painting, a news item, or a religious or social atti-tude. He knew that he did this. When I challenged him about it he said he knew he spoke about general matters a good deal more than most good analysts. I think this matter is worth some discussion and thinking about. This talking about many topics of psychologi-cal and social interest was clearly consonant with his nature, but he also believed that it had an important role in the psychoanalytic process. One aspect of it is quite clear: that he believed that the transference was so powerful a process that it was not disrupted by the sorts of exchanges I am describing. I can only remember one occasion when I felt a discursive comment to be insensitive.

Until now I have spoken as if these discursive forays were *totally* disconnected with the interpretative work that was going on, and if I have given this impression then it is a mistaken one. They were usually, though not always, *connected* with interpretative inter-change. I have always derived a lot of self-understanding from reading, and my own emotional development has been aided considerably through reading. When I was in analysis quite a lot of material from me came in the form of a dialogue with the author of whichever book I was reading at the time. On one occasion I was reading Somerset Maugham's *Of Human Bondage*, and some-thing had crystallized for me. It may have been a narcissistic satis-faction in discovering Maugham's statement that all weak men lay exaggerated stress on not changing one's mind. Whatever it was, I remember Klauber saying that he thought *Of Human Bondage* was Maugham's greatest book. I think I went on to say quite a lot about *The Moon and Sixpence,* and if I remember it rightly I think he thought *Of Human Bondage* was head and shoulders above the rest of Maugham's books. Although I thought it was a great book I also thought *The Moon and Sixpence, Cakes and Ale, The Summing-Up,* and some of his short stories of equivalent worth. I believe that these conversations had the effect of linking psychoanalysis and the interpretations that he made into the web of life, so that life and psychoanalysis interpenetrated. After a Klauber analysis I could only with the greatest difficulty put psychoanalysis into one mental compartment and the rest of life into another. These conversations, which were a kind of dual free-association–interplay, embedded psychoanalytic insight into the pattern of my own relationships and value system. I think that Klauber also trusted the psychoanalytic process deeply and that these conversations were generated by it.

In the last few years of his life, Klauber said quite often at Scientific meetings that when making interpretations the analyst needed to keep in mind the day when the patient left the consulting room for the last time. I regret that I never asked him how this factor influenced specifically the structure of his interpretative work, but my surmise is as follows. He believed that the aim of psychoanalysis was to foster the development of the patient's own individuality, creativity, and attitude to life. He was also aware that the psychoanalytic procedure was one through which the patient was greatly influenced and that it was impossible for the patient not to incorporate some of the analyst's own attitudes. In particular, he thought this was the case where the patient was an analytic candidate, because in these cases the analysand is following the career of his mentor and taking up the same role in relation to his or her patients as the training analyst has in relation to him or her. Therefore, he saw as a danger a patient's identification of psychoanalysis with the particular form in which he or she had experienced it. He believed that, although it could not exist without the agency of the analyst, the process of psychoanalysis was to be differentiated from the particular tonal qualities that it receives inevitably from each individual analyst. Therefore, as much as possible, the patient needs to be helped to differentiate between the process of analysis that is being purveyed through the agency of many analysts of differing attitudes and the particular colouring that it is receiving from this particular analyst. I believe it was for this reason that he favoured some grasp by the patient of the analyst as a person with his own prejudices and attitudes. My own experience has been that this revealing of himself had some beneficial effects for me. I think it has helped me to separate analysis from my own analyst to some degree. It may not seem so from what I have said so far, but in fact I felt, and still feel, in considerable disagreement with him over certain attitudes of his both in terms of psychoanalytic technique (e.g., his non-use of the "part of you" interpretation) and more general attitudes. Another very important fruit of these conversations was that I was able to see some areas that he was unlikely to be able to analyse well. I can think of one area that was not analysed at all, really, and I sensed from what I knew of his character that he was not likely to be very successful in attempting it. This is true of all analysts, but I think that these conversations of his meant that it was not hidden and therefore was more truthful. And for Klauber it was the truth that healed. In the introduction to his book *Difficulties in the Analytic Encounter* he says, "I believe that truth is the great corrective by which, with the analyst's help, patients heal themselves" (Klauber, 1968, p. xiv).

I suppose that every analyst has areas that he or she thinks particularly need to be analysed. Klauber was particularly determined to analyse successfully paranoia and paranoid ideation. I think that he felt paranoid groupings were particularly damaging in social life. He believed, I think, that paranoia always masqueraded under a façade of idealization, and he tackled idealizing tendencies on all fronts. He recognized, of course, that some idealization was necessary in life and that a man's illusions and dreams are a powerful motivating factor, but if he detected *belief* in the idealized image then he tackled it. In particular, he tackled any idealization of himself or of psychoanalysis. Here again lies the paradox: that he believed very deeply in psychoanalysis. But I believe his "conversations" and admissions about himself contributed considerably to reducing paranoia. If the analyst colludes with the patient's part-object image of him, then he colludes with the patient's paranoid phantasies. Paranoid phantasies are the coinage of a part-object relationship structure. If the analyst is a part-object to the patient, then the paranoid phantasies remain and are colluded with. This is why Klauber believed that real but denied perceptions of the analyst should be interpreted. In the paper "Elements of the psychoanalytic relationship and their therapeutic implications", he says,

> In order to reduce the split between the analyst of fantasy and the analyst apprehended in detail by the ego, a constant aim must be to facilitate the integration of the two images by the interpretation of the patient's warded-off perceptions of reality and, sometimes, in my opinion, by the acknowledgment of their accuracy by the analyst. [*ibid.*, p. 59]

Klauber believed that it was necessary to allow aspects of the analyst's real character to emerge in treatment, especially towards the end. He says this most obviously in his paper "A particular form of transference in neurotic depression", and I think it is worth quoting him in full here,

> The liberation of the aggression in the context of love results in a diminution of the distance between the self-images and the object-images. The object-images no longer appear so unattainable. This enables the patient to feel freer to evaluate the analyst's character. In particular he seeks out his weaknesses, and thus attempts to test the reality of his degraded self-images against the reality or other-wise of the omnipotent object-images. It is therefore necessary to the reality testing and cure of the depressed patient that this process should not be impeded. He needs to gain confidence in his reality testing and to be allowed to affirm such real weaknesses in the analyst's competence and personality as he has been able to observe. Only if he can see that the analyst is sincerely prepared to recognise them, and, if inescapably confronted, to admit them, can he gain the confidence necessary to tolerate the degraded parts of his own personality.
>
> In the typical case the patient will bring this aggression directly, and will confront the analyst with many of his most painful diffi-culties. In my opinion it is an error to interpret such confrontations in terms of transference without first acknowledging the possibility of the reality. This may be exceedingly painful, and I believe most analysts will have encountered such experiences.

While the patient brings some of the analyst's weaknesses openly, he brings others in disguise. It is essential that the analyst should be on the watch for hidden implications painful to himself in the patient's transference and should not hesitate to interpret them. This will, again, not merely be painful but to some extent impossible, and the analyst must also avoid the danger of masochistic confession. But insofar as he can achieve their recognition, courageous interpretation of the patient's secret thoughts is necessary if the patient is to leave the analyst with an adequate confidence that he can pursue his ambitions in spite of his deficiencies. [*ibid.*, pp. 106–107]

In this context it was clear that Klauber did not believe that any analyst was capable of analysing everything, and he says that a second analysis always reveals some things that the patient did not feel he or she could say to the previous analyst.

Before leaving the subject of the therapeutic elements of Klauber's personal style, I will just give you a few examples. I was born and brought up in Oporto in Portugal and my father, uncles, and most family friends were in the port-wine trade. I talked about port quite a bit, especially early on in the analysis. I said one day to him that I had the feeling that he was rather partial to port and he acknowledged enthusiastically that he was. On another occasion I told him that my father always liked picnics in the Portuguese style: i.e., with tables and chairs and so on, and he immediately said that was the way a picnic should be. He was also clear on his views on certain aspects of religious beliefs and so on. He talked quite a lot about a painting by Lhote that was on his wall. It is my impression that all this did not in itself diminish in any way the transference phantasies and, in fact, I think enabled him to interpret more subtle differentiations within the transference than would otherwise not have been possible.

A valid question can be asked about this aspect of his technique, which is this. How does the analyst decide, in the face of a communication from the patient, whether to interpret or respond in some other way? The answer can only be that it must rest entirely upon the analyst's own inner judgement. This is the only thing that the analyst has to rely upon. Rules and principles are invoked in the absence of inner judgement. How on earth can you educate someone in the business of judging? A powerful superego cripples such judgement. A sense of mutuality, on the other hand, helps such judgement to come to birth. Clinging to rules or theories are manifestations, I think, of what Bion called *beta elements*. The capacity to make judgements is a manifestation of *alpha function*. (*Beta elements* are untransformed by the inner creative agent that Bion called *alpha function*.) I think that often both analyst and supervisors intensify the inner superego and help to cripple judgement.

I just want to mention three further aspects of Klauber's style that I think were therapeutically beneficial. The first was absolute fairness, and this came out in all his dealings. The second was that he did not make a "big" interpretation until what he wanted to say was clearly crystallized. It just was not possible to persuade him of something. If it had not crystallized inwardly for him then it was wasted breath. The third thing was his conviction that truth was paramount and that psychoanalysis was a servant of truth or it was nothing: not that it possessed the truth, but was the servant of it.

*   *   *

In all of what I have been saying I have been giving you some of my experience of him and conjectures as to why he analysed in the way he did. I want now to place what I have been saying, and in particular his "conversations", in the context of his theory of analysis as a process of mourning and detraumatization. In effect, Klauber says that a trauma occurs when a patient enters analysis. When he lies on the couch, he lets go of the presence of the analyst through his eyes, loses touch thereby with the facial and gestural response of the analyst, is thrown back upon his archaic inner images, and is overwhelmed by the analyst of phantasy. Klauber is insistent that the first requirement of analytic technique is to facilitate the patient's capacity to communicate his feelings and thoughts as fully as possible. It was Klauber's view that secret hostile thoughts are frequently harboured by the patient and that this explains the not infrequent violent revolt by people towards analysis some time after the analysis is over. If the patient is too overwhelmed by the analyst of phantasy then it will block the patient's capacity to communicate feelings and thoughts. Klauber thought that the traumatic quality of the analytic situation could not be mitigated by interpretation alone. I think Klauber was here trying to encourage analysts not to behave in abnormal ways but to be as natural as possible. If you walk down a corridor at the Tavistock and look into the consulting rooms as you go by, you can immediately detect those analysts or therapists who are waiting for a patient to arrive. There is a marked stiffness of pose and attitude. This can only have the effect of stiffening the patient's attitude also. Klauber had the view that the patient's trauma could be relieved by responsiveness *and* interpretation. The patient can only effectively mourn their analyst if they can assess the analyst's real attributes and slowly separate out those phantasies that they have projected on to the analyst from their real perceptions of the analyst. When the patient has had the experience of the analyst containing these projections they are able to reintegrate them in a modified form. They are able to leave the analyst as a more or less ordinary person and manage their own phantasies in the future. When I think of my own experience of being analysed by Klauber and the difference between before and after, I think most essentially it would be that I seem to have within me a kind of shock absorber which is able to manage a greater quantum of anxiety than was possible before. I think Klauber's method enables the patient to mourn the illusions and phantasies in the face of a good-enough real analyst. In this way the process of detraumatization and mourning are parts of the same process. In fact, the patient usually resists very violently the process by which the analyst tries to wean the patient from long cherished illusions and phantasies. At the beginning of analysis the patient is plunged more deeply than ever into a narcissistic world and the analyst, through his responsiveness and interpretations, drags the patient out of it. In this way there is a similarity between Klauber's view and that of Fairbairn, who said in his 1958 paper that it was part of the analyst's task to crash into the narcissistic inner world. In his later years Klauber began to question the desirability of the couch. Again I think that this was in the service of detraumatizing and forcing the patient to mourn his illusions more actively. He did not favour very long analyses.

I want to emphasize three things here. I may have given the impression that Klauber softened the cutting edge of analysis. This was not so. His whole aim was to speak the truth; this was his central guide and he never let sentimentality get in the way of saying terrible things. I believe that because he knew he would have very painful things to say he ensured that the analytic environment was right for it to be received emotionally. Second, the focus on the transference, together with his responsiveness (of which the "conversations" were a part), made for a very rich experience and I think that this ultimately was the transforming factor. Expansion of one's emotional experience is a crucial analytic ingredient. Last, I think I have changed as much, if not more, since finishing analysis as during it, and I think this is testimony to the efficaciousness of his method, which was orientated to the day when the patient left the consulting room for the last time.

To make emotional contact was more important than making interpretations. The making of emotional contact comes from only one place: the creative centre of the individual person. For this reason Klauber emphasized spontaneity. Spontaneity, to be distinguished from impulsiveness, springs from the ego, freed from the dictates of the superego. Of course, to say that spontaneity is an essential concomitant for analysis is an appalling stumbling-block for any committee involved in student training because, by very definition, it is something that is totally outside its control; it is something that it cannot legislate for. What a scandal for a committee whose self-esteem is so bound up with laying down rules for others!

He was thoroughly against forcing his viewpoint upon a patient. He did not think that he necessarily knew what was the best way to live a life. On one occasion I had started to see a patient who had had therapy beforehand on several occasions. The patient's history showed that it was likely that he would not stay with treatment for very long. I said, "He is not taking his treatment seriously", and Klauber replied, "He will probably leave treatment, come back to it, leave it again." I said, "But don't you think that is the wrong attitude?" Klauber replied, "It's his life, not yours." That is a remark I shall never forget.

It is in this context of spontaneity and freedom that the deepest emotional contact takes place because it opens up the areas of reverie in the analyst and the patient stimulates it through his own free expression. Rigidity is part of the psychotic area within the personality and it means that this area is not available to make contact with the patient. Freud recommended "free floating attention", Bion recommended the state of "reverie" and Klauber recommended spontaneity, which is nearly synonymous. I say "nearly" because I think conversational exchange is implied in the word "spontaneity", which is absent in the other two. Spontaneity was so important to Klauber that he thought it better for the analyst to give expression to things than to hold back. I believe he extended the frame necessary for spontaneity too far, but I am sure it was an error on the right side of the dividing line between rigidity and licence.

Klauber was dissatisfied with the received classical theory and it remains a question mark as to whether he would have tried to create a theory in his further lectures had he lived to give them, but somehow I doubt it. He was critical of the received theory and technique. He thought it was too reductionist. He thought it did not give sufficient account of the personal elements in the bond between analyst and patient and the centrality of emotional contact did not have a proper place theoretically. So why did he not forge a new theory? The answer to this question must lie in some element in his personality.

In every individual there is a struggle between the individual and the collective within, as Jung emphasized. John Klauber felt that he could be spontaneous with safety as long as he respected the society of which he was a part and its voice within him. He was very conscious of these two sides of himself and gave expression to it on a variety of occasions. He believed deeply in the importance of listening to the inner light and said on one occasion that he thought those who had had a Quaker upbringing had the potential for being good psychotherapists and, on the other hand, he had a reverence for the group, the collective. This was manifested in his exaggerated reverence for the genius of Freud. He said once that we analysts are all working in the shadow of a genius. It seems that he was opposed to tampering with the theories of the founder of psychoanalysis. He clearly recognized the enormous advances in understanding that had come about since Freud but thought that no one had come up with a plausible replacement for his metapsychology and he did not like attempts to alter it. On one occasion Dr Dennis Duncan gave a paper at a scientific meeting at the British Society in which he tried to re-cast theory in the mould of intersubjective knowing, but Klauber criticized him for "tinkering about with theory". He did not like Ellenburger's book on the Unconscious because he thought it unfairly demoted Freud. I suspect that he felt that none of us ordinary mortals could reach the profundities of Freud's mind and thinking and it was a mistake therefore to "tinker" with his theory. It was as if he felt that until someone of Freud's stature emerged it was better for all of us to accept the inheritance that Freud had bequeathed to us. Klauber knew himself well, which means that he knew his limitations. He was dissatisfied with the theory and the technique that was closely wedded to it. He criticized it vigorously, but it seems that he was wary of trying to change the theory. He was prepared to take up his own personal approach to patients and justify his stance. Perhaps it is that he was not willing to found a new school of theory within psychoanalysis. In this he was like Ferenczi, whom he admired, and also like Balint and Winnicott. In this he was the epitome of the Independent Group of analysts within the British Society. The members of this group are against the founding of schools.

Freud felt betrayed when Jung took issue with one of the central tenets of his theory. In a similar way Melanie Klein felt betrayed by Paula Heimann. This can only mean that the theory is felt as their creation and to have it criticized is a personal attack. They feel as sensitive about it as Michelangelo was when one of the cardinals criticized his nude figures in the judgement scene in the Sistine Chapel. There is, however, an added element in that Freud wanted the mental attitude of his followers to be moulded according to his own conceptualizations, and in this Melanie Klein was the same. Now perhaps we can see something of Klauber's dilemma. If he becomes a forger of new theory he goes against one of his own deepest principles: that it is *good* for individuals to find their own free personal expression. With such a view how can you want to forge others into your own image and likeness? That is the dilemma of the person who espouses freedom in a deep way. That was Klauber's dilemma as it has also been the dilemma of those who believe in personal freedom. Isaiah Berlin, in his book *Against the Current*, instances some of the few brave thinkers within the European tradition of ideas who have set themselves against the great monocausal systems of thought: Vico, Herder, Montesquieu, and a few others, but their names will never be as famous as Descartes, Karl Marx, or Freud.

It seems, then, that to be individually wedded to freedom may mean "living within the shadow of a genius", that it is necessary to be a follower in order to have an internal and interpersonal life because to be the moulder of the lives of others is intolerable for one who believes in freedom. But this leaves a wound at the centre of his being. Rousseau felt this dilemma when he said in exasperation that men must be forced to be free. But I think it may be that it is those who have felt this wound at the centre of their being who have the capacity to heal. Klauber was a very good healer. I think he would have been satisfied with that epitaph.

Thoughts thirty years after

When I think of my experience with John Klauber and read through some of his papers, I am struck with amazement at his stress upon the person. The development of the personhood of the patient and of the analyst is central for him and yet has largely remained hidden because his statements, some of which are quite staggering, are embedded within a psychological soil that repudiates the personal, that extols blind forces as primary in the personality, and there suddenly, embedded in this determinist system, is a perspective that is deeply personal. It is analogous to the espousal of faith by Hume, who was such a thoroughgoing rationalist. These winking diamonds within a muddy field were not missed by the German Romantics, Hamann and Jacobi. It has taken me a long time to isolate this perspective in Klauber and to try to plant it within a philosophical garden that is congenial to it. It is clear to me that he stressed this personal element against an attitude that favoured systems and anonymity.

When he defended his "conversations" he did so, I believe, because he had an intuitive sense that they were essential to the development of the personal. I think he was trying to get at this from several angles. I have become more and more interested in the nature of the human person. What is a person? What is different about a person from a mere individual? Is it that in the person there is an inner imaginative and spontaneous response whereas in the individual this is lacking? This imaginative response occurs at a deeper stratum of the personality than that of language. Klauber's conversational response was the linguistic manifestation of something much deeper. I believe that this emotional reciprocity is what creates the person. I think Klauber knew this, but was not fully aware of it. Becoming a person is something avoided because it is the person who feels sorrow, feels shame, feels regret, and feels guilt. An individual in whom the person either has not developed or only exists in embryonic form does not feel these things. There is frequently an instinctive veering away from the personal and I think a whole psychoanalytic methodology may be governed by this very dread. I think it took courage for Klauber to take a stand against a widespread technique whose basis was to avoid the personal.

This, for me, was John Klauber's central virtue, and, although without fully realizing it, I have spent many years trying to surround this outlook with a psychology that is consistent with it. After this, the two most valuable principles that I have retained is his instinctive respect for the freedom of the individual and his oft-stated dictum that the analyst's first job is to make emotional contact with the patient. These two are handmaidens of what I have referred to as his "central virtue". The ability to make emotional contact with another is not a capacity that everyone has. This communicative ability is formed, I believe, in that forge of the mother–infant bond. Because it is dependent upon this capricious factor it is often not well established. Some psychoanalysts and psychotherapists suffer from this early damage and "making an interpretation" becomes a compensatory mechanism to replace the inability to make a relationship. Freedom is a necessary ingredient for someone to make a relationship.

So, looking back today, twenty-five years after Klauber died and twenty-one years after this paper was written, my conclusion is that he was able to make a relationship in a profound way but he did not sufficiently understand the psychology of how this is formed and I think that was partly due to his over-valuation of Freud's system, which did not support his personal perspective. For instance, I think his concept of anxiety as an impulse-seeking discharge is too mechanical and does not really fit with his own stress on the ego and the analyst's value system. I think this is a great pity, because the analyst's own person and the way this influences the process was central to his way of practising psycho-analysis. In fact, his paper "The psychoanalyst as person" (Klauber, 1968, pp. 123–139) precisely focuses upon this exact point, but

I think this perspective requires the kind of philosophical under-standing that has been elaborated by people like John Macmurray, Kierkegaard, Merleau-Ponty, Jaspers, Berenson, Max Scheler, and others. The ego's job of integrating those aspects that are ego-alien is not quite the same as saying that there are impulses seeking discharge. In the former, the ego is seen as the factor that structures the personality, whereas in the latter the accent is upon the agent-less impulses. I think that Fairbairn, for whom the personality was the ego and from whose schema the id was banished, and Bion, who formulated an interaction between container and con-tained, do better service to the primacy of the personal than Freud's more mechanical model. Through his study of history Klauber was influenced by Collingwood, who had this perspective to some extent. What Klauber did intuitively was contrary to what he subscribed to theoretically. I think this is why there was a somewhat mournful note in his comment that we are always working in the shadow of a genius, as if he longed to throw off that shadow and don a theory that complemented his intuitive understanding more closely.

At the time I thought that Klauber did not understand that area of the personality which has been described variously as *prim-itive, pre-Oedipal, pre-verbal*, whereas I believed that the Kleinians had, and after qualifying as an analyst, I went to fortnightly clini-cal seminars with Herbert Rosenfeld and I learned a great deal about this area from him. It was a Kleinian claim that they did understand this area of the personality. However, with the passage of time, I came to the conclusion that they did not understand it either.[1] There were some notable exceptions. When I came to realize all this I felt more warmly again towards John Klauber. Let us say that to analyse a patient there are two essentials: first to be able to make a relationship and second to be able to analyse the emotional patternings that generate the distortions that we associate with psychosis. John Klauber was certainly able to do the first, and I believe that he also did the second. His stress on spon-taneity and his active engagement with it therapeutically was addressing the psychotic area of the personality from the perspec-tive of that which is contrary to psychosis. In other words, he cul-tivated a garden in which the weeds of psychosis would in good time be banished. Psychosis, which is a structure governed by the superego, is characterized by rigidity, dogmatism, and systematizing. Spontaneity is the antidote of this.[2] Klauber, I think, knew this, and therefore through this knowledge was able to unsettle the psychosis and allow the patient to develop in its place free spontaneous inner action, which is the hallmark of sanity. Making emotional contact with the patient is the foundation stone upon which the analytic process is structured. The personality stabilizes if this foundation is securely established and the work of analysis can then proceed.

Klauber believed that the truth was the great healer and he was faithful to this ideal. He gave me enough to be able to build upon in later years. It is now thirty years since I finished my analysis with him and my emotional development and analytic understanding have grown spectacularly since then. I believe I have, in large measure, him to thank for starting me on that journey. As the years pass I become more and more grateful to him—for being who he was. It was a great privilege to be able to share in the light of his wisdom and understanding.

My gratitude to him for his respect for my freedom is immense. He also was thrilled when good things happened to me in my life later, after the analysis had finished. I remember being in the library of Mansfield House shortly after Joan, my wife, had become pregnant with our second child. He came in unexpectedly and I told him this news. He physically and literally jumped for joy. I told him that it was to be another boy and he said that when he first had news that their second baby was a girl, like the first, he was disappointed, but then he said to me, "But when the birth happened I was overjoyed and it did not matter." I remember going away with joy in my heart. His humanity was unmistakeable to anyone who knew him well.

Notes

1. This is clearly not true of Bion, Rosenfeld, Sohn, and Segal.
2. I am indebted to Dr Mark Howard, who drew my attention to this important factor.

PART II

EMOTIONAL FREEDOM
IN THE ANALYST

Introduction

"Speak what we feel, not what we ought to say"

(Shakespeare, *King Lear*, Act V, Scene 3, line 324)

The following papers were, in fact, written before the one on John Klauber that forms Chapter One, but in terms of my development as an analyst they come after that one. When I wrote the paper on Klauber I was retracing my steps to a point before the following four papers.

These four papers are all of a piece. Their focus is upon the conviction that it is emotional freedom that puts the analyst in touch with the most primitive area in the personality that has variously been called *the psychotic, the pre-genital, pre-Oedipal, area of the basic fault* or simply the *primitive*. Although these papers were written at the very beginning of my career as a psychoanalyst, and I have developed a great deal since then, they embody an outlook that has changed only in the philosophical background into which they are now placed in my mind. What has come later is a context that fits them better. I came slowly to realize that they did not fit the theoretical schema that I had been taught when I did my training, so I slowly developed another over many years. Today, these papers fit much better into my new outlook and, therefore, I understand them much better than I did when I wrote them.

The first of these papers, "The patient makes the analyst", tells the story of a treatment that confronted me with the problems whose solution is then elaborated in the following three: "The analyst's act of freedom as agent of therapeutic change", "Phantasy effects that which it represents", and "Maturity and interpretation as joint therapeutic agents". These papers were seminal for the way I think and have governed my practice ever since.

I have reflected more recently upon that analysis that makes up the paper "The patient makes the analyst", and two years ago I gave a renewed version of it that I called "Waking from dogmatic slumbers". I have included some of the points that I alluded to in this latter lecture in the endnotes to "The patient makes the analyst".

CHAPTER TWO

The patient makes the analyst[1]

"All right," said the Cat; and this time it vanished quite
slowly, beginning with the end of the tail, and ending with
the grin, which remained for some time after the rest of it
had gone. "Well! I've often seen a cat without a grin,"
thought Alice; "but a grin without a cat! It's the most curious
thing I ever saw in all my life"

(Carroll, 1974, pp. 63–64)

I had finished my analysis. My two training cases had satisfied
both my supervisors and the Education Committee of the
British Psychoanalytic Society, so now I was a qualified analyst.
I had changed greatly in my own analysis, so I knew from personal
experience that psychoanalysis is able to bring about profound
changes in the personality. That judgement was made from the van-
tage point of my emotional life at the time. Then I was confronted
with someone my analysis had not equipped me to deal with.

She came to see me hot on a hallucination in which, while
merged with her mother, she was strangling her boyfriend. She had
been turned down by two prestigious psychoanalytic clinics before

27

being referred to me. I was working at the time in a little-known psychotherapy centre. She was angry at not being taken on by either of these clinics and realized that I was her last resort. If she turned me down she knew that no other treatment would be available for her. She was extremely poor and private treatment was out of the question. So, there she was, stuck with me, whom she found cold and severe, but what options did she have other than accept what had been dished up to her? Oliver Twist did not get on too well when he asked for a second bowl of soup.

She started early in January, just after New Year and for the three months until Easter an easy harmony ruled the treatment and the young analyst felt very pleased with himself. I imagined that things would continue on this note until the treatment was successfully completed, but after the Easter break I was in for a shock.

I think that in those first three months she was testing the water to see if she dare risk entrusting to me her mad self. I learned that some patients do make just such a scrutiny of their analyst in the early phase of treatment. It also gives the analyst an opportunity to assess whether he/she is prepared for a more searching challenge.

Why I passed that test I cannot say, shut off as I was from such crazy madness. In retrospect I think she intuited potential that had not been actualized.

After that first break I was precipitated into a clinical world that was new and frightening. My analysis and supervision had not prepared me for such a fright. I shall try to tell you what now confronted me. She came in and after a long silence said, "Gnome".

Then there was a ten minute silence. She looked at a spot on the floor and said, "Toy".

I was flabbergasted by this sudden change in direction. I was not qualified for an analysis such as this. Surely there was someone else who could see this patient? But who, I asked myself. This was a question she had certainly asked herself. I could run to a supervisor but something spoke inside me and told me to face the music. I was attending a fortnightly post-graduate clinical seminar with Herbert Rosenfeld at the time. Now, here, surely, was the place to present this patient and yet, when my turn came, I chose to present a woman whose obsessions veiled a hidden psychosis. I also had a presentiment that I must follow my intuition and was, at the time, too borderline not to be thrown off course by a renowned authority.

How was it then that I later dared to present her to Bion? I think it was that I was able to differentiate knowledge from wisdom. So I reached a resolve: I will see this patient through thick and thin. I said one thing to myself: "Whatever she says and does I must stay in communication with her", so, having said "Gnome" and then "Toy", I fumbled into my mind and said, "You feel a small child and want to get down on to the floor and play with your toys and you want me to play with you."

I did not get any confirmation or disconfirmation. Session after session she communicated in this way. I had nothing to rely upon other than my own imagination, and on this faculty I put all my trust. I was very glad to discover in later years that Kant said that in imagination lies the core of understanding. I learned from my own experience that imagination is *the* tool of the analytic endeavour. Through imagination I linked what I came to call her "telegraphic bits"—these images with no sentence structure to give them a linguistic context. When I look back to the way I linked them I am ashamed at my naiveté. I am sure that seventy-five per cent of what I said to her was wrong, but I continued to weave a pattern or a narrative tale out of the material she gave me. I think she knew I was a novice who could not do better than he was doing. However, she was determined that I should do better, and believed that I could. This judgement of hers was correct. She enjoyed this time of narrative pattern-weaving; I knew this because sometimes there was on her face the hint of a smile.

You are probably frustrated that you have no transcriptions of these early sessions. They were so bizarre and disjointed that they were impossible to record. They were all of the nature of telegraphic bits. She would stare very intently at a spot in the room and say "Blue circle" and then ten minutes later stare elsewhere and say "Giraffe", and so on. This disturbing process had been going on for about a month when I realized from the intense way that she looked towards different points in the room that the telegraphic bits were objects which she "saw" in my consulting room. I then knew she was hallucinating (see Commentary, point 1). Strange how comforting such a realization was to me. Why? I think it must be as Bion said, quoting Milton,

The rising world of waters dark and deep
Won from the void and formless infinite (Bion, 1970, p. 88),

that when something is won from formlessness to form it is a great comfort to home-seeking human beings. It was similarly comforting when, later in her analysis, it dawned on me one day that I was in the grip of a psychotic transference.

Many of the hallucinatory objects in my consulting room were animals, suggesting to a colleague that my room had become the abode of Noah's Ark. I also observed that she never looked *at* me. She began to see a devil above my desk. I realized intellectually that this was a displacement of what she did not dare to see directly in me. When later the devil jumped inside of me, I was in for a hard time.

I learned that what is described in the initial interview about the crises in a person's love affair become re-enacted in the transference. I had experienced this before, but I had not expected that this would be true of the hallucinatory experience she had had of strangling her boyfriend while in unison with her mother.

I was looking at her one day when I was suddenly gripped by a very odd fear. I had once or twice thought she looked a little like a girlfriend whom I had once known. In this session I suddenly thought it *was* her. I tried to tell myself not to be so silly but the delusion persisted: "It *is* her".

Was I right or was I mad? My head raced around in drunken stupor. Then in the very next session I was gripped by the same horror. During this early part of the analysis she was still coalesced with her boyfriend, David (whom she hallucinated strangling), but only later did she tell me that in those early months of treatment she had thought *I was* David. She further had a vivid recollection of when she had become disabused of that conviction and I realized that it was in the very week when I had believed that she *was* this past girlfriend. It was a very unnerving experience. Another piece of comfort emerged when I was able to label it a "psychotic countertransference". Because it was such a frightening experience, I came to understand why we all shrink from taking on psychotic patients and began to think that perhaps the two clinics who had passed her on were wiser than I knew. I also understood better that at the beginning she had been testing to see whether I would be able to bear the violence of her psychotic projections.

Thrusting these telegraphic bits at me went on for about five months. For instance, on one occasion, she came in, looked intensely at the wall and said, after a silence of ten minutes, "The Cheshire cat—its smile."

I said, "The body plus the face of the cat, the last session, has all gone. Only a trace remains: something that gave you pleasure."

I had no idea whether such an interpretation was right. The only thing I knew was that it came from inside me—out of my own madness. I turned to *Alice in Wonderland* to get me into the right gear—that was my only textbook. I thought once that if colleagues had been watching this strange encounter through a one-way screen then both she and I would have been carted off to the nearest lunatic asylum. One thing I did learn about psychosis from these weird events: only those communications that come from within the analyst, from the very depths, from his own true self, have any effect. The very moment when the patient needs most desperately a communication from the personal heart of the analyst is the very moment when the analyst is most likely to run to a supervisor. Of course, it is all right to run to a supervisor as long as the analyst is able to stick to his or her own intuitions and be prepared to say to him or herself, "Although this supervisor's name is Rosenfeld I think he is wrong."

At that time I was not resilient enough to be able to say that to myself. It is only in later years I came to realize that the psychotic patient is tortured by the dictates of a voice that commandingly says, "Do this", or "Do that; say this, say that".

The sensitive intuition of a psychotic patient such as the woman I am describing knows instantly when I am speaking what I think and when I am speaking what I have been told to think.

Bion then came to London on one of his trips from California and I went to him for supervision. He had that rare gift of being able to make comments without interfering with the me-ness of interpretations. I hardly started presenting her when he said, "And she had the idea that you would be able to help her?"

I mumbled with embarrassment that I supposed she did. He said it without a hint of condemnation. I think he really was wanting to draw my attention to her phantasy that I, this exalted being, would be able to help her. The phantasy of the analyst as a divine being is, I believe, always present in the psychotic part of the personality. It is a projection of the omnipotent part of the personality into the analyst. When I explained to Bion her telegraphic bits, and that I knew not a whisper of what happened in her life outside the consulting room, he said to me, "You must say to her that if you are to analyse her she must keep you informed."

There was I thinking I ought to be able to decode this cryptic language. Bion made me realize that I was only colluding with her phantasy of me as divine. He said another thing to me, which made me sigh with relief. She had been communicating in telegraphic bits for about five months. I was beginning to get fed up with it. I had somewhere read, perhaps in a philosophical treatise, perhaps in one of Bion's writings . . . but somewhere . . . that consciousness is the patterning into a whole of discrete primitive imagery. Then I had the sudden thought that I had been obligingly fulfilling the role of consciousness for her and I was tired of this role that she had pushed me into. This was about two years before I went to those supervisions with Bion, and I had no guide other than my own feelings combined with that thought that I had become for her the agent of consciousness. There was nothing I could detect in the content of her communications that counselled a change in direction except my own feeling plus that thought. I decided, for better or worse, to act upon this feeling. So, in the next session, when she started with her first telegraphic bit, holding my breath, I said to her, "You want me now to weave this into a meaningful narrative for you, because you believe that you are not able to do it for yourself."

That was the end of the honeymoon. Her loathing and detestation of me began in earnest. I learned that a patient is never liberated from narcissism and its psychotic components without first having a long-lasting period where she hates the analyst unremittingly. This is because what is hated is the reality of the "me", the reality of the other, which now encroaches upon an illusory self-enclosed world. When I explained this interpretation and how I had no evidence for it other than my own feeling of fed-upness, plus the thought of what consciousness is, Bion asked me what her response had been. I relayed to him her undiluted rage and hatred and his owl-like eyes looked at me while pondering for what seemed an age and then his deep rumbling voice spoke, as if pulling truth from its ancient lair: "I think that was a correct interpretation."

The devil that, until then, had been safely lodged on the wall above my desk, was well and truly deposited inside of me. This led me to go to pieces inside. At that time I did not have the wherewithal to sustain an attack of psychotic fury, and I fell back upon cliché interpretations. They were mostly interpretations similar to those that my own analyst had made to me. I will give you the record of a session that occurred shortly after that crucial intervention of mine.

"The only thing is I detest you. You're completely inhuman."

There followed a very long silence, and then she said, "And just elaborations of the same theme. Like it's just like being with a computer—understanding but no feeling."

Another silence, and then, "And a housewife's robot doing the cleaning."

Another silence, and then I said, "You experience me as computer and this makes you feel a robot."

Another silence: "I don't know who is a robot."

Another silence, and then she said, "I always wonder how those monkeys do so well on those cloth frames."

A long silence, and then she said, "And violence and destruction."

And silence, and then she said, "And a play in which school desks were being smashed."[2]

Silence, and then I said, "Your hatred is because of the frustration that you get no feeling from me."

She answered, "Ye-es", with a slight smirk, followed by another silence, and then she said, "No wonder I amuse myself with hallucinations."

And there the session ended. (See Commentary, point 2.)

In many subsequent sessions she complained bitterly about having to be responsible for my reactions. It was only later that I realized that she was paralysing me, and that here I was giving only "mirroring" interpretations that were woefully inadequate, if not useless. When she said she was responsible for my reaction that was absolutely accurate. I was not answering out of my own freedom, but in fearful reaction to her emotional rage. I gave the mirroring interpretations that I have just quoted because I was too frightened within to respond with vigour to what she said. She was in very dire straits at the time and terrified of the violence in her.

She feared she might do someone an injury, especially her boy-friend David. I did not connect with any of that, but just mirrored her comments to me like a frightened rabbit. I now think that mirror interpretations usually flow from this inner paralysis. Such interpretations never advance an analysis, but in a patient who is psychotic they make things worse, because they induce guilt. She, the psychotic patient, knew that these mirroring interpretations came from an analyst whom she had disintegrated inside. Analytic progress in this analysis depended entirely upon the synthetic process going on inside my own psyche. She needed more from me, and the more she sensed that she was having this paralysing effect upon me the more panic-stricken and sadistic she became. So, when I related all this to Bion, he said with characteristic wit, "Sadism only works when the victim is helpless."

What I came to realize through the process of this analysis is that what is of concern to the patient who is psychotic, or to the psychotic part of every patient, is not what the analyst says but rather the emotional attitude in his heart. That this patient was in tune with my inner emotional states was certain. I came to realize that the *place* where psychoanalysis occurs is in the inner life of the patient and the inner life of the analyst, and that language is only the medium of exchange between these two.

I will give an example from another session that came later, but while she was still hateful towards me. The session was just before Christmas. I started by reminding her that it was the last session before the break.

> She said, "A girl's face that I don't like; a talking alarm, and a device to stop people stealing motor-bikes."
>
> I replied, "That you don't like my face since I have absorbed you. I am a talking alarm when I tell you this is the last session; and you need a device to stop me stealing sessions from you."
>
> She said, "Ingenious."
>
> I replied, "But perhaps true."
>
> She said, "Well, the first part about the girl's face is."
>
> I asked her a question, "What did you not like about her?"
>
> She replied, "She was absorbed into a girl with a face behind."

I said, "That since I have taken you in, as we were saying . . ."

She said, "Yes, that I disappeared into you long ago."

Then she said, "Just a sticky continuum."

There followed a long silence after which I said, "It implies that I cannot extricate myself without talking down to you."

After saying this I realized that I could not bear this stuck transference.

Then she said, "I cannot feel you."

I replied, "That there is just me and that there is no way out."

To which she immediately replied, "I saw an image of a head at that moment."[3]

I replied, "Out of sticky me floats thoughts."

And she said questioningly, "Me?"

I replied, "Or sticky 'you-and-me' fused together floats thoughts."

She answered, "Yes, that's it."

There was a pause and during it I shifted my position in my chair and she said, "You needn't be so impatient. You only have to bear it for fifty minutes."

I felt immensely sad, and said, "Whereas you have to bear it all the time."

She replied bitterly, "And not because I professionally want to."[4]

And there the session ended. I think you will see from this session that I was more in touch with her emotional state and communicated better. I have rarely felt such sadness for someone. I had come to understand that she was mentally fused with me and could not separate herself. This led to confusion for her but it was also extremely difficult for me to get in touch with what *I* thought and felt and it was precisely this that she was most anxious to discover.

*   *   *

As I suppose it would also be possible to name this paper "The apprenticeship of an analyst", I will slip in another incident that was associated with this patient. During the first three years of treatment I was seeing her at a small psychotherapy centre in central London. We were a staff of four non-medical analysts. Once a fortnight one of our medical colleagues, also an analyst, used to come and attend our clinical meeting. I presented this patient a few times at this venue. When he heard my presentations of this patient he said several times, "You need to speak to her from the shoulder about her self-destructiveness. When people are being self-destructive it is necessary to speak to them about it from the shoulder."

I do not think those were his exact words, but that was their import. He said it several times and it was quite apposite and he correctly picked up my timidity. I was director of the clinic and had engaged his services and we organized medical cover for our patients around the fortnightly presentations. His visits were important. He began to be delinquent: missing sessions, coming late, ringing at the last moment to say he could not come, and on a couple of occasions appeared in a dishevelled condition. I had also heard on the bush telegraph that was, as always, active in the psychotherapy world, that he was behaving provocatively at the main clinic where he worked and so on. One day when he said yet again, "You need to speak to her from the shoulder about her self-destructiveness . . .", I suddenly realized that he was talking of himself. I had the ideal opportunity to do what he was so clearly asking for because, as director of the clinic, with him breaking his contractual arrangements with us, I had the ideal opportunity. However, I didn't, but I regretted it bitterly when a few months later he committed suicide. I learned two things from this sad event: (1) to be tuned to unconscious communication, not only in patients but in the wider social spectrum; (2) in that dilemma—to speak or not to speak—that the former alternative is usually to be preferred to the latter, however hard it might be. I need hardly add that I have frequently rejected this self-administered advice.

*   *   *

For a year she castigated me for not attending to the things that urgently needed attention. If only I knew what these things were! She spoke in elliptical phrases and believed that through them I knew the full content of her mind. I understood from what Bion told me the importance of being kept informed of what was happening to her, yet she hated putting things into words: "Oh, the divinity of words . . ." she once said with disdainful scorn. It was excruciating for her to reveal the intimacies of her inner states to me. She felt it was disgusting.

She reproached me for not being sympathetic to women's problems; she said she should be with a female analyst and that I was prejudiced against her. These complaints were not delivered in a coherent pattern of sentences but in bits, in short sharp salvos. I had two thoughts about this complaint: (1) that she was being sadistic to me, the hated male; (2) that her complaint was correct—that I was not in touch with her.

Hindsight suggests that both these were true. She pounded me so insistently that I doubted myself. As I doubted and wavered so the power of her sadism soared. Finally, I asked a female colleague to see her for a second opinion. My colleague reported back to me that in the two interviews that she had with her, my patient spoke flowingly and in the most coherent way. Although this does not surprise me now, it was a shock at the time. Only then did I realize that I was experiencing a psychotic transference. My colleague was herself in doubt, but on balance she favoured my continuing with the treatment. At the same time I had this surprising thought: "I never say to myself, 'Perhaps my wife would do better with someone else'."

I reproached myself for having any truck with such wimpish promptings. Thereupon, I resolved to carry on with the analysis and had no further self-doubts on that particular issue. I learned at this time a very important lesson, but I will tell you first how I arrived at it. She used to say quite frequently, "I cannot move until you move first."

I asked myself, "What does this mean?"

She would say also that I needed to try different approaches. I thought she meant that I needed to try some other form of psychotherapy, or that she was requesting an interpretation. In one way she did mean this, but it was not on the level of words. Then at one point she started to take up a position behind my chair in the consulting room and I found it disconcerting to interpret with her standing behind me. As I was walking home one day after a session a determination arose in me to tolerate this no longer. In the next session when she did this I moved to another chair across the other side of the room and she turned on me in fury, but later calmed down and some good work came about. There were many other such inner resolutions in the course of that analysis. I have so far given two: (1) when I decided not to continue functioning as her consciousness; (2) when I resolved that I was *going* to continue conducting her analysis myself.

And now here was a third: I would not tolerate trying to interpret with her standing behind my chair. (See Commentary, point 3.)

Then one day, in a sudden flash, I realized that she meant she could not move forward emotionally until *I* had made such an *inner* move myself: "Attend to yourself", and "You need more analysis", but, most crucially, "I cannot move until you move first."

I now realized that when I made one of these inner moves she was in turn able to move forward emotionally (see Commentary, point 4). I formulated this understanding some years later in a paper entitled "The analyst's act of freedom as agent of therapeutic change" (Symington, 1983).

I would like to take the opportunity here to emphasize that what I meant and still mean is an *inner* act of freedom. This inner act clearly has outer manifestations, but it is the inner emotional act that is therapeutic. I have been understood to mean some outer act of intervention, and what I have said has been misused in this sense. For many years I believed that the inner act alone sufficed, that it was not necessary to interpret its content, but I agree now with Rosenfeld (1952, p. 76),[9] who writes that this is not sufficient and that the matter needs to be interpreted for the patient.

I have chosen this patient to report upon because I saw her early in my psychoanalytical career before (happily) any dogma had set hard and because I derived insights from the treatment of her that have structured my thoughts ever since. Many other patients have expanded this understanding, but this patient did something more radical. She taught me that analytic work resides in inner resolutions in the mind of the analyst, and I also learned from her that psychotic patients are able to intuit the existence of these inner states; that there is unconscious knowledge and communication operating all the time in analysis. This *is* the analysis. I certainly did not know this until it finally sank into my brain in about the third year of this patient's analysis. I was an analyst in name when I was elected to Associate Membership, but in reality only some four years later in a hard apprenticeship with this patient.

*   *   *

A central problem was her terror of violent sadism towards males. This referred to the male within her and also towards men outside. In particular, should she give birth to a baby boy at some future date, she feared she would torture him in the cruellest way. I came to realise that I was for her that boy whom she attacked cruelly but also challenged to adulthood, both analytic and emotional. At a later stage in the analysis, after a change in her from hate to love when guilt reigned supreme and she was reproaching herself for her treatment of me and her fear of her cruelty to male babies, I said to her, "You have mothered this baby extremely well", and I meant it. She eyed me with doubt, but I think she took in an emotional understanding of the comment.

I was able to manage her attacks more easily when I realized that I was this "man-child" and that when she said she could not move until I moved first she was also saying that she could not give up sadistic behaviour until I had passed through my own inner resolutions. She monitored my analytic progress and at each new resolution she was able to move ahead. What is sadism to someone broken up inside is the medicine of healing to someone in whom synthetic integration is occurring. Kierkegaard is the only thinker I have come across who sees this two-edged sword in the phenomenon of punishment. Her punishment of me had a healing effect. That is what I meant when I said that she had mothered this baby very well.

I now realized that she thought I was *deliberately* withholding and was therefore the focus of an intense paranoia. Yet this is not entirely correct, because she *also* knew that I did not because I could not, so the paranoid and the depressed rode shoulder to shoulder, side by side. When she realized, through some interpretations I made, that she had to wait for me, that I could not turn these changes on at will, she became sad. Here she was with an ordinary bloke, not some divine being. Even at her most paranoid she had some hidden intuition that I was struggling. Once, in the midst of another orgy of castigation, she reproached me for being switched off in yesterday's session and then said, "Your interpretations were quite off the mark. Usually they are rather accurate."

I smiled to myself. Even in the midst of the bitterest battle human generosity struck through. I remembered an incident in the Peninsula War during the Retreat to Corunna. As the French guns were blazing at the British troops fleeing to their ships, a courageous Englishman stood up and made of himself a clear-sighted target so that he might draw the bullets to himself, thus allowing more of his compatriots to reach the boats in safety. The French lowered their guns and left their easy target unharmed. She also lowered her guns, not because she detected valour but because she knew intuitively that her adversary-cum-helper could not manage unless she did so. The other time she lowered her guns was when she had been reproaching me one day for being just like one of Harlow's wire monkeys. Then the next day, in the middle of the session, she said in a dreamy voice, "Surprising how well those monkeys do on those wire mothers."

I believe she knew that I was a novice and that without the odd word of encouragement I might not stay the course.

She was not only anxious about cruelty to a possible future baby but about her present cruelty towards the man within her. I think Jung's theoretical schema of *animus* and *anima* is insightfully accurate: that a woman cannot be a woman unless she loves *animus* within and a man cannot be a man unless he loves *anima* within and no marriage can occur between man and woman unless that inner marriage is first cemented in solemn consummation. When I revolted and decided I would be consciousness for her no longer, she experienced the hatred inside her of which she had not been aware before. That was the beginning of a process that begins in unconscious hatred, changes to conscious hatred, and ends in love. The move from unconscious hatred to conscious hatred was a step forward, because she was now engaged with the other and no longer insulated within an imprisoning chrysalis.

She complained bitterly that I had not helped her to communicate with people outside the consulting room. She again lowered her guns for a moment, though, and let me know that I had helped her to communicate better with me. I think that when she said I had not helped her communicate outside she was saying that I had not helped the development of the male in her, but she did make a start in this direction. I have already quoted this incident in another paper (Symington, 1990, p. 101) but will quote it here now:

She said, "You have not helped me one bit to communicate outside this sacred room. Oh yes, you will help me to communicate with you but not with anyone besides the wonderful you."

The next day she came in and pranced around the room (me nervously eyeing a flowerpot she was stroking with her right hand) and then she looked at me piercingly and said, "Now I have found someone who is *really* sympathetic to women. I spoke to him yesterday and he understood the predicament of women, he understood how a woman feels."

As on the day before, my inner anatomy was a surging millrace and also a fury at her insinuations. I was about to point out her destructive attacks on me and her attempt to denigrate the work that had been done, but I held it. I did not hold it easily; there was a tug of war inside me: one side was saying, "Point out her denigration" while the other side was saying, "Hold it". The "hold it" side won and then calmness began to come over me and out of that state came a clear thought, which I voiced thus: "You are letting me know that things have improved since yesterday; that now you *are* able to communicate with others outside the consulting room."

Again the two-edged sword: a clear message, but clothed in a provocative tone that initially prevented me from hearing. This was good mothering within a bitchy frame.

The cruelty towards herself was also lessening in her professional life. When she started her analysis she was a statistician: when she ended her analyis she had become a painter. She was making in the analysis a major emotional transition. A figure cruelly intervened to prevent man and woman coming together. There were two opposite impulses, one pushing me away and the other clamouring for me to come closer. The clamour for me to come closer was clear to hear if I could shut out its provocative clothing— like someone who is a good mother but outwardly looks a sexy tart.

When she came to me she had had a psychotic episode with hallucinations and in the analysis she broke down back into the primordial elements out of which the foundation of our mental life is fashioned. What I referred to as "telegraphic bits" were composed of visual images. Each of these bits encapsulated an intense but discrete emotional experience. In those three months when she was speaking the images that appeared on my consulting room walls I was plunged into a weird world that was unnerving—a meaningless world that disturbed me greatly. She projected these images on to the consulting room wall in front of us. At least here was something solid and concrete—no symbols there, but when I explained it to Bion, he said to me, "That's the wall between the two of you."

That remark of his blew my mind. I realized deeply in me what he meant. The wall was constructed out of her provocation and my narcissism. That made a very solid wall indeed.

Shortly after I made that intervention when I refused any longer to function as consciousness for her, she reported her first dream:

> She came into a room where the body of her mother lay. It was made of polystyrene. She touched it and it exploded into a mass of particles.

When she told me that dream I experienced enormous relief. The weight of the world seemed to slip from my shoulders. I realized instantly that the mass of particles were the hallucinated images of those first few months which had now come together into a dream and held within her. I had come out of a bizarre Kafka-esque world into a place of freshness and light. I think that dream represented a moment of synthesis. It was an experience unlike any other that I have had in my clinical practice. Shortly after that came this session, which I think encapsulates this early problem that she was struggling with. She had lived it; now it began to be possible to understand it and to transform it into words.

> She said one day, "My thoughts are elsewhere—just what a gooey mess human beings are."
>
> Then she said, "I am thinking of a story of Doris Lessing."
>
> I asked, "Could you tell it to me please?"
>
> She said, "It is about the problem of meaning. A black man leaves his culture and goes to the land of the whites. It is all mysterious and he has not got the tools and implements."

She expressed perfectly what the problem was in that last sentence. She was in the world of sensuous images and she did not have the tools with which to express it. She was moving into the territory of language: where symbols express these powerful inner emotions. She did manage at last to bang this into my head and I think I began to have some dawning understanding of it.

Since then I have had other patients who hate words that seem so out of harmony with the inner emotion. There was another very important thing that this patient taught me: simplicity of expression. Any interpretations in the mode of "I think you are trying to tell me . . .", etc., were a dead loss. I learned that I had to speak the obvious in simple language. I had to interpret the visual message. So, for instance, towards the end of the analysis she came in looking quite different. She was well dressed and had taken possession of her beauty. Yet she was saying how awful she felt and how bad things were. By now I had learned to trust simple observation so I said to her, "You are *looking* extremely well, so in your feelings you are cut off from the way you are."

You will realize that I took her at her own words and took the visual—the sensuous—as expressing the true her. I had begun to realize that I must not be beguiled by the words.

It was only towards the end of the analysis that her extreme negativity came to the fore. In the past she had so consistently accused *me* of negativity that only now was I able clearly to see it in her.

There was one other incident, which I related in *The Analytic Experience* (1986):

> She had been castigating me session after session, week after week, month after month and I had been busy defending myself against attack and pointing out her destructiveness. She went to a country town and spoke to the counsellor she had first seen and confided her anxiety about the way the analysis was going. She told me what this woman said to her: "He can't hear a crying baby." When she said this it struck a chord which went right through me. I suddenly heard the session after session, week after week, month after month in a different light. I heard a desperately crying baby. I was thunderstruck. I said to her: "What she told you is entirely correct", and she burst into tears.

She came to me because she was desperate. I saw her on the National Health Service in England. Very few analytic vacancies are available in England in hospitals and clinics. She had no money; she was on the dole. I had offered to see her; she accepted me because she had no alternative. She had been turned down by two clinics. I was a last resort. She also knew I was not mature enough professionally or emotionally to manage her. She realized that her only option was to force me with all the strength in her being to be the analyst she needed. Before seeing her I had no idea what analysis was. When I had finished her treatment I began to get the first glimmerings. It also set in train emotional developments that were favourable to areas of my life other than professional.

She wanted to stop. I had been seeing her for nearly six years. I do not know whether it was right to agree to that termination, but I suspect it was. I think she had reached into me for all the resources and knowledge that were available at the time. In the last session she brought me a drawing she had done of a woman in a recumbent position. In that session she said she could be a woman now that she was able to acknowledge the man in her.

On one occasion I was with a group of people who were discussing how best to bring adolescent boys through a homosexual phase to heterosexual maturity. There was a young middle-aged Frenchwoman in the group. After a great deal of refined intellectual discussion this woman stridently spoke up: "I was once a governess to a young boy called Pierre. When he reached the age of fourteen I explained to him all about sex and lovemaking . . ." Then she looked around at all of us, puffed out her bosom with pride, and said, "But when he reached sixteen—on his sixteenth birthday—I made him a man."

I had had an analysis, had my cases supervised, and attended many clinical seminars. I had been told how to conduct an analysis, but my experience with this patient made me an analyst.

Commentary

When I look over this analysis many years later and reflect upon it, the following thoughts come to me.

1. Bion spoke of the way internal sensuous images are expelled through the eyes, ears, or pores of the skin. Her startled eyes might have given me a clue that she was hallucinating. I think there is a

positive reason for hallucinating: to get rid of an overload of imagery in order to clear a space for a re-ordering within. I think this is what she meant by a play in which school desks were being smashed. She came to me as a statistician. She could only find the space to become a painter when those statistic desks had been destroyed.

I have also found it helpful to think of the transference as a particular form of hallucination. I have had patients since this first one who have turned me into a parent especially when a mother or father has died when the patient was a child. When I have realized this it makes sense of many seemingly trivial things are reported—just the sort of things a child would tell his or her mother. In such cases I think the analyst becomes the hallucinated mother who integrates those elements of experience that until then have been in disarray. Winnicott speaks of this:

> An example of unintegration is provided by the very common experience of the patient who proceeds to give every details of the week-end and feels contented at the end if everything has been said, though the analyst feels that no analytic work has been done. Sometimes we must interpret this as the patient's need to be known in all his bits and pieces by one person, the analyst. [1958, p. 150]

Recently Thomas Ogden has emphasized what Winnicott means when he uses the word "interpret" here:

> Winnicott is using the word "interpret" to mean *not to give verbal interpretations to the patient*, and instead, simply, uninterruptedly to be that human place in which the patient is becoming whole. [Ogden, 2004, p. 1352]

So the very receptivity has a therapeutic function. I think this means that the analyst is receptive to the hallucinatory projection.

2. You will notice from this that I made two interventions and, please note, they are not interpretations because they are given by me in a state of inner dismay. Her attack threw my inner psyche into disorganization. When she says "and a housewife's robot doing the cleaning", I reply "You experience me as a computer and this makes you feel a robot." This does not come from someone who is sufficiently in possession of himself to wonder about the

meaning of a housewife's robot doing the cleaning. It is clear to me today that she is automatically cleaning out dirt and rubbish preparatory to a new mode of encounter or communication. But, rather than receive some elucidation of this, she meets instead a timid mouse trying to defend himself. It is also very narcissistic and dictatorial: *You experience me as a computer*—how do I know, for heavens sake? And why am I so focused on myself as if she does not have inner concerns that are much greater at that moment and then I continue and say: ". . . and this makes you feel a robot." What arrogance! How in hell do I know that she feels a robot; and if she does, what is the point of saying it? When someone feels something they know it; it is part of consciousness. Our job is to bring the unconscious to consciousness, not to pronounce to someone something that, if it is true, is already known anyway. And I do just as badly with my second intervention. She says, ". . . and a play in which school desks are being smashed" and I reply, "Your hatred is because of the frustration that you get no feeling from me." Here again it is the reply of the frightened mouse. I am defending myself under attack and so self preoccupied that I cannot ask myself why school desks are being smashed. If I had stopped to think about her, that she was a statistician working in a research laboratory, which was not right for her, I might have understood that the work of transformation was beginning—smashing up those old school desks first before a studio with painter's easels took their place.

Perhaps, however, I should be kind to myself. I was a novice, a beginner, but I want today to use the way I was then as an object lesson. The problem then was that under attack my psychic response is a defence of myself. Why I say that both my comments are interventions rather than interpretations is that my words are pushing her away to protect myself. I have not digested the attack; I am too disintegrated to be able to see what is happening *to her*. The real problem is that my words are pretences. It would have been far better had I said to her, "I am feeling shocked and dismayed by the heat of your fury and I shan't be able to give what you have said my proper consideration until things have calmed down inside me." It would have been better because then the words would have corresponded reasonably closely to the reality of what was happening between us. It clearly would have been better to have digested the attack and then tried to elucidate her statements, but it would have been better than what I did do because the truth heals and generates trust. So she ended that session with the words "No wonder I amuse myself with hallucinations", meaning, I think, that with such self-defensive replies she is better occupied spending her time with hallucinations—cleaning up her inner house is more profitable. In many subsequent sessions she spoke bitterly about having to be responsible for my reactions. She said she felt she might be causing these but it is only possible to cause something to occur in another if there is some sympathetic echo in that other. It was only much later that I realized that she was in touch with my inner state; that she knew that I was frightened and emotionally disintegrated inside. She needed to be able to hate or be aggressive without having to nurse a wounded boy with his pitying cries. Today if I make a mirroring interpretation (or intervention) or find myself telling a patient that he or she is feeling this or that, a little Symington supervisor taps me on the shoulder and tells me to take a mirror and attend to myself.

3. I believe I acted rightly in this scenario. It would have been a betrayal of psychoanalysis had I indicated that she should be sitting down in her usual chair. It would have been even worse if I had said that she was trying to unnerve me. It takes two to tango—it was my job to unnerve myself. So I moved across the room into another chair, which I was free to do. Freedom as the contractual baseline was something I had learned in my analysis with Klauber, but it was greatly reinforced by coming to know and understand the emotional position of Bion.

Also, out of freedom comes certainty. So, when she said to me that I had moved my chair in order to control her, I was certain that this was not the case and therefore replied, "Can you think of no other reason why I might have done it?" Today I am reasonably happy with that reply, though there may be a hint of disparagement in the word "no": "Can you think of *no* other reason". Now, with the calmness of hindsight, I would be happier if I had said, "I do not think you are right. I moved my chair for a different reason." However, I am reasonably happy with what I did say because after I had said it there was a long silence and, as the silence progressed, the atmosphere changed and a peace settled over the room and then she said, "I don't know about you, but I am feeling better."

4. I want to make five interrelated points about these moments of inner integration:

(a) A moment of inner integration communicates itself to the patient. That is *the* place where communication happens. Speech is the surface manifestation—it is not *the* place of communication. It is the inner coming together of disparate parts that fashions communication. Communication nurtures the two people.

(b) These moments of integration are the creation of a person or the further establishment of a person. The creation of the person in me allows the creation of a person in her. The person is not a given, but a creation.

(c) Therefore, the focus of psychic attention needs to be on *my* own processes of integration or disintegration.

(d) The good effect upon the patient is not the aim, but a happy outcome of my own inner construction.

(e) Doing good to the other is a missionary activity. It is also a tyranny.

There is a Benign Headmaster listening to this paper and he says to me:

"Neville—it is not right to call this area of the personality *psychotic*. It has negative connotations and everything you have said indicates to me that a very important work of reconstruction was going on—that this lady had the courage to rebuild her life from the foundations. I know that superficially it might look as if it is destructive but, after all, you are an analyst. I think you should look at things more deeply and see below the surface. In those hallucinations she was sweeping something away that needed to be re-ordered inside of her. Her hatred was her pain. Don't you hate pain? So please don't call it *psychotic* or any other of those terms you seem to have learned from a psychiatric textbook. What you are witnessing is not a disease but a remarkable metamorphosis. So can we agree and call it an area of renewal and regeneration?'

Notes

1.   I wrote this paper about fifteen years ago, which was about twelve years after this analysis took place. I still have no doubt whatever that

I became an analyst through the treatment of this patient. I based my paper "The analyst's act of freedom as agent of therapeutic change" (Chapter Three) upon the understanding that had come about through treating this patient.

2. I think this is an example of the type of re-ordering that the hallucination allowed the space for. She came to me as a statistician. She could only find the space to become a painter when those statistic desks had been destroyed.

3. I think she had this image because she sensed that I was beginning to think.

4. I have never forgotten that moment. In it I realized the intensity of her pain. Psychosis is an attempted anaesthetic against pain. I have always kept that as a baseline assumption and the attitude that it generates changes the nature of the interaction in a radical way.

The analyst's act of freedom as agent of therapeutic change[1]

> "Freedom is, I am assured, the pearl of great price for which, if we are wise, we shall be prepared to sell all our possessions, to buy it. The ancient and widespread belief that the supreme good of human life is happiness—for all its persuasiveness—is false. Freedom has a higher value than happiness; and this is what we recognise when we honour those who have been ready to sacrifice happiness, and even life itself, for freedom's sake"
>
> (Macmurray, 1949, p. 2)

I n this paper I intend to explore a phenomenon with which all analysts are familiar. I will first describe it and then examine what its implications are for theory. I shall refer to it as the "x-phenomenon". I shall start with some clinical examples.

I was charging a patient whom I shall call Mary a little more than half what my other patients were paying. She had been a clinic patient and I used to sigh to myself and say inwardly, "Poor Miss Mary, £X is the most that I can charge her."

I did not, in fact, articulate it as clearly as that. In my mind it was like an acknowledged fact that everyone knows, like the unreliability of the English weather. It was part of the furniture of my mind and I had resigned myself to it in the same way that I reluctantly resign myself to the English weather. So the analysis went on and on with that assumption as its unquestioned concomitant until one day a startling thought occurred to me: "Why can't Mary pay the same as all my other patients?"

Then I remembered the resentment she frequently expressed towards her boss, who always called her "*Little* Mary". A certainty began to grow in me that I was the prisoner of an illusion about the patient's capacities. I had been lassooed into the patient's self-perception and I was just beginning to extricate myself from it. I then brought up the question of her fee and in the course of a discussion she said, "If I *had* to pay more then I know I would."

She had now clearly told me that she had the capacity in her to pay more and that this could be mobilized if I changed my inner attitude towards her. A few sessions later I said to her, "I have been thinking over our discussion about the fee. I charge most of my patients £X, and in our discussion I have not heard anything that makes me think that I should not charge you the same."

For two sessions she cried rather pitifully, but then became resolved that she would meet the challenge. Soon she found a job that paid her one third more than her previous salary. In moving jobs she extricated herself from the patronizing tutelage of the boss who called her "Little Mary". She had been able to do this because she had first been freed from the patronizing attitude of her analyst. Shortly after this she finally gave the push to a parasitic boyfriend. Again, I think, she had been able to do this because she had been able to give the push to a parasitic analyst. These two events were soon followed by other favourable developments. I think the source of these beneficial changes was in that moment of inner freedom when I had the unexpected thought: "Why can't Miss Mary pay the same as my other patients?" I am calling this act of inner freedom the "x-phenomenon".

Now I want to take another example. This patient was an obsessional man who used to hesitate sometimes in the middle of telling me something, usually as he was about to tell me some thought he had had since the previous session. As he had often expressed his apprehension that I would think him pathetic, I would say to him something like, "I think you are afraid that if you tell me about the incident in your mind I shall think you are pathetic."

Of course, I was thereby clearly implying that I would not think him pathetic. With this assurance he would then obligingly tell me the thought in his mind. Then one day I was reading the following passage from *Four Discussions with W. R. Bion*:

> Q. . . . She wouldn't be put off by what you suggest; she would get irritated with your reply and insist that you call her by her first name.
>
> B. Why not the second one? Why not whore? Or prostitute? If she isn't one, then what's the trouble? Is she wanting to be called a prostitute or a whore? If not, what is the point of the story? What convinced her that her father was right?
>
> Q. She wants sex with other men besides her husband, therefore in her view, she must be a whore. She's afraid that if she got a divorce from her husband she would run around and have sex with all sorts of men—behave like a free whore.
>
> B. In view of what you are saying I think I would try to draw her attention to the way in which she wishes to limit my freedom about what I call her. It is just as much a limitation if the patient wants you to give the correct interpretation. Why shouldn't I be free to form my own opinion that she's a whore or that she is something quite different? Why be angry with me because in fact I am free to come to my own conclusions?
>
> Q. Her fear is that your conclusion will be that she is a whore.
>
> B. Why shouldn't I be allowed to come to that conclusion?
>
> Q. So you conclude she is a whore—now where are you?
> B. But I haven't said that I do. The point I want to show is that there is a wish to limit my freedom of thought . . . [Bion, 1978, pp. 15–16]

As I read this I had a moment of illumination about my obsessional patient. I had been a prisoner of this patient's controlling impulses and at the moment of reading this passage from Bion I had a new understanding in which I felt freed inwardly (though this had outward concomitants). The next time he expressed his apprehension that I would think him pathetic I said to him quietly, "But I am quite free to think that."

He was much taken aback. It was possible then to see how much he operated by controlling my thoughts and the thoughts of others. A great fear was that if he allowed me to think my own thoughts then I might have the thought: "How nice it would be to get away from Theodore".

This led on to his feeling that no one ever *wanted* to be with him, which was linked to childhood experiences where his parents never wanted to be with him but farmed him out with child-minders while they pursued their business interests in various parts of the world. We were able to look at his need to wind himself around me like a boa-constrictor and try to substitute my thinking and feeling for his, to make me into his ego, as it were. It was then possible to link his failure to be able to think and feel with the absence of a mother or analyst who wanted to be with him. The foundation of the thinking capacity seems to lie in the internalization of this maternal desire. Again, the source of all this interpretative work and insight started from the moment of my own inner act of freedom. So this was another case of the x-phenomenon. The remaining examples I want to take are from a patient whom I have described in my paper "The patient makes the analyst", to whom I shall refer as Annabel.

Annabel was referred after an episode of hallucinatory psychosis. I took her on largely because of her strong motivation to get better. She regularly hallucinated in the sessions and communicated with what I have called "telegraphic bits" (see Chapter Two). It may have been a regression to holophrastic speech. After a long silence she would just say "crocodile" and then some minutes later she would look at some point in the room and say "blue circle". I found myself reading *Alice in Wonderland* to help me into the right gear. I abandoned myself to crazy fantasy through which I linked these discrete elements. This phase of treatment progressed satisfactorily and eventually the hallucinations disappeared and she was able to address me, if not as a person, at least as a distinct entity. I learned later that until that point she had not been able to distinguish between me and her boyfriend, and in fact thought that I was him. From the moment that she saw me as distinct the honeymoon period of treatment was over for me.

I quickly became the target of her sadism. Her sadistic attacks were subtle, unrelenting, and certainly threw me off balance. She honed in on those areas of my own vulnerability with a devastating precision and she was relentless. For instance, for a long period she said she felt I was not the right person for her and she began to investigate other possible therapists. She twice sought the advice of a female colleague. In all this she reiterated frequently that in my attitudes, tones of voice, gestures, and in my manner of dressing I conveyed male chauvinist attitudes and that I was unsympathetic to the needs and predicaments of women. This was not articulated neatly like that. It was hinted at on occasions, raged about at others, and only slowly was it possible to decipher what she was saying. At other times she would scream exasperatedly at me, and so intensively that I was unable to think. She would reproach me with fury for not attending to matters that she had insistently brought to my attention. I was usually quite in the dark and realized that she probably thought she had asked me something or told me about some thought or event but had not in fact done so or had told me so elliptically that either the phenomenon itself or its import had escaped me.

Now, in her persistent accusation that I was dominating towards her because she was a woman and I was a man, I was aware of two things. In the first place I knew that she was sadistically attacking me and, second, that operating at a psychotic level of perception she was more sensitive to my own unconscious attitudes than a patient in a classical transference neurosis. My problem, therefore, was on the one hand not to allow myself masochistically to become a victim of her sadism and yet not to dismiss out of hand the content of what she was saying. Yet, of course, in that hesitant and divided state of mind, I was the perfect victim. The treatment went through a particularly bad patch that lasted for about a year. I thought to myself that perhaps I was not the right person for her, perhaps she did need a woman, perhaps my male chauvinist attitudes were getting in the way of clear interpretation, and so on. And the more I wavered inwardly the more furious and attacking she became. During this time she also complained regularly about rigidity, that I needed to be more flexible, I needed to consider other approaches or needed more analysis myself. For a long time I wavered inwardly as if I were standing on marshy ground.

Then, as I have described in "The patient makes the analyst", about three years into treatment she adopted a new manner of behaving in the sessions. Instead of sitting in her normal chair (she did not use the couch) she walked past me and sat in a chair behind me. I resolutely remained in my chair. Sometimes she pulled her chair right up behind mine and on one occasion she poked my arm with her finger. Then, instead of sitting behind me, she took to standing behind me and I continued to keep to my chair determinedly interpreting and continued to do this for some eight sessions.

Then one day I became uncomfortable with this procedure. I did not feel at ease and I was not able to respond spontaneously. Although I was interpreting, it was not out of an inner freedom but defensive in character. I decided the next time she walked past me and stationed herself behind my chair I would move across to the other side of the room. I could not say quite why I decided to do this but I knew that I could not interpret freely when I felt this discomfort. So the next time she took up her standing routine I got up calmly and moved to a settee on the other side of the room. As she saw me do this she turned and said in tormented fury, "Why did you move?" (it had a tone which denoted that I had no right to move as I had just done) and at the same time she moved back to her own chair and I moved back to mine.

"What thoughts do you have about why I moved?" I asked.

"Just sheer male dominance", she said in defiant rage.

Now, at this point I had an inner conviction that it was no such thing. I felt an inner certainty that I had not possessed before. I felt quietly confident that I had not acted out of any such motive and that I was not reacting to her sadistically.

"Can you think of no other possible interpretation of my action?" I asked her.

"No", she said, "it's just sheer male dominance."

Thereupon I said that it seemed we had reached a deadlock and then there was a tense silence and an atmosphere that was pregnant with fury. Then, at the end of about twenty minutes, the atmosphere began to ease and I felt that we both had come through a crisis like two swimmers who had just managed to cross a turbulent river and reached terra firma. Some ten minutes after that she said, "I don't know about you but I am feeling better", smiling slightly.

That composite moment when I acted, and then when in response to her I experienced an inner certainty that I had not had before, is another instance of the x-phenomenon. She was more able to listen from then on, and in certain ways communication became easier and there was greater clarity, although a great deal remained obscure and communication was still badly impaired.

With the same patient there was another instance that is less easy to describe, but I shall attempt to do so. I had a very clear notion that my role as analyst was to interpret to the patient my understanding of the unconscious import of what lay behind her manifest communications, but a stage was reached with her when she could not bear any interpretations. She screamed that she could not sort anything out unless I accepted the surface meaning of what she said and also unless I accepted responsibility for what belonged to me in the process. She could not sort out what was her, could get no insight into herself, until she was clear who she was and who I was. In other words, she needed to separate out the two elements that made up herself and me from the agglutinous mass that they were for her at the time. At this stage the only way in which it was possible for her to do this was, at various junctures, for me to express what my feelings were. It was important to her to know that they were really mine; several times she asked me if these were my feelings or those of all analysts; I told her that they were mine. Sometimes she would ask whether these were feelings shared by all analysts and I told her truthfully that I did not know.

After a period of this type of communication it became possible for her to express some separateness and then it was possible to interpret in the normal way again. There was a transitional stage when I would couch interpretations in this sort of way, "I want to express to you the thought that is in my mind . . .", and then I would go on with the substance of the interpretation.

Finally, I was able to interpret what I thought was in her mind. I understood this as being a transition from being a fused object in the transference to being a separate one, and that the interpretations had to be in a mode that was acceptable to the different psychological states that accompanied those phases. Again, when I acted from personal freedom rather than follow some specific technical regulation that is supposed to be followed in an analysis, therapeutic shifts occurred and, I might add, a great deal of insight and learning in the analyst. (I hope it will not be inferred that I am scorning analytic technique; this would be the very opposite of what I intend to say. After all, the soul of analytic technique is to free analyst and patient from the normal social constraints and so favour development of the inner world. The problem is when "classical technique" becomes the agent of a new social constraint.) I hope that these illustrations of the x-phenomenon are sufficient to convey my meaning.[2]

My contention is that the inner act of freedom in the analyst causes a therapeutic shift in the patient and new insight, learning, and development in the analyst. The interpretation is essential in that it gives *expression* to the shift that has already occurred and makes it available to consciousness. The point, though, is that the essential agent is the *inner* act of the analyst and that this inner act is perceived by the patient and causes change. Even the most inner mental act has some manifest correlate that is perceptible, though this perceptibility may be unconscious and probably is. The psychotic is particularly sensitized to these minute changes. I will give two examples of this from the last patient that I took my clinical material from. In the first example it was an instance of an inner emotional state and in the second a specific inner mental act. Shortly before seeing my patient one day, I received news that another patient of mine had committed suicide and I was upset, to put it mildly. There was a silence for the first twenty minutes of the session, then she looked at my desk and I made an interpretation that I cannot now remember but I shall not forget her response, "I am not taking stick for your bad experience."

She was in tune with my emotional state in relation to which my interpretation bore little importance and she sensed this. She perceived it in the atmosphere. I am quite sure that she had no external knowledge of what had occurred.

The other occasion was when I was trying to decide on which day to finish prior to Christmas and I was thinking about this during a silence. At the precise moment that I said to myself inwardly that I would make Tuesday the last session, she said, "You have interrupted my thoughts, you have just stolen something from me."

I had, of course. Instead of being in reverie with her I had stolen a chunk of shared thinking in favour of an administrative decision. As far as she was concerned I might just as well have spoken my thoughts out loud because she felt my inner act so that even an inner judgement has some perceptible external correlate. I do not think that the mental, emotional, and sensational spheres ever exist in isolation. The most inward mental act reverberates through the sensational and perceptual spheres. The psychotic patient is tuned in to these inner spheres in a way that is not so of neurotics or normal people. The psychotic is not cut off from reality but, rather, one minute aspect of reality is enlarged so that the rest of the mental or emotional field is crowded out. It is like the zoom lens on a television camera that swoops down on one object of interest and that one object then takes up the whole television screen. I am insisting, therefore, that the inner act of the analyst affects the patient; especially is this so in the psychotic and borderline patient. The focus of this paper, though, is that the analyst's inner act of freedom causes a therapeutic shift in the patient. To account for this further contention it seems that some theoretical ramparts are needed to support it.

I think at one level the analyst and patient together make a single system. Together they form an entity that we might call a corporate personality. From the moment that patient and analyst engage in what we call an analysis the two are together part of an illusory system. Both are caught in it. Recent literature stresses that the analyst is not just a mirror, but this is a gross understatement. The analyst is lassooed into the patient's illusory world. He is more involved in it, more victim to it than the average social contact. As the analytical work proceeds the analyst slowly disengages himself from it. In this way transference and countertransference are two parts of a single system; together they form a unity. They are the shared illusions that the work of analysis slowly undoes. Psychoanalysis is a process that catalyses the ego to ego contact: that area of the personality that is non-corporate, personal, and individual. In this way psychoanalysis is working in the opposite way to religion, whose central social function is to bind people together into corporate entities. We need to look at this corporateness as belonging to a part of the personality where fusing takes place and how we can assimilate this to psychoanalytic theory.

In all the instances of x-phenomenon that I have given, the analyst's personal feelings have been shrouded by illusory feelings, emanating from the patient's unconscious superego. This could be formulated by saying that the feelings belonging to the superego have cloaked the feelings belonging to the ego. However, the term superego needs to be amplified in the way that the sociologist Talcott Parsons (1952) has done:

> The place of the superego as part of the structure of the personality must be understood in terms of the relation between personality and the total common culture, by virtue of which a stable system of social interaction on the human levels becomes possible. Freud's insight was profoundly correct when he focused on the element of moral standards. This is, indeed, central and crucial, but it does seem that Freud's view was too narrow. The inescapable conclusion is that not only moral standards, but *all the components of the common culture* are internalised as part of the personality structure. Moral standards, indeed, cannot in this respect be dissociated from the *content* of the orientation patterns which they regulate. [p. 23]

These illusory feelings in the patient are partly the internalized values of the family of origin, of his class and national allegiances together with the impulses, especially the destructive ones, from within. The impulses from within are strengthened and supported by the cultural values. At the beginning of the analysis (and often for a long time) the patient and analyst are held in thrall by the power of this personal–cultural illusion. This is possible because the patient and analyst become part of a system through which communication takes place. In his passive role, where he does not assert his own view of the world, the analyst allows himself to be swept into the personal–cultural contents of the patient's superego and interprets within that framework. Analyst and patient are part of a system and are joined through the superego parts of their personalities. It is through the superegos that a corporate personality is effected. When the patient first comes to the analyst's consulting room it is probable that a fusing takes place of the analyst and patient via the superegos of each. Transference and countertransference are emotional expressions of this fusion.

If this model is accepted, then it follows that within the corporate personality there is a process of resistance and transference occurring in the whole entity; in other words, in the patient and analyst.[3] There is, however, also a process of analysis occurring in both persons, in the total entity. The process of analysis is the guarantee that there can be movement out of a locked situation. A female patient once asked me, "What guarantee have I that something in your unconscious will not block my progress? You may unconsciously envy my desire to have a baby and my capacity to have one and therefore block me subtly."

I observed that it seemed that she assumed that all the analytic power lay with me. She immediately retorted that it did not lie within her. I pointed out that she seemed to feel that if it was not in her and not in me then it did not exist at all. This linked to her view that I had possession of the process. When she began to realize that this was not so she felt grief, and realized that neither she nor I had control over the speed of development. She often said she could not move until I moved first.

For a very long time I did not understand this. Only after about three years of treatment did I suddenly realize that she meant that she could only move when an inner act of freedom had occurred within me. I had not realized at this stage that she was able to "know" when such an act occurred. She was reliant on the x-phenomenon but for a long time she had the fantasy that it was within my power to summon it at will. She became sad as it began to dawn on her that I had to wait, just as she did. So, in the corporate entity there is a shared illusion or delusion (transference–countertransference) and the shared resistance, and there is also a process that we call psychoanalysis, which fights a slow but persistent battle in both against the shared resistance and illusion. The analytic process catalyses the individual to individual existent reality. The x-phenomenon is a product of the analytic process. The latter works at a deep level, at a preverbal, primary process level. It finds its verbal expression in interpretation. Interpretation expresses this deep change and effects the final consummation of it at the conscious and manifest level. The sudden access of personal feeling in the analyst that breaks another bond of the illusory stranglehold in which both patient and analyst are held in thrall is immediately experienced by the patient and exists prior to insight. It implies a form of communication between analyst and patient that supersedes man's methods of perceiving the non-human world. The analytic procedure capitalizes on this special form of human communication.

It could be argued that what I am describing is a particular instance of projective identification, but I do not think this does justice to those psychological events which, for want of a better term, I have called the x-phenomenon. Projective identification means that feelings, which belong to the patient, are projected into the analyst and lodge there like a foreign body. What I am describing is a joint process in which the real feelings of the analyst and patient are aroused by the resistant process. The analyst's feelings are *his* feelings, even though they may have been stirred up by the patient. Patient and analyst are responsible for the feelings that are generated in the situation. Often the patient is "blamed" for feelings that are experienced by the analyst, and this is called projective identification. This type of description implies that there are only two blameable objects in the room: patient and analyst. There is a third term: the process in which both are involved.

What I have said so far may seem to contradict Freud's view that our only knowledge of the external world is through perception, mediated consciously by the ego. In nearly all Freud's writings he followed the scientific view of his day, which was that man's knowledge of his fellow man is via his senses and does not differ essentially from his knowledge of the non-human world. Before Freud formulated the structural model he ascribed this type of knowledge to consciousness and thought that the unconscious did not have *direct* access to the external world. When he came to formulate the structural model he thought that the agency whose role is to mediate the external world to the organism is the ego and that the superego and id do not have direct contact with it. Now, he does not specifically say whether he considers that this mediating role of the ego is just the conscious part of the ego, but there are two passages that contradict all his other assertions on this matter:

> I have good reason for asserting that everyone possesses in his own unconscious an instrument with which he can interpret the utterances of the unconscious in other people. [Freud 1913i, p. 320]

> It is a very remarkable thing that the *Ucs.* of one human being can react upon that of another, without passing through the *Cs.* This deserves closer investigation, especially with a view to finding out whether preconscious activity can be excluded as playing a part in it; but, descriptively speaking, the fact is incontestable. [Freud, 1915e, p. 194]

He is here talking about a special type of knowledge that exists between human beings that does not pass through the normal sense organs or through that conscious part of the personality inhabited by word presentations. This particular type of knowledge therefore antedates any interpretation that the analyst may give.[4]

That there is a special type of knowledge by which human beings know each other that is quite different from the way in which men know the physical universe was, I think, first articulated by Giambattista Vico. Until Vico, all knowledge had been divided into three different kinds: metaphysical or theological, deductive, and perceptual. Under this last category were included empirical observation and experimentation. To these three types of knowledge Vico added another: knowledge that we have of ourselves and other human beings. In the case of human beings we are not just passive observers, he said, because we have a special knowledge "from the inside", and we have a right to ask why it is that human beings act in the way they do. This type of knowledge is active and not passive because we can only know something from the inside if human beings have created it. God is, therefore, according to Vico, the one who has perfect knowledge as he is the creator of all, but in the case of the special knowledge that human beings can have of each other it is a similar type of knowledge: it is knowledge *per caussas*. But Vico has not had a great following among thinkers within the human sciences. What he asserted has been taken for granted by all great writers of prose and poetry but has not been studied seriously within the social sciences. Probably Max Weber, the sociologist, is the best-known follower of Vico's viewpoint. He distinguished between ordinary knowledge by which we know the physical universe, which he called *wissen*, and that special type of knowledge proper only to the knowledge of human beings, and this he called *verstehen*. Although this special type of knowledge has been central to clinical work in psychoanalytic practice, there does not seem to be a metapsychology to account for it. The idea that a scientist might take this type of knowledge seriously is also scorned by almost all schools of thinking within academic psychology.

Vico said that it was possible to enter into the world of past cultures "from the inside" by studying the poetry and myths that belonged to them. To gain this special type of knowledge man needs to be equipped with *fantasia*. Vico considered that this type of knowledge was superior to the knowledge that we have of the non-human world; this is because human culture has been created and can therefore be known from the inside. Now, this idea that culture is a human creation and can therefore be known from the inside can, I think, be applied to the sort of knowledge that we have of a patient in the psychoanalytic situation. Once we accept clearly that there is the "constitutional factor", or the biological given with its associated drives, then the rest of what we are concerned with is the product of human creation. What we analyse is the product of the inner fantasy life in interaction with first the mother, then the mother and father, siblings, and finally the whole social environment. Theoretically, it would be possible for all these elements to be analysed and understood. This understanding is of a special kind and arises through an act of insight that has been generated and made possible by the analytic process. We need to get some clue as to how this act of insight occurs.

Let us say I take hold of Kant's *Critique of Pure Reason* (1781) and read this statement: "If we have a proposition which contains the idea of necessity in its very conception, it is a judgement *a priori*" (p. 26), I may understand it straight away but, on the other hand, I may not. If I do not it is because I have a false idea and this blinds the intellect. I will be able to understand when I can banish the false idea and allow the idea that Kant is proposing to be grasped by my intellect. I may be quite resistant to doing so because it may mean I have to give up many fond ideas that are comfortable to my way of life or habit of mind. To understand Kant I need to adopt a passive attitude so that I can become receptive to his ideas, but I must actively be prepared to banish mine. At the moment of understanding I become Kant, as it were, through an action of ego, whereby I dispel my superego contents and because of this I remain separated and become slightly more of an individual. At the moment of understanding, activity and passivity come together and form a single psychological event.

Now, in the psychoanalytical situation, something very similar occurs. The patient's communications and the analyst's feelings and thoughts become the raw material out of which understanding arises. The analyst does not only have his own false ideas to clear away but needs to be passive to the analytical process and combating the resistance that he and the patient are locked into. The attempt to understand is being continually sabotaged by a parallel process that stimulates and fosters false ideas. Received theoretical positions may be used by the resistant process, as they may also be used by the benign psychoanalytical process. The patient and the analyst as a corporate entity are involved in these two processes. Belief in the psychoanalytical process seems to be the essential ingredient for both parties. However, it seems that it may be the special role of the analyst to carry this belief for the patient as well as for himself, especially early on in treatment.

The act of understanding is rooted in what is most personal, in the ego, but the false ideas are located in the superego. At the moment of insight, expressed in interpretation, the illusions or false ideas are banished in both analyst and patient. A personal, ego to ego, contact is established and replaces an illusion or false belief that held the two together until that time. This belief that held both together is the social glue in the microcosm that binds together the numerous communities and groupings of society. This type of togetherness is quite different from the ego-to-ego contact that occurs at particular moments in analysis. This type of contact is a revolution because new reality, new growth, begins. In fact, it is the only true revolution that does occur within human affairs, because subsequent to this personal act of understanding new concepts have to be imported into the superego in order that the latter agency can now reflect the new changes that have taken place in the ego.

In order to separate, the patient needs to get access to the analyst's core feelings. His interpretations need to flow from here to as great an extent as possible if the patient is to be able to extricate him/herself. This is most especially true for the psychotic patient whose fusion at the superego level is greatest and whose need for ego-to-ego contact is also greatest. It greatly concerned one patient whether what I said to him was what *I* thought or felt or was just a received dictum of the psychoanalytical tradition and, therefore, just a superego content. Each time a resistance was overcome it was then possible to reach further into what I truly thought or felt and then he was able to separate himself a bit more from the analyst and from his maternal object intrapsychically. My greatest problem in his analysis was to reach those feelings that were most truly mine. In the case of that patient the problem was particularly acute, but on reflection I think this may be a central problem in every analysis.

The psychoanalytical setting is concerned to foster a particular type of communication, which is demonstrated most clearly in those moments that I have called the x-phenomenon. This level of communication occurs from the very first moment when the patient enters the consulting room and with it a certain patterning of unconscious knowledge. The goal of the interpretive work is to make this conscious. At the same time there is another process at work, in both the analyst and the patient, whose goal is to sabotage the analysis. This process is located in the superego and makes use of illusions and cultural myths as its instrument. We call this process resistance, but I have wanted to emphasize that this is a system in which both analyst and patient are involved, not something that is just located in the patient. The x-phenomenon implies that there is knowledge that is preverbal and that it is anterior to speech and, therefore, to interpretation. At this level of knowledge the patient knows unconsciously the analyst's internal attitudes. If, for example, the analyst is unconsciously envious of the patient in some particular way, then the patient perceives it and only a change in the analyst's inner attitude will enable the patient to move forward psychically. The moment the analyst is freed from it, then the patient perceives it. That is to say, he or she perceives a change within the self and may make declarations to that effect without knowing the cause. The interpretations that follow the x-phenomenon become conscious articulations of a change that has already occurred unconsciously at the ego-to-ego level. The interpretations help them to re-establish the superego so that its myths and values change and become tuned into the changes that have occurred within the ego.

With the exception of Winnicott, I think that most analysts operate on the assumption that people are separate entities. I think that the x-phenomenon and the particular form of knowledge that it must imply means that people are individuals and yet part of a corporate entity. Because we are parts of a corporate entity, then as soon as analyst and patient come together in the same room there is an immediate adaptation and fusing. The corporate entity instantly establishes itself. Socially, this occurs when two people meet, but in this case ego-to-ego contact is kept to a minimum. In psychoanalysis the latter is enhanced, but only, so to speak, so as to hypercathect it and work through it, and give place to the personal.

Notes

1. This paper was published in the *International Review of Psychoanalysis* in 1983. I had given it at a Scientific Meeting of the British Psychoanalytical Society on Wednesday 5 May 1982. Before giving it I asked myself "Am I mad?", because I had not heard the thesis I was proposing put forward before, though I had heard on one occasion Herbert Rosenfeld making an anecdotal comment that suggested this line of thinking. I had in me a deep conviction that I was right but, after all, is that not what all mad people believe? What is the litmus test that will tell me whether I was mad or sane, acid or alkali? I think it is the capacity to manage or not the group's reactions to novelty. A new discovery puts a demand on the inventor to give emotional support to his dawning illumination. The fresh spring of translucent water requires from his emotional reservoir all its contents, to the very depths, if the garden beds of his personality are to burst forth with new growths. If he is not able to do this then he goes mad. I had only been an analyst for five years. I was a new boy but I had had a very intense emotional experience in the treatment of a patient who was referred after a psychotic episode. (See the paper "The patient makes the analyst".) The present paper was written much later, but contains much of the clinical interaction that led to the insights embodied in this earlier paper. This clinical experience radically altered my understanding of the psychoanalytic process. So I gave the paper on that Wednesday and I gained confidence in both the delivery of it and during the subsequent discussion. I believe that the paper had quite an impact upon those who were in attendance. It has also been reprinted twice in symposia and has quite often been quoted and referred to (e.g., Kohon, 1986; Scharff, 1996).

2. I note here that later the paper was sometimes the subject of misunderstanding. Nina Coltart gave a paper at the English Speaking Conference in London in October of the same year entitled "Slouching towards Bethlehem", in which she referred to my paper thus:

> One day, without really thinking it out clearly, I suddenly demonstrated an example of what Neville Symington has called "the analyst's act of freedom". I simply and suddenly became furious and bawled him out for his prolonged lethal attack on me and on the analysis. I wasn't going to stand for it a second longer. I shouted, without the remotest idea at that moment of what alternative I was proposing . . . [Coltart, 1982]

It has been similarly quoted by other analysts. What I refer to in my paper is the way an *inner* emotional act affects the patient. What Nina

Coltart describes here is different from what I was delineating. I was referring to an internal act that came about as the resolution of an anxiety state generated from the superego and that its inner quality was one of calmness and certainty, which was reflected also in its external manifestation. Nina Coltart, in this example, was in a highly charged emotional state. I am not making any comment about the clinical value of an intervention like Nina's, but want to point out that her emotional state and mine (*the one I described?*) were quite different.

3.   I would today stress "the personal" and would not talk of ego-to-ego contact. I would not now invoke the concept of "corporate personality", but rather invoke the reality of the infinite, the absolute, or existence itself, in which we all participate, and would contend that the personal is grounded in this. What I refer to as the superego structure I would today see as partly a hallucinatory system built to protect us from pain, especially the pain of absence. What many patients want is a personal life, a personal relationship, but the person sees things as they are whereas the hallucinated image both of the other and the self protects from the pain of absence, of not being understood, of loneliness, of shame, of guilt, and so on.

I would today see the superego, which I refer to in this paper as part of the debris thrown up by an early infantile trauma, and the kind of attachment which I refer to as "corporate personality" as an embodiment of the superego.

4.   I was at this time still working within Freud's determinist model, on to which I had pasted Vico's theory. I had no theory to explain why the analyst's act of freedom led to therapeutic change in the patient. I had a conviction that it was so from my clinical experience, but it did not fit Freud's epistemology. He believed that all knowledge came about through a processing of the senses. In this way he was in the tradition of Locke. However, as he himself says in the two quotes I give in the paper, there is a source of knowledge that bypasses this form of gaining knowledge. So, in this paper, I just quote those two passages from Freud to back up my claim but do not embed them in a theory with which they are consistent. I rely in this paper on Vico's theory as it has been passed on to us by Isaiah Berlin (1980). I do say in this paper that I think Vico's theory is a more accurate account of human communication than that of Freud, but it meant revising Freud in a fairly radical way which I had not fully grasped at that time. I have since tried to do this and I hope this may become clear as the document of this journey becomes clear.

CHAPTER FOUR

Phantasy effects that which it represents[1]

"Suspicion creates its own cause;
Distrust begets reason for distrust"

(Thompson, 1913, p. 3)

Phantasy creates a response in the social environment and this is a constituent part of it. When the social environment ceases behaving in a particular defined and familiar way then the phantasy is no more. It has passed into non-existence; it has been worked through. It no longer blocks the healthy psychological act in the subject. I am going to give some examples.

Clinical examples

A female patient had the phantasy that men just use women as objects to satisfy their sexual impulses. When psychoanalysis was recommended in the consultation she believed that the analyst just wanted to gratify his own narcissism. She had a prolonged affair with a man who lived in another country but came to London on business about once a month or once in six weeks. He used her sexually on each visit. She was furious about it but continued with the affair. After some years a moment occurred when she believed that the analyst wanted her welfare and did not only want to gratify his narcissism. She finished with her intermittent lover; she began to feel more feminine and then some time later developed a fully satisfying love affair. The phantasy that men just use women as sex objects evaporated.

A patient had a phantasy that she did not exist, or at least that she did not exist in the minds of others. She belonged to a rambling club and was going for a week to the Lake District with several other members. When she arrived at the coach terminal she discovered that the organizer had forgotten about her and had no seat marked for her on the coach. When I came to write this paper I found that I had forgotten her name and it took me some minutes to recall it, although I know her name well. The phantasy is still active; it is not dead; it has not been worked through.

From reconstructions it seems that a man had been suddenly dropped by his mother emotionally when still a young baby. It left him with the feeling that he was worthless, that he must be someone who was fit only for the rubbish heap. He worked in a bank where people dumped all the humdrum jobs on to him. For the first year of analysis he expected me to say he was not worth treating and he would have accepted it with a shrug of the shoulder. On one occasion the bank invited him to give a speech after an important dinner. He had carefully prepared the speech when, an hour before he was due to leave for it, the organizer rang him and said that he hoped he did not mind but he had asked someone else to make the speech instead of him. Evidently he acceded in a nonchalant tone. I might mention that he had come for analysis partly because his wife was exasperated because he repeatedly missed promotion. People used to refer to him as "Good old Tom", who was always obliging on all occasions. As the analysis proceeded, this phantasy that he was a worthless piece of rubbish began to recede. At work people no longer referred to him as "Good Old Tom". One day he overheard a secretary at work saying to one of his colleagues, "I wouldn't ask Tom to organize the Christmas party this year. He's been bloody-minded recently." He was promoted at work and received recognition in his career. The light of the phantasy is not extinguished, but it is much dimmer.

A patient has a very powerful superego. He is exceedingly inhibited. He feels that he is very damaging and murderous. His defence against this is to be very obliging, always willing to be helpful and afraid of causing any inconvenience. It became clear in the analysis that he was destructive and damaging to those around him. He murdered their own individual feelings. The feelings of others were mercilessly shut out. I have a large oval table by the door of my consulting room and on it are a few *objets d'art*. He had been coming to me for two years, then one day as he walked into the consulting room I noticed his head jink in the direction of the table. When he lay on the couch he said, "Is that new? I have never seen it before." It was symbolical of the intensity with which he had obliterated me as an individual with my own feelings. When his son had his twenty-first birthday he turned to his father and said to him that he had destroyed his life. The phantasy continued to be active but was less strong than it had been at the beginning of treatment.

Nature and definition of phantasy

The phantasies I have described block development; they are destructive to the subject and to others. They are destructive of healthy development in both the subject and in the other. In the first case of the woman having a sexual affair with the man from abroad, the phantasy was destructive of her own potential for love, emotional closeness and feminine creative capacity. At the same time it fostered in the man the idea that women are just sex objects. In the second case of the girl who had the phantasy that she did not exist, her resentment towards those who disregarded her, like the organizer of the rambling club holiday, prevented that harmony with others which is essential to the development of the life force. One can assume that, in the club organizer, it favoured his narcissistic view that existence was centred in him and not in the other. In the third case of the man with the phantasy that he was worthless, it blocked development in the particular field in which he had great expertise because so much of his energy went into accomplishing the humdrum tedious jobs that colleagues at the office dumped upon him. At the same time it encouraged the notion in his work colleagues that they were more worthwhile than others, and gave strength to their sadistic impulses. In the fourth case of the man with the powerful superego, his phantasy of damaging others so mutilated his own feelings that he had no basis of confidence in himself, so he could never take a step forward and remained stuck, and it also encouraged others to abrogate their own responsibility and individual feelings so that growth was stunted in them as well as in him. So these phantasies have the function of blocking development both in the patient and in those closely involved with him or her. This may be because the phantasies have been summoned into the service of a destructive, anti-life force. This brings us to the second feature of these phantasies, which is their static quality.

A phantasy of the kind described is immobile. It is like a photograph that sits on the mantelpiece and never changes. It is not a living, changing reality. There is an analogy between such a phantasy and a fanatical belief. It resides in the personality but creates the social environment to conform to its stasis. Its capacity to mould the social environment to a static image or representation is an essential part of the phantasy. If it loses that capacity the phantasy crumbles and vanishes. This fixed static phantasy screens the ego from change. It throttles what lies in potency within the individual. By the phrase "in potency" I mean the special way in which the oak tree can be said to exist already in the acorn. For the acorn to send out a shoot it must have access to soil, water, and sunlight. The phantasy is like a barrier that prevents sunlight or water reaching the acorn. It prevents the life force reaching those elements that can make it flourish. It therefore absorbs into its structure the defences. When the analyst makes an interpretation that gets through the defence and makes contact with a living nucleus he can then observe something beginning to move in the personality. The locus of the phantasy is in the individual and in the group.

Phantasy is real, though it is a strange type of reality. Its reality is similar to the reality of a dream or a hallucination. Freud named this "psychic reality". Susan Isaacs (1952) has stressed that phantasy should not be contrasted to reality in such a way that it is thought not to have existence:

> Again, the word "phantasy" has often been used to mark a contrast to "reality", the latter word being taken as identical with "external"

or "material" or "objective" facts. But when external reality is thus called "objective" reality, this makes an implicit assumption which denies to psychical reality its *own objectivity as a mental fact*. Some analysts tend to contrast "phantasy" with "reality" in such a way as to undervalue the dynamic importance of phantasy. A related usage is to think of "phantasy" as something "merely" or "only" imagined, as something unreal, in contrast with what is actual, what *happens* to one. This kind of attitude tends towards a depreciation of psychical reality and of the significance of mental processes *as such*. [p. 81]

Her emphasis on the fact that phantasy has an existence and is therefore real is crucial, but I think that defining phantasy as a *mental* fact conjures up the idea that its locus is situated within the boundaries of an individual's mind. It also assumes that the mind is a separate entity to the body.

The mind–body problem has been the subject of passionate debate since the time of Aristotle and Plato. It may be assumed that the philosophical position that someone takes on this matter has no bearing on clinical work, but I believe that this is not the case. For instance, if an analyst has a Platonic view of the relation between mind and body he will tend to collude at some level with the obsessional, who so strongly repudiates bodily functions and impulses like defecating or a desire for comfort. Aristotle had the view (and this was further elaborated by Thomas Aquinas in the thirteenth century) that the psyche, the anima, or the soul was the principle which endowed the individual with all his or her characteristics from the colour of hair to the smell of faeces to the most abstract reasoning and cultural strivings. At no point did the mental exist independently from bodily happenings. My clinical experience leads me to endorse this viewpoint. I do not think that even the most abstract thought takes place independently of some bodily registration. Therefore, the most secret thought is picked up or is capable of being picked up, even though unconsciously, by someone attuned to the person who executes the so-called inner act. In the psychoanalytical situation the patient is frequently just so attuned to the analyst.

Konrad Lorenz tells of an instance where his parrot was just so attuned. Whenever he was leaving his sitting-room to go out of the house his parrot gave a particular squawk, so he then *pretended* to be going out of the house but the parrot did not squawk. He even took the pretence to the extent that he put on his overcoat and hat and left the room but the parrot did not squawk. Only when he was *actually* leaving the house did the parrot squawk. He never discovered what the subtle cue was that enabled the parrot to distinguish the true exit from the fraudulent one. I can think of several cases where a patient has registered a thought that I thought was quite private. I have also supervised trainees who would tell me that they were planning this or that but then hastened to add, "But of course I did not say anything to my patient about it", but then it was perfectly clear from the clinical material that followed that it had been picked up by the patient. So it is not only that the mental does not exist as a solitary realm but also that the psychic acts of one individual cross the boundaries of his own personal space to that of another.

In line with this thinking, therefore, the phantasy is an entity that stretches from the innermost parts of the psychosomatic entity of one across and into the object area of the other. Psychic reality is different from a wooden table or a hippopotamus, but it is not solely mental. Phantasy coheres in a communication system between people and derives its power from the fact that it draws its sustaining energy from a source deep in the personality structure of two people (or more than two) in communication with each other. The phantasy has its roots deep in the personality but, for that very reason, is pervasive on the surface of the personality. Defences then become the manifest aspects of the phantasy. The patient who expected me to say he was not worth treating, and whose after-dinner speech was cancelled at the last moment, was behaving defensively and hid the fact that there was a worthwhile core of him, but the external nonchalant shrug of the shoulders that says, "If you tell me that I am not worthwhile treating then that's fine by me", comes from a deep phantasy that he is just a piece of rubbish. So the phantasy pervades the external representation of the person-ality and crosses the boundary of the individual to the other, so the deep unconscious phantasy exists in the most open manifest levels of the communication system between people. The phantasy is active and creates its own response. It is particularly this point that I want to focus upon.

The phantasy has the power to create that which it *imagines.* In the first case the phantasy that men merely view women as sex objects is imagined inwardly and created outwardly. The phantasy creates that which it imagines. In the second case the girl who has the phantasy that she does not exist finds that the club organizer has forgotten her existence and so has not allocated a seat for her on the coach and her analyst finds that he has forgotten her name. This raises the interesting question "How does the phantasy create that which it imagines?" I wish I knew the answer to that question. The only formulation I can give it is that the phantasy has the power to stimulate the areas of potential phantasy in both actors, to use a sociological term. It is able to keep its life going through the fact that there is a supply of readily available victims.

Smallpox can only exist if there is always a ready supply of non-vaccinated hosts that it can continue its life in. If a stage is reached when all human beings are vaccinated, then the smallpox virus perishes off the face of the earth, as it almost has done. In other words, the phantasy has to have available non-vaccinated people, or, in other words, areas in people that are susceptible to its stimulation. To keep in being, a phantasy has to find in each person an area susceptible to its stimulation. These stimulations that emanate from the phantasy and find their source in it are very subtle and are usually below the threshold of awareness. We shall come to this again when considering some of the clinical consequences in the next section. The phantasy in the man who thought he was a worthless piece of rubbish created a consonant response in the bank organizer who cancelled his after dinner speech. The man who had a phantasy that he was very damaging effected what he imagined and feared, and his son told him that he had ruined his life for him.

Now I want to attempt to define phantasy: phantasy is a psychic reality located intrapsychically within the preverbal human communication system, whose goal is to muffle truth and throttle development. I want now to pass on to the clinical repercussions germane to this way of conceptualizing phantasy.

Clinical consequences

The analyst is not in the position of the person who has been vaccinated against the smallpox virus. He or she has areas that are susceptible to the subtle stimulation of the phantasy. I think it likely that whenever an analysis is "stuck" it is because the analyst and patient are victims of a particular phantasy that stimulates both of them. In the analyst there are areas that are susceptible to particular stimulation. In a paper written by Steiner (1982) he describes how he was susceptible to just such stimulation.

> There were in fact many occasions when I failed to stay sufficiently in touch to make him feel understood, especially I think at those times when I could not resist clever, witty interactions with him which I think he experienced as me abandoning his real needs to collude in a perverse way and gratify *my* narcissism. [p. 248]

Jung (1935) particularly has stressed the way in which patients are adept at finding precisely those points of greatest vulnerability in the analyst:

> The emotions of patients are always slightly contagious, and they are very contagious when the contents which the patient projects into the analyst are identical with the analyst's own unconscious contents. Then they both fall into the same dark hole of unconsciousness, and get into the condition of participation . . . You probably all know certain patients who possess a diabolical cunning in finding out the weak spot, the vulnerable place in the analyst's psyche. To that spot they seek to attach the projections of their own unconscious. One usually says that it is a characteristic of women, but that is not true, men do just the same. They always find out this vulnerable spot in the analyst, and he can be sure that, whenever something gets into him, it will be exactly in that place where he is without defence. That is the place where he is unconscious himself and where he is apt to make exactly the same projections as the patient. Then the condition of participation happens, or, more strictly speaking, a condition of personal contamination through mutual unconsciousness. [pp. 140–141]

Here is a clear expression of the notion that the phantasy finds a host area in the analyst. A point that I have made in a previous paper (1983)[2] is that interpretations sitting on the base of an active phantasy will not be effective and that the analyst has to become free of the contaminating phantasy. This is the prime way in which the analytic setting becomes contaminated. The phantasy stimulates part of the object area of the analyst's mind and then his or her attitudes receive their colouring from this underlying base. Fundamentally, this means that interpretations rooted in this structure become slanted in an anti-developmental direction. Klauber (1968) has stressed that analysts are not free in their inner acts of judgement. He makes the point in his paper "The psychoanalyst as person":

> In practice it is difficult for the psychoanalyst, when confronted with the imminence of a decisive choice by the patient, not to find that his own system of values inevitably comes into operation. For example, a woman suffering from sexual inhibition was married to a successful husband who suffered from severe unreliability in respect of both his sexual function and many aspects of his character. The result of her first analysis in another country was to give her greater freedom of sexual expression, but she could obtain no satisfaction from her husband, and she started a liaison with a man of lower social class. The first psychoanalyst's interpretations were directed toward stopping the liaison, which was rightly regarded as an acting out of transference fantasies. At this stage it became necessary for the husband's career that the couple should move to England. The patient began a second analysis and commented early that the second analyst's view of the liaison was quite different from that of the first. While he agreed that it expressed transference fantasies, his interpretations acknowledged the increase in the ego's capacity for decision which had accompanied the liberation of her sexuality and sympathized with her need for sexual fulfilment. [pp. 131–132]

Interpretations always have a direction, but I want to add to Klauber's point by saying that the values that give psychological orientation to interpretations may themselves sit upon a base constructed of phantasy. In the first case of the girl who was having the intermittent affair with the man from abroad, I interpreted for a long while from the angle that this was self-destructive behaviour. Then one day I said to myself that after all it was her life and although I did not feel that it was a very satisfactory form of living, if she wished to live it in that particular mode then it was her choice. In other words, I let go of a possessiveness that the patient had been stimulating. Once this had occurred the patient shortly gave up this affair and sometime later started a more fulfilling and satisfying relationship. That patient, before she could engage in a fulfilling love affair, needed to know that her analyst was able to allow her the freedom to make her own emotional liaisons, which was something which neither she nor her mother had been able to allow.

It seems that in cases like these the analyst needs to overcome in him or herself that area that is accessible to the stimulation of phantasy. This analytical task antedates techniques of interpretation. This stimulation can be very subtle and, in the case of the patient whose name I forgot, it is to this day not clear, or at least not clear enough for an accurate interpretation to emerge. In the case of the man who perpetually shut out my table in the consulting room, I found that I was colluding with the phantasy by not forcing in front of his eyes facts that he knew or that he at least thought about. My colluding with the phantasy was favoured in his case by the analytical value that the patient is anyhow not supposed to know certain facts. When I once pointed out to the patient that he was pushing away some facts that he knew, he replied that my way of behaving had given him the idea that he was not supposed to know these facts and had therefore pushed them away. Only when this phantasy began to be laid to rest did this patient begin to come in touch with his own feelings and to gain some confidence in his life.

It takes me a very long time to become aware of these subtle stimulations. The only way I know to come to this awareness is the method used by Charcot and so admired by Freud (1893f), "He used to look again and again at the things he did not understand, to deepen his impression of them day by day, till suddenly an understanding of them dawned upon him" (p. 12).

The analytical process working in the unconscious of patient and analyst breaks through in the form of insight after months or years of staring at the clinical phenomenon. I think this must be one of the factors differentiating psychoanalysis from psychodynamic psychotherapy. The deeper the phantasy, the more all-pervasive it is on the surface; the more the analyst is subject to the phantasy, then the longer it takes before the moment of insight is arrived at. I think the awareness of this kind of phantasy is likely to be obstructed by interpreting everything because emotional space is necessary for it to occur. The psychological mode most favourable in the analyst is that of reverie or free-floating attention. Through reverie he makes contact with the analytical process, which ultimately unseats the phantasy from its tenacious hold in the object area of the patient and analyst. The state of not seeing, prior to insight, is actively fostered by the phantasy. The psychological insight finally dispels the phantasy, but it takes a long period of gestation during which there needs to be emotional time and emotional space.

The phantasy does not exist just in the patient or just in the analyst, but is in the communication system between the two. The clinical consequence of this is that interpretations focusing on the agency of the patient or that of the analyst are not reflecting the truth. It is not possible here to discuss the origins of phantasy, but it will become clear from the drift of this paper that the phantasy does not originate either in the mother (or mother and father) or in the child, but has arisen in the communication system between parents and child. This has an influence on the orientation of interpretations in that a situation is not seen as the result of what the mother has done towards the child or vice versa, but as the result of both activities in the phantasy.

My clinical experience tells me that most patients come in a struggle to get free from the throttling phantasy. A recognition of this gives strength to the healthy side of the personality and helps it to overcome the phantasy. If the analyst is being stimulated by the phantasy then it leads to persecutory interpretations. This is a sign that he is under the stimulation of the phantasy. An instance of this is clearly described in Kohut's (1979) paper, "The two analyses of Mr Z". In the first analysis of Mr Z, Kohut describes how he interpreted according to the tenets of classical theory. He viewed the patient as the centre of his own independent initiative and as wanting to hold on to his own childish gratifications. In the second analysis some years later, his focus was on the patient's struggle to disentangle himself from a noxious self-object. In the first analysis his interpretations were condemnatory, and when the patient came for a consultation again some four and a half years after the termination of the first analysis, Kohut realized that the neurosis had only been displaced into a different sphere. It had temporarily been driven underground but was now reappearing again. In the first analysis the interpretive schema was under the dominance of phantasy; the stimulation of the phantasy was on the side of an anti-life force, although he had a dignified theoretical heritage to support what he was saying. Phantasy can make use of any theory for its purposes.

The other important area for clinical work is the recognition that the phantasy is active and effects what it imagines or represents. In other words, the patient's collusion with the phantasy is really effecting his social world. This effects the way in which the analyst executes his interpretations. A patient was describing how she was not going to visit her family for Christmas. From previous associations the analyst realized that this was due to her fear of damaging her family, and so said, "You consider not going to your family for Christmas because you have a phantasy that you may damage your family"; but in this statement there is the implication that this is just in the imaginative inner world and that in fact no damage is being done. After supervision the analyst altered this statement to "You are not going to your family for Christmas because you sense that you are doing something damaging to them".

This is an illustration of Susan Isaacs' point about the reality aspect of phantasy. In the patient's relation with the analyst, it means that there is important work to be done aside from interpretation. This other work might be called the analyst's psychological stance in relation to the patient. This psychological stance is the product of the psychological process and rests on that rather than on phantasy. When interpretations rest on phantasy instead, then analysis does not really take place. More important then than interpretations is the analyst's task of overcoming the activity of phantasy. If the analyst allows the patient to deprive him, exploit him, bore him, attack his thinking, pressure him, then it is this activity that needs to be tackled. Only when the phantasy ceases to create that which it represents does it collapse. Phantasy has this strange quality that when it collapses it seems to vanish as when a soap bubble pops, but while it is active it is real enough. Both aspects of this strange phenomenon need to be grasped in the clinical encounter. The giving of interpretations without overcoming the phantasy will not produce lasting psychic change, though it might produce the appearance of it. I want now to pass on to some theoretical considerations.

Theoretical implications

The thesis of this paper is that phantasy has an active force that effects that which it imagines or represents. But phantasy is in the object part of the personality, so there seems to be some contradiction. This section is an attempt to resolve it.

The human psyche is made up of a subject part and an object part. There is the subject that acts, which we call the ego, or, in English, that which is denoted by the personal pronoun "I". Then there is the object part of the personality. Internal objects, good objects, bad objects, persecutory objects, introjects, "parts of the self", projected parts, the external world, the past and the future, are all constituents of the object aspect of the psyche. The subject, the ego, is in the present and is the source of actions. This would seem to be in contradiction to the way I have been speaking about phantasy in this paper. I have spoken as if phantasy is its own source of action. This is true, and I have spoken of a part of the self acting autonomously. I think a truer way of conceptualizing the matter is to consider that a part of the personality can only act, as if with its own ego, if the ego will agree to it. The object part of the personality is like a businessman who can only set up a new company and market a new product as long as the bank manager remains friendly and will guarantee an ongoing loan. The ego loans, as it were, some of its subject-energy or libido-energy to different parts of the personality. Now, in this sense phantasy is located in the object part of the personality, but can only exist provided that the ego continues to supply ego–libido and also a host object in another personality. To return to the simile of the businessman, he needs not only a guaranteed loan from the bank manager but also the good will of a local borough council that will agree to his factory, offices, and marketing to take place within its boundaries. Without the cooperation of both the bank manager and the borough council the scheme evaporates. When we use the term "unconscious phantasy" it means that the ego is loaning its energy, which only it can provide. (It is the sole agency in the personality that is possessor of ego–libido.) And the bank manager and the borough council are in cooperative activity together so that when the borough council withdraws its permission for the businessman's activities, then immediately the bank manager withdraws overdraft facilities. As soon as the phantasy has no hold in a host object it collapses. The psychoanalyst cannot alter the ego's policy by attacking it, but only by removing himself from the position of being a host to the phantasy's activity.

I have used the word "phantasy: in a pejorative sense through-out this paper. It is, therefore, closely allied to the concept of a bad internal object. It differs from it, however, in that "phantasy" is not only internal. The bad internal object is the imagined representation of the phantasy. It is logically separable, but not really, because with the collapse of phantasy so also the bad object collapses. What, then, is the difference between activity fostered by good objects and the activity characteristic of phantasy?

I approach this question by reflecting on my own subjective experience, especially when exposed to a patient in analysis with me. When I am under the dominance of phantasy I feel worried, I am in a state of some unease, some sense that all is not right, know-ing that I am not understanding, feeling that I have been obtuse, that I have made some interpretation that has upset the patient. It is a state of anxiety that is related directly to a particular patient (though I may not be aware of this locus) and the fundamental sense is that I am not properly in touch with the patient. There is a sense that something is coming between me and the patient, that something is blocking contact.

I think that in this subjective experience there are two crucial elements: the feeling of *not* being in contact with the patient, and that there is some interference that is *extraneous* to my ego and that of the patient. There is a sense that the ego has been scooped into some alliance with something that is not true to its nature. And in this sense the bad object appears to have ego characteristics in that it seems to have some source of action that is able to lure ego–libido into its service. The bad object as a constituent of phantasy has this same twilight quality. It seems to be an object and yet to have no ego characteristics. Yet, when the ego is able to "work through" the phantasy, it collapses and passes into non-existence. But while operative it is destructive, so much so that it can lead to suicide. It has the power to throttle truth and block development and yet seems to vanish into non-existence. Good internal objects are quite different.

The good object does not have this extraneous quality. It is felt to reside in the ego, give it substance, and be identified with it so that it is not felt to be alien to the ego. It is identified with that centre of the ego that is truthfully open in the social communication system. Under the influence of the good object the ego can act freely. Also, the ego is brought into direct communication with that free centre of the ego of the other. A direct emotional contact is established. In these two ways the good object is the opposite to the bad object that is the representative constituent of the phantasy. The psychoanalytic process endorses the development driven by the good objects. It is a process that is deeper than the phantasy level of operation and at the same time it is expressed on the surface and carries across the boundaries of the self and makes contact with the other, but in the area of the other marked out by the centre of the ego. Psychoanalysis is a process that operates at this direct ego-to-ego level. It is a process that renders insight and is absolutely essential for living. When this process breaks down, the individual's psychological equilibrium is hampered and he or she experiences symptoms and distress.

When this situation arises in the modern city, the person may consult the expert who specializes in pathologies of this function. We call these experts psychoanalysts. I once had a patient from a working-class background who prided himself on the knowledge of himself and the world that he had achieved through insights derived from formal psychoanalysis. Then one day he came to his session in a state of great surprise to find that his father, who was a commissionaire in a large firm in the City, had such insight and perspicacity without psychoanalysis. It was a shock to him to realize that he had come to formal psychoanalysis because he was defective in this function whereas in his father it seemed to be reasonably intact. It was a source of envy in him. It is the cripples who come for formal psychoanalysis, not the healthy. There is no doubt that this function is absolutely essential if the individual is to survive in the modern city. It is this process which is interfered with by phantasy. Phantasy locks the psyche into a rigid, unadaptable formation and becomes anti-developmental when one phantasy does not give way to another. Especially today, with the rapidity of social change, to be stuck in a particular mode is to spell psychological disaster.

Most of my patients have a veneer of sophistication but, after a little analysis, it is clear that they are fixated in a complex of quite traditional values and attachments and have been unable to make the transition necessary to live happily in the modern city. The analytical process moves through using good objects as its counters.

The good objects to the analytic process are as the internal combustion engine is to the motorcar. Formal psychoanalysis re-establishes the quality of the good objects or moves them from potential existence to actual existence.

Phantasy is an active process and it effects that which it represents. How does its activity work? How does it effect that which it represents? How is it that an analyst feels uneasy in a session? How is that feeling generated? What is passing between the patient and the analyst and how does it occur? I take it for granted that I *feel* something although nothing may have been said. It must mean that the feeling registers the presence of a particular form of existence. I cannot see it otherwise than that the object areas of the two personalities come into contact and this contact is registered as feeling. When feeling is a constituent of phantasy, it seems that this is only possible on condition that there is narcissism residing in the object part of the personality. It is while the host personality bears the same culture that the phantasy can find a place. I can only say that then there is a merging, and in that state of affairs the activity of the phantasy has a fertile arena in which to operate. We are not surprised that the phantasy can be operative within one individual. It should not surprise us that, through narcissism, which obliterates "otherness", it can operate in two. The feeling that occurs when the contact is made via a good object in the other to the ego is not that of anxiety but emotional satisfaction.

Phantasy is a strange phenomenon within the human condition. It exists, but can pass into non-existence. It blocks development and throttles truth. It seems to be intrinsic to human nature and yet is extraneous. Psychoanalysis sets out to overcome its destructive aims.

Notes

1. This paper was published in the *International Journal of Psychoanalysis* (*66*: 349–357) in 1985. I had previously given it at a Scientific Meeting of the British Psychoanalytical Society on Wednesday 18 January 1984. This was eighteen months after I had given the "Act of freedom" paper. It has never, unlike the latter paper, been reprinted in any symposium or caught the interest or imagination of analysts or

psychotherapists. None the less it is, I believe, just as important, though perhaps less dramatic in its statement.

2.   See Chapter Three, "The analyst's act of freedom".

CHAPTER FIVE

Maturity and interpretation as joint therapeutic agents

"I always have a distrust of something I can do easily"

(Henry Moore, in Jones, 1966, p. 93)

In a previous paper (1983) I said that an inner act of freedom on the part of the analyst led to beneficial changes in the patient. One analyst was very critical of this as she felt it devalued interpretation. This has led me to study more closely the relation between the emotional state in which acts of freedom take place and interpretation. I shall call this emotional state "maturity". Maturity is not to be understood as an achieved state of affairs but a developmental process that is named by its final cause.

To say that maturity in the analyst leads to therapeutic change in the patient is threatening, because when an analyst is blocked, it implies there is underdevelopment in the analyst that frustrates the process. It means that the analyst has to wait for the maturational process in him to develop. The analyst is subordinate to this process and is not in possession of it. This can be galling to self-esteem. He feels particularly under pressure when a patient is attacking him for his immaturity. Much aggression from patients is attributable to their perception of real areas of diminishment in the analyst. I believe it is a mistake to ascribe it too readily to transference. An analysis is central to a psychoanalyst's formation because its goal is to liberate the patient from fixations so that the maturational process can develop unhindered. Analytic societies recognize that this is necessary in an analyst because his or her therapeutic work is deficient without it. Yet, despite this, interpretation is thought by many to be the central agent of change, but logically there is an inconsistency here. I believe that there are two reasons for this inconsistency. First, there is a resistance to the truth that maturity is an agent of change, and second, there is a desire to stress the importance of interpretation. In this paper I want to look at this resistance and explore the reasons why interpretation is so important.

If maturity is an agent of change then the analyst is subservient to the process. It is humbling to know that the instrument that effects change is not in our possession. Self-esteem is closely linked to professional skill and mastery of a craft. For an analyst it is inextricably linked to his or her relation to the maturational process and greed, envy, or impatience can interfere with it. It is always precarious. The analyst can never say, "I have it." Yet, if it is true that our professional competence and even livelihood depends upon psychical realities that are never certain, it is not surprising that we resist such a conclusion. It is very uncomfortable to live with lack of certainty, yet, in this regard, I think the analyst's lot is the same as that of the artist, writer, or composer. The practice of analysis is a creative art rather than a craft, and like all true art is intimately dependent upon moral qualities.

If maturity is an essential ingredient of therapeutic change then I think this conclusion is resisted for another reason. An analyst can never have the maturational factors necessary for the requirements of all his or her patients. In a consultation a patient will nearly always make it clear that he or she needs the analyst particularly to possess a certain quality. One patient made it obvious that her mother and a past therapist had been frightened of her. It was essential for her that her new analyst should not be afraid of her; "My bark is worse than my bite," she said, showing that it appeared from her external behaviour and presentation that she was dangerous but that she did not actually harm. Another patient showed in consultation how much he was able to get under people's skin and that it was essential for him not to meet a paranoid response. With some patients it will be required of the analyst that he or she develop if the needs of the patient are to be met. This places a considerable psychological burden upon the analyst. I think it is the most challenging and yet rewarding aspect of an analyst's work. Again it is a moral quality that is being required of the analyst and, therefore, he or she cannot be certain that it can be met.

It is made more difficult by the fact that there are institutions and establishments whose job it is to teach people how to psychoanalyse or do analytic therapy. They cannot teach people the maturational process, but they can teach theory and suggest interpretations. This reinforces an inner wish to believe that interpretations are the central agents of change, but this is not so.

Another major reason why the notion that the maturational process is itself an agent of change is resisted is because it lifts a central element in psychoanalysis out of the consulting room into the maelstrom of daily life. I cannot claim as an analyst that I am the sole possessor of the maturational process. It is a psychological process happening in all mankind. It means that psychological healing is one of the spontaneous effects of human relationships. Initially, I find it unnerving to discover that my window-cleaner can have a therapeutic effect on a friend of his when I have undergone a ten-year training to acquire just this very quality. Harold Searles (1975) has said that a psychotherapeutic striving is innate in all men. And we all know that healing work goes on spontaneously among human beings. Psychoanalysis taps a natural resource and refines it for the benefits it confers just as an agricultural zoologist will breed a certain type of mallard duck so that it will provide more meat than the wild variety. In other words, it is the artificial cultivation of elements already existing in the social environment. Although considerable expertise has gone into the cultivation of this personal skill, it is disconcerting when we discover examples of native therapeutic ability that surpass our own.

Another related reason is that if change in others can be attributed to the maturational process itself then responsibility for the wellbeing of others is transported out of the consulting room into all other spheres of social and professional life. The destructive character of another puts a challenge to change upon me just as it does in the consulting room. I will give two examples of this, but each reader will be able to provide others. In marital therapy a couple complained of the sulky nature of their daughter. For instance, when the parents had made an effort to give her a nice time then at the end of the day she would ask if she could stay up for the dinner party when some friends of the parents were coming. The parents would say "no", and then the little nine-year-old girl would sulk and say she had not enjoyed the day. The parents would remonstrate and say how selfish she was, and so on. In the marital therapy sessions it became clear that the parents were provoked by this spoilt self-indulgent behaviour partly because they were guilty about self-indulgent aspects of themselves. On each occasion when this happened they became roused and, in a sense, the daughter knew she had got under their skin. Then the parents saw this clearly and made a resolve between themselves not to be roused on future occasions. They did this and checked each other when one saw that the other was about to lose control. They just demonstrated an impervience to the girl's sulky taunts. By the end of the week they noticed that their daughter's behaviour had changed markedly and, what is more, it remained as a constant in her character.

The other example was told to me by a friend who is a banker, to whom I was explaining this notion of mine. He told me that in his bank there were factions who were differentiated according to differing attitudes to investment policies. There was one very difficult man who was in charge of investors in Britain from the Middle East. This man would rouse people to a fury because, from the way he talked and especially from the way he criticized the board of directors, it was clear that he was implying that the bank had been very foolish not to have appointed him on to the board. As a result of these innuendoes that he was constantly making he roused his work colleagues to paroxysms of fury. They ostracized him, and on each occasion that this man was slighted he took revenge in subtle ways and ways that were not so subtle. When my friend joined the bank he found he was roused to fury just like the rest, and he could not bear this man. However, one day he was talking to this *bête noir* of his, who preened himself with a self-complacent smile. My friend could not bear it but at the same moment he had a disturbing flash of insight into himself. He saw a self-complacent side of himself that he was quite horrified to experience. From this moment he was able to enter into more friendly relations with this man. By managing to come to terms with a narcissistic part of himself he was able to tolerate his work colleague with greater equanimity. On one or two significant occasions after this moment of insight the man was about to embark on a destructive and provocative course of action when this friend of mine was able to humour him out of it. He was able to do this because he was no longer so hateful towards the self-complacent component of his character and through this more tolerant attitude the man experienced himself as more accepted. These are just two examples, but I hope sufficient to illustrate the maturational process outside the consulting room.

At this point someone might fairly ask whether the maturational process is enough of itself. Is there any need of interpretation? I have no doubt that there is and that it is crucial in any psycho-analysis. It first needs to be said that in the two examples quoted, although there were no statements which an analyst would call an interpretation, there were communications that demonstrated a changed tone and attitude that one might call "foetal interpreta-tions", i.e., not fully born interpretations but nevertheless on the way to becoming so.

An interpretation, conjoined to the maturational process, is heal-ing because it is a creative act. I will try to explain what I mean. In an interpretation there is something that is put into words. This "something" is an emotional happening that begins to be seen either dimly or clearly. This is a mental act. The work of putting this into words is a creative act. It is something that the analyst has to *do*. Sometimes, when a patient has complained that I only talk but do not *do* anything for him, he is rightly remonstrating because he is not experiencing this creative activity from me. There is an anal-ogy between painting and making interpretations. The artist sees something and then he transposes this act of seeing on to the canvas. The result on the canvas brings other aspects of himself to bear, other than just the seeing. His motor skills, his colour sense, and so on all come into play. It is not true to say that the finished painting is as the artist sees it. It is what the artist is able to create from what he sees with the medium at his disposal. In a similar way the analyst sees something in the emotional field and goes about transposing what he has seen into words. Frequently he will not be able to make that transposition for a long time. The analyst is frequently not satisfied with his result, though sometimes he will be. It is this personal creative act that is therapeutic. It is so because the patient knows that it is the product of an emotional experience that has been generated by himself and the analyst and this sense of mutuality is healing and helps to build an inner sense of trust in the self. There is considerable personal struggle in creative work and the patient develops respect for the fact that this is being done for him. Also, the finished product, the interpretation, has an emotional impact upon the patient and the patient comes to try and change the structure of his emotional responses.

Yet interpretations have their root in the maturational process. In the absence of the maturational process there are words that look like interpretations but are not. When the painting is studied closely it is discovered to be only a clever reproduction. A psychoanalysis demands that the maturational process be converted constantly into interpretations. It is the conjoint activity of the two that makes an analysis.

*   *   *

Commentary

The core of this paper argues for something that I have only come to implement about twenty years later. It is that an interpretation is the transferring of my own emotional experience into language. What I refer to as a reproduction rather than the original is when the analyst acts a borrowed part rather than do this personal creative work. Today I believe that communication rather than interpretation is the essence of the psychoanalytic process. What I have referred to in this article as "maturity", or the emotional state of the analyst, is also the foundation-stone of communication. First, the transferring of emotional experience into language is communication within the self, but, at the same time, to the other as well. It is a sharing of one's own personal emotional life with another and that is healing.

PART III

THE INFLUENCE FROM TREATING PSYCHOPATHS AND THE MENTALLY HANDICAPPED

Introduction

"Does one who has been all but lost in a pit of darkness complain of the sweet air and the daylight? There is a way of looking at our life daily as an escape, and taking the quiet return of morn and evening—still more the star-like out-glowing of some pure fellow-feeling, some generous impulse breaking our inward darkness—as a salvation that reconciles us to hardship"

(Eliot, 1976, p. 866)

A psychoanalyst is formed by his own experience of being analysed, his experiences of analysing others, and through thinking and self-reflection upon these experiences. I have already indicated the influence of being analysed by John Klauber and the experience of having a psychotic patient in analysis. The three papers "The analyst's act of freedom as agent of therapeutic change", "Phantasy effects that which it represents", and "Maturity and interpretation as joint therapeutic agents" were attempts at extrapolating from those experiences. The next three papers chart further experiences that have been influential. There is great emphasis within the psychoanalytic movement upon thought and reflection upon experience, but I believe not enough is spoken or written about experience itself. It is, I believe, life-enhancing to plunge into some more extreme experiences, frightening though these may be, as they open the personality to new areas within. These areas that lie dormant are beckoned into life, endowing the personality with new vitality. The first two of these experiences, working with psychopaths and the mentally handicapped, occurred in London.

While I was doing my psychoanalytic training I held a position as psychotherapist at Grendon Prison in Buckinghamshire. It was a psychiatric prison whose governor was a psychiatrist. Consequently, I spent time endeavouring to understand the mind of the psychopath. I read Edward Glover's book *The Roots of Crime*, Freud's *Criminals from a Sense of Guilt*, and some of Melanie Klein's references to this subject. Although I found these helpful, I felt none of them had put their finger on the central problem. Then one day I read for the first time Emily Brontë's *Wuthering Heights*. It blew my mind apart as I thought that Emily had understood the soul of the psychopath better than any psychoanalyst whom I had read. It so happened that, shortly after, I was asked to give a paper at a day's symposium at the Institute of Psychoanalysis in London called *The Mind of the Criminal*, and at this I gave the paper entitled "The response aroused by the psychopath". This was in 1979. The other two participants were Dr Hyatt Williams and Dr Mervin Glasser, and the day was chaired by Mrs Edna O'Shaughnessy. Later I submitted the paper to the *International Review for Psychoanalysis* and it was published in 1980. It is a paper that has been noted a few times by forensic psychiatrists and has been reprinted in a book called *The Mark of Cain* (Moloy, 2001).

Many years later in Australia, on a day's symposium on psychological aspects of crime, I gave a further paper on the subject of criminality entitled "The origins of rage and aggression" (Symington, 1996a) and, as it is of a piece with the paper on psychopathy, I have included it here.

The experience of working with psychopaths at an early stage in my development as a psychoanalyst helped me understand better the remorseless acts of psychopathic individuals. People are often mystified when a brutal murderer is sentenced in court and shows no remorse for what he has done. If the individual had been able to feel remorse it is unlikely that he would have committed the crime. There is an absence of reflexivity that is a crucial element in remorse. The psychopath is behaving at the level of motor action and not at the level of emotion; and remorse is in the emotional field. Another way of putting this is to use Bion's formulation and say that the psychopath is dominated by *beta elements* that he is discharging and that *alpha function* is very undeveloped but these *beta elements* have an agglomerated form. They are what Ferro (2005) calls *balpha elements* (p. 3). I think one of the reasons why the psychopath has great difficulty in unfurling his emotions is that if he does he has to confront enormous guilt for the damage done to himself and others in the past. This explains why it is difficult to dissolve the psychopathic condition once it is established but it does not explain how it started off in the first place. I think that all pathologies are emotions that have solidified into a particular mould. Psychopathy is, I believe, an intense sadness that has become crystallized into a hard rigidity in the personality. The psychopath assaults those around him in a way that is extremely distressing and sad-making for others. This is a sign of the "stuff" out of which the psychopathic condition is constituted. So, close engagement with psychopaths was the first of the two experiences; the second was the treatment of a mentally handicapped man.

After leaving Grendon Prison in 1975 I took a job as a psychotherapist at The Personal Consultation Centre (later re-named the Camden Psychotherapy Unit) that was located near Russell Square. After a year's probation I was appointed director of the unit. Apart from one-to-one clinical work we also did consultations to social service projects within the London Borough of Camden. One of these was a sheltered workshop for the mentally handicapped. The junior staff at this centre were distressed because they felt that some of the denizens of the workshop had more mental ability than their work tasks suggested. There was one particular man who fell into this category. I decided to see him for psychotherapy once a week. I thought I would thereby learn about mental handicap. After two years of treatment I gave a paper on it at the Applied Section of the Institute of Psychoanalysis in London. The topic awakened interest in several institutions. I subsequently gave a talk on it at the Portman Clinic, the Cassel Hospital, the

Child Guidance Training Centre, the Tavistock Clinic, and the British Association of Psychotherapy. I then submitted it to the *British Journal of Medical Psychology* and it was published there in 1981. Of all my published papers I have never had so many requests for reprints as I did for this paper. Many requests came from behind the Iron Curtain.

CHAPTER SIX

The response aroused by the psychopath

"How can I be substantial if I fail to cast a shadow? I must have a dark side also if I am to be whole; and inasmuch as I become conscious of my shadow I also remember that I am a human being like any other"

(Jung, 1984, p. 40)

What do we mean by "psychopath"? We need to know this before we can understand the response that he arouses. The term "psychopath" or "psychopathic" covers a wide range of observable phenomena but there is one common denominator: the overriding determination to attain certain goals, and these by flouting the values that society holds sacred. This was a point made succinctly by Edward Glover (1960): "Moral obliquity is in fact the hallmark of the psychopaths who engage the attention of the courts".

It was, for instance, a value of this country to accumulate wealth by hard work and saving and correspondingly taboo to obtain this by robbery or fraud. But this alone would mean that all revolutionaries are psychopaths, so there is another important diagnostic criterion: the criminal psychopath always acts in isolation. This is why Karl Marx saw the criminal as a reactionary and not a revolutionary.

On the subject of psychopathy, the standard psychiatric and psychological literature is unrewarding. The psychoanalytic writings are more helpful, and in particular that of Freud, Melanie Klein, Glover, and Hyatt Williams, but an important aspect of psychopathy, though noted, is underemphasized. I think this lacuna is supplied by Emily Brontë in her novel *Wuthering Heights*. The protagonist of the book, Heathcliff, is a psychopath. Characters of his kind are often found in novels. The arch-villain is a well-known stereotype and in fact Emily's sister, Ann, writes about such a one: Lord Huntington in *The Tenant of Wildfell Hall*. But here the villain, as is usually the case, is described "from outside" and the writer's purpose is to arouse our disgust and condemnation. In *Wuthering Heights* the reader is left with no illusion about Heathcliff, but Emily's aim is to enlighten the reader and to evoke neither condemnation nor praise. I will give a resumé of the story for those who have forgotten it or do not know it.

The action takes place in two properties on the Yorkshire Moors—Wuthering Heights and Thrushcross Grange—which are separated from each other by a distance of three miles. Wuthering Heights is the estate of the Earnshaw family and has been in the family for some generations and similarly Thrushcross Grange belongs to the Linton family. One day old Mr Earnshaw goes on a trip to Liverpool, and while there picks up a young gypsy brat who is homeless. He is adopted by him and his wife, much to the latter's annoyance. His origin, background, and name are unknown, and so he is simply called "Heathcliff". He grows up together with the two Earnshaw children, Hindley and Catherine. Old Earnshaw has special affection for Heathcliff and he exploits his position. From Hindley he gets things he wants by blackmail. On one occasion old Earnshaw brings home two colts and gives one to Hindley and the other to Heathcliff. A few days later Heathcliff's becomes lame, so he demands that Hindley swap, saying that he will show the old man the bruises Hindley has given him if he refuses. Hindley submits. The children grow up and Heathcliff, we discover, loves Catherine, but when she is of age she decides to marry Edgar Linton. By this time old Earnshaw has died and Hindley, master of the home, humiliates Heathcliff and has him reduced to servant status. Catherine tells her confidante, Ellen Dean, an old family retainer, of her decision to marry Edgar Linton but Heathcliff overhears and disappears for three years. In the meantime Hindley's wife has a child, called Hareton, and she dies, and then Catherine marries Edgar Linton. After three years Heathcliff, unexpected and uninvited, appears on the doorstep of Thrushcross Grange, having gone to lodge at Wuthering Heights. Although Hindley hates Heathcliff, his greed for money overcomes his natural sentiments. Heathcliff is an expert at playing on people's weaknesses. He now has some money of his own and is a fully-grown man. He becomes a regular visitor at Thrushcross Grange and Edgar allows it for Catherine's sake. It is not long before Heathcliff starts to flirt with Edgar's sister, Isabella, who becomes totally infatuated with him. Catherine sees them kissing in the garden and there ensues a row between Heathcliff and Catherine in which the former abuses the latter. Ellen Dean rushes off to fetch Edgar Linton, who rushes at Heathcliff, but Catherine, instead of defending her husband, goes to the defence of Heathcliff. Eventually, with the help of two labourers, Heathcliff is ejected from the house and banished from it. Catherine, who is now pregnant, declares that if she cannot have Edgar and Heathcliff she will make sure that neither of them can have her and she determines that she will die and so she starves herself and becomes delirious. Heathcliff elopes with Isabella and marries her and then returns with her to Wuthering Heights. With the help of Ellen Dean, Heathcliff sneaks in to see the dying Catherine and they declare their love for each other. Catherine dies, but not before a baby daughter is born to her and she is also named Catherine.

Heathcliff is now governed by one ruling passion: to possess everything that belonged to Catherine and to oust all other contenders. He is determined to become owner of both Wuthering Heights and Thrushcross Grange. When Hindley Earnshaw dies of drink, it emerges that Heathcliff is now owner of Wuthering Heights. Hindley had mortgaged his property to pay his debts incurred through gambling, which Heathcliff had encouraged. The mortgagee of the property is, of course, Heathcliff, so on Hindley's death the property becomes his. Isabella flees from Heathcliff to the south of England and there she has a baby boy whom she names

Linton. Twelve years later Isabella dies, and Edgar Linton goes to collect the young Linton and brings him to Thrushcross Grange, but hardly has he arrived in the house when Heathcliff sends to claim his son, so the young Linton goes to his father at Wuthering Heights. Despite strict instructions from Edgar Linton, Heathcliff manages, when the two children are of age, to bring Catherine and Linton together through various deceptions. Then he captures the two and forces them to marry. Edgar Linton, now dying, realizes that unless he changes his will all his property will go to Catherine and therefore fall into Heathcliff's hands, so he sends messengers to summon his solicitors but Heathcliff sends contrary messages and so Edgar dies before the solicitors reach him. So now Heathcliff is also master of Thrushcross Grange. All that was associated with his beloved Catherine now belongs to him. Now his goal is achieved but, instead of satisfaction, life becomes an empty abyss and all he wants now is to die. Like his beloved Catherine he starts to starve himself, but he first desecrates the grave and makes a place for himself next to Catherine. Then he dies and is buried next to his beloved tormentor, Catherine. His son, Linton, had died shortly before him, so the final irony is that the whole estate of Heathcliff passes to Catherine Linton and Hareton Earnshaw, who marry at the end of the book.

Heathcliff's relationship with Catherine is the key to an understanding of his character and makes Emily Brontë's formulation a precursor of object relations theory. Explanation, which focuses on the death instinct, guilt, impulses, and tension cannot be left out. It is impossible to give an account of psychopathy without taking account of this, and Emily Brontë was well aware of it. Where Heathcliff came from, what his parentage was, and even his nationality is deliberately left unknown. The biological organism with its genetic inheritance, impulses, and instincts is therefore given recognition, but on to this foundation Emily grafts a character structure that is a product of his relationship with Catherine. The relations between Heathcliff and Catherine need to be understood both as symbolical of an intrapsychic conflict *and* the early relationship of infant with mother. The internal relations within the unconscious can only become literature by translating them into adult love relationships. In this way great novels frequently describe an intrapsychic conflict.

Heathcliff and Catherine become close friends when Hindley goes off to college for three years. The bond between them was all the stronger because Catherine's mother had died some years before. Catherine becomes quasi mother to Heathcliff. The relationship of Heathcliff to Catherine symbolizes the bond between infant and mother at a very early developmental stage.

While they are in their early teens, old Earnshaw dies, and Hindley returns with a wife whom he has secretly married. He is now the master of Wuthering Heights and puts Heathcliff to work on the farm, treats him as a servant, and humiliates him in various ways. Heathcliff swears revenge. Then comes the biggest blow for Heathcliff: Catherine decides to marry Edgar Linton of Thrushcross Grange and we get a crucial insight into the psychology of the relationship between the two. Ellen Dean, who narrates the story, asks Catherine why she is going to marry Edgar Linton and she answers that Edgar has position and money. Ellen Dean asks, "What about Heathcliff?" Catherine's answer is staggering:

> It would degrade me to marry Heathcliff, now; so he shall never know how I love him; and that not because he's handsome, Nelly, but because he's more myself than I am. Whatever our souls are made of, his and mine are the same.

And a few minutes later she says,

> I cannot express it; but surely you and everybody have a notion that there is, or should be an existence of yours beyond you. What were the use of my creation if I were entirely contained here? My great miseries in this world have been Heathcliff's miseries, and I watched and felt each from the beginning; my great thought in living is himself. If all else perished, and *he* remained, I should continue to be; and if all else remained, and he were annihilated, the universe would turn to a mighty stranger. I should not seem a part of it. My love for Linton is like the foliage in the woods. Time will change it, I'm well aware, as winter changes trees. My love for Heathcliff resembles the eternal rocks beneath—a source of little visible delight, but necessary. Nelly, I *am* Heathcliff—he's always in my mind—not as a pleasure any more than I am a pleasure to myself—but as my own being—so don't talk of our separation again—it is impracticable.

And later in the book ,when Catherine has just died, Heathcliff says of her, "I *cannot* live without my life! I *cannot* live without my soul."

Heathcliff, the psychopath, is merged psychologically with his primary love object and separation from it is unbearable. He says his love for Catherine is a thousand times stronger than the love Edgar Linton has for her, but it is a love that will suffer any behaviour in the beloved just because it is a product of the loved one. Heathcliff says that if his and Edgar's positions were reversed he would never have raised a hand against Edgar, even though he hated him, for as long as she had regard for him but then he says, "The moment her regard ceased, I would have torn his heart out, and drunk his blood!"

This can only mean that he is furious with Catherine for her attention to Edgar Linton, but he will always protect her from his own violently vengeful feelings; but as soon as Catherine is dead he is determined upon Edgar Linton's downfall and he also brutally attacks her brother Hindley, which he would not have done while she was alive. The revenge of the psychopath is so intense that he is terrified of experiencing it towards his primary love object with whom his own survival is so intimately bound up. The needs of survival do not allow him to attack his primary love object. Talking of the baby's dilemma, Bion (1962) says, "Fear of death through starvation of essentials compels the resumption of sucking. A split between material and psychical satisfaction develops" (p. 10).

So, desire for revenge becomes displaced from his primary love object on to other figures. He protects this one figure with all his strength and destroys all others in order to do so. What the world sees is the figures whom he destroys but not the invisible figure whom he protects. When treating a psychopath, the analyst frequently becomes this protected figure in the transference, and I think one of the reasons this type of patient is so difficult to treat is that if interpretations begin to bear on this protective screen the analyst becomes a focus of paranoid fury that is not expressed verbally but acted out either towards people outside of the treatment situation or towards the analyst in some concrete way, like burgling his home or attacking him or a member of his family. Until this paranoia is laid bare I do not think the patient's psychopathy can be treated more than superficially, and this creates a difficult problem. But surely in prison the problem can be tackled with safety? But how many would allow themselves to become the focus of a determined vendetta that might put the analyst's family at risk? It was no surprise that weapons were smuggled in to the Baader-Meinhof group in Stuttgart Prison. Officers protecting these prisoners would know that their families and themselves would be at risk from the group's confederates outside if they had not done so. I do not offer a solution, but it is healthier to recognize that very often we collude with the criminal psychopath for our own safety, and we should not deceive ourselves about it or blame others for doing so. In *Wuthering Heights* one of the most fateful aspects of the novel is that all, even Edgar Linton, submit to Heathcliff's undying determination.

It is often asserted that the criminal psychopath is amoral and not bound by any ethical system; nothing could be further from the truth. He is intensely moral and generally speaks in puritanical terms. Hatred for the primary love object is displaced and acted out in external behaviour, so feelings of guilt are frequently displaced on to something quite venial. A criminal once borrowed two pounds from a forensic psychiatrist; a few days later he battered an old lady and nearly killed her. Some time later he was enormously guilty at not having repaid the money to the psychiatrist, but had no apparent remorse about the elderly lady who was his victim. The criminal's ethical system is built around an internal figure. The end justifies any means but there always is an end. In the story of Heathcliff we see an example of this where he marries Catherine's sister-in-law, Isabella, to take revenge on Edgar Linton. His ethical goal is individual, personal, and remains unseen by those around him and by himself also. Klein (1934) has given expression to the way in which the positive factor is not seen by those in his social environment:

> One of the great problems about criminals, which has always made them incomprehensible to the rest of the world, is their lack of natural human good feeling; but this lack is only apparent. When in analysis one reaches the deepest conflicts from which hate and anxiety spring, one also finds there the love as well. Love is not absent in the criminal, but is hidden and buried in such a way that nothing but analysis can bring it to light . . . [p. 260]

I want to dwell further on internal objects and ethical systems. Within the psychical system there is a subject that is the ego and objects to which it relates with feelings of love, hate, or a mixture of both. Subject and object are used in the grammatical sense of subject and object of a sentence; in fact objects are usually figures of people experienced internally. These are the significant caring figures of childhood, but altered according to the infant's own perceptions and feelings so the internal mother may be quite other than that consciously experienced. So the psychopath consciously may proclaim his mother to be a saint but unconsciously feel her as a bitter persecuting figure. It is these internal objects or inner figures that mobilize energy; someone will cross the world in pursuit of a loved one and also in search of a hated enemy. Motivation flows from the presence of these inner figures but they have a conscious representative in the external world. So a man is devoted to the improvement of conditions of some minority group, like the Maltese or the Cypriots, has a loved figure within that he wishes to care for, and in analysis this can be traced to the minority group that becomes the conscious representative of the unconscious inner figure. Then there is the man who dedicates his life to combating some evil, like racism, which he vehemently hates, and again the emotional force comes from a persecuting inner figure. In these cases the internal object has undergone a process of sublimation, but with the psychopath, due to failure in symbol formation, this has not occurred. He is dedicated to an inner unseen figure and in pursuit of her destroys all objects in his path. All the world can see is that he sweeps aside the values that most people hold sacred, as Glover (1960) has observed,

> in order to obtain an accurate picture of the "criminal psychopath" it is essential to keep constantly in mind that the main feature of criminal psychopathy, viz. moral obliquity, is estimated by social rather than clinical considerations. The lack of "moral fibre" is measured by the degree to which the criminal psychopath ignores and contravenes social codes.

For Heathcliff, the motivating inner figure is the dead Catherine, who yet remains alive for him. When Catherine dies, his only way of taking hold of her is to possess entirely all the material possessions which were associated with her: Wuthering Heights and Thrushcross Grange. But the point is this: it is he who has killed her and he is so guilty that he has to keep her alive. By keeping her alive he does not experience the guilt for her death. When he does finally own all that belonged to Catherine he feels he is in an empty abyss and says, "Be with me always—take any form—drive me mad! Only do not leave me in this abyss, where I cannot find you! Oh God! It is unutterable!"

He has one last desire: to die and be buried next to Catherine, so he starves himself and makes sure that he will be buried beside her. What he pursues so ruthlessly is a lost object that has become persecuting to him. The persecuting figure is similar to the one Freud (1917e) describes in "Mourning and melancholia", but there are two important differences. The depressive persecutes his object mentally inside himself; all is conducted within the mental sphere. The depressive is suffering from a loss that has occurred later developmentally when symbolization has been satisfactorily established. The psychopath's loss has occurred earlier, when the infant is still stretching for his object and holding it to himself in a tactile way, and before he can internalize it within the unconscious. The psychopath has suffered a loss that occurred when mother and infant were still a unit. In Kleinian language, the infant has sustained a loss while in the paranoid–schizoid position. The projective and introjective mechanisms by which the infant separates himself from mother have not completed their work. So the infant has not lost just mother but a part of himself. It is precisely this that Heathcliff poignantly describes when Catherine dies.

The envy and destructive forces towards the primary love object are so powerful that they have to be deflected both from the self and from the object. The psychopath cannot say, "I feel I would like to kill my mother", because unconsciously he has killed her and the guilt and depression about it is so enormous that it is projected powerfully into those significant others of his environment. He *is* mother, and if for one instance the depression comes home, as it were, he kills himself.

How do people respond to the psychopath? Let us listen first to how those surrounding Heathcliff responded.

Ellen Dean says of him as a child, "From the very beginning he bred bad feeling in the house."

One of the most evident signs of psychopathy is the presence of confusion and bad feeling. One person is set against another and suspicion is rife. But the cause is never rooted out. In these days, when it is fashionable in institutions to analyse group phenomena on a systems theory basis, the presence of psychopathy is often missed. It is thought that all can be resolved if everyone's role is clear and that by "talking through" harmony can be reached. This may work in the absence of a psychopath, but not when one is present in a group. The psychopath scorns such genteel methods of dealing with problems. He will create more confusion out of it so that "talking through" will provide no solution.

Another time Ellen Dean says, "I wondered often what my master saw to admire so much in the sullen boy who never, to my recollection, repaid his indulgence by any sign of gratitude."

People expect that the psychopath will respond to goodness and kindness and show gratitude in the end. This is a pious wish; the experience of those working with psychopaths is the opposite. Experience belies the wishes and longings of those brought up to adhere to the Christian ethics of Western society. After the incident where Heathcliff blackmails Hindley, Ellen Dean says of him, "I persuaded him easily to let me lay the blame of his bruises on the horse; he minded little what tale was told since he had what he wanted."

He did not care as long as he got what he wanted. Material gain sweeps all other considerations aside. Ellen Dean also notes that he did not seem to mind being abused physically or verbally by Hindley, and she says, "He complained so seldom . . . that I really thought him not vindictive . . . I was deceived completely, as you will hear."

The psychopath is extremely vindictive but does not show it in word or gesture at the time of the injury. He stores it up and responds in action later. When normal people tell a lie it is registered on a GSR, but not with a psychopath. The psychopath does not belie his feelings. People around do not feel him to be vindictive and vicious. I once refused a request to a psychopath and he just said blandly, "Oh, that's all right, don't worry", went off cheerily, and burgled my flat the very next day. The rage and vindictiveness is so split off that people do not believe he has done what he has, even when the evidence is incontrovertible.

Even Catherine says of him to Isabella who was later to marry him,

> He'd crush you like a sparrow's egg, Isabella, if he found you a troublesome charge. I know he couldn't love a Linton; and yet he'd

be quite capable of marrying your fortune and expectations. Avarice is growing with him a besetting sin. There's my picture; and I'm his friend.

And soon after Isabella has married him she writes to Ellen Dean and asks, "Is Heathcliff a man? If so, is he mad? And if not, is he a devil?"

It is possible to classify the responses aroused by the psychopath under three headings: collusion, disbelief, and condemnation.

In the novel, after Isabella has married Heathcliff and is living at Wuthering Heights, Ellen Dean goes to visit her, in response to a forlorn letter from her. There she meets Heathcliff, now banned from Thrushcross Grange, but he persuades Ellen Dean to help him sneak in unseen to visit the dying Catherine; against her better judgement she agrees, because she feels that if she does not, worse will happen. She is also afraid of Heathcliff, who threatens her. The psychopath is so desperate that he persuades people with a pressing urgency to carry out his wishes. To obtain what he wants is all important, and he will seduce, cajole, and threaten in order to obtain it. The despair and ultimate emptiness calls forth a collusive response in those to whom he appeals. A beseeching call for help that only you can answer is difficult to resist. It revives in us early feelings when we also were totally helpless. In treatment, the psychopath will try every means to get us to do something other than give interpretations. He makes a desperate appeal to us to lend him money, give him longer sessions, get him a glass of water, allow him to use the telephone, and so on. In themselves these requests are harmless enough, but to collude is to spell disaster; it is equivalent to agreeing that it is impossible for the patient to introject a good object and, ultimately, to give the analyst up. Once a patient tried to persuade me to go for a drink with him after the session, telling me he needed to feel I was human. I did not accede to his request. Later it was possible to analyse that he hated me for my happiness with my family and friends. In taking me for a drink he was wanting to lead me into drunkenness, then drugs, and so destroy the happiness I had. On this occasion the word "human" was not so benign as first appeared. In treatment the cry of the psychopath is frequently "You give me absolutely nothing—give me something concrete."

It is essential to help the psychopath pass through this "dark night of the senses" and that we do not, from our own anxiety, prevent him from doing so.

There is another type of collusion that is more difficult to define but which haunts the atmosphere of *Wuthering Heights* from start to finish. It is that ultimately it is hopeless to resist the determination of the psychopath. In the novel this is typified by Edgar Linton, who becomes helpless in the face of his rival. He forbids Heathcliff entrance to his home yet he is defied; he forbids his daughter to go to Wuthering Heights but Heathcliff subtly interferes and thwarts his plans. He goes to fetch his nephew, Linton, when Isabella dies, but when Heathcliff demands the child he submits without a murmur. Finally, Heathcliff kidnaps his daughter and forces her to marry his son. Edgar Linton's only response is to die. All the people close to him die: Catherine, Isabella, Edgar Linton, Hindley, and his own son Linton. The psychopath projects his own inner despair into those around him and achieves his short-term goals in this way. He controls those around him through powerful projective mechanisms. He makes others feel what he dare not feel himself. Only at the end of the book does Heathcliff himself cry out with despair, and then it is his turn to die. When I have made an interpretation to a psychopath that gets in touch with his despair there is a momentary flash of horror accompanied by some statement such as: "I'd bloody kill myself if I thought that", and then the projective armour clashes to again. What he says is true: there is a symbolic equation between the ego and the hated object in the unconscious. If the depression comes home it leads to an actual killing, so he has to push it away.

Through strong projective mechanisms, the psychopath stirs our own primitive sadism and this leads to a twofold response: either disbelief or condemnation. These are two ways of dealing with our own sadism. This attitude of disbelief is expressed commonly enough in such exclamations as "Surely he can't be as bad as that". Yet, when Heathcliff elopes with Isabella, he gives her clear evidence as to his character. As the two are leaving Thrushcross Grange he takes her favourite dog, puts a rope around its neck and hangs it from a tree, and yet she still adheres to an illusory picture of him and he despises her for it. The psychopath despises the person who holds on to an illusion that he is good; unconsciously he knows that it is a rejection of an important part of him. It is the renewed experience of a mother who could not contain his sadistic impulses in the first few weeks of life. Despite the evidence, Isabella keeps a protective screen around him. Just as Heathcliff maintains a protective screen around his Catherine, so he arouses the same response in relation to himself. Remember he *is* Catherine; that is not a literary metaphor but a psychological fact. Because the psychopath hates unconsciously the person who has an illusion about him he will always give a strong clue about the hidden side of his character. Some years ago my flat was burgled one weekend when I was away, and it seemed certain to have been done by one or more ex-prisoners that I had been concerned with. Two men had been observed climbing up a ladder into my flat on the Saturday night, so it was known that two men had been involved in the burglary. A day or two later an ex-prisoner came to see me, slapped me on the back and said, "Oh I know, Neville, we've had the odd rows but I really think it's diabolical when someone burgles your flat after all you do for us."

I had an immediate presentiment that he was one of the culprits. Consciously it was the old trick; I was bound to say to myself, "It can't be him", but unconsciously he was telling me the truth, using a reaction formation defence. Shortly afterwards the police arrested him for the crime. One of the objects stolen from my flat was a cheque book. Another man whom I knew quite well came to me and said with pride, "Look, I've opened a bank account and here's my cheque book", and he showed me his new cheque book. He was showing me that it was he who had stolen *my* cheque book. He was the other man who was arrested. This need to leave evidence of his real character is the unconscious determinant of clues left by the criminal that lead to his arrest.

To adhere to the evidence rather than disbelieve requires us to accept our own sadism, which we deny all the harder when it is being stirred by the psychopath. Our disbelief is reinforced by the Christian value system that says that man, like God, is good. We are all familiar with the counsels "Blessed are the meek" and "Blessed are the merciful". Our desire to be acceptable in terms of these standards puts additional pressure on us to deny our own sadism. If we accept what we see in the psychopath then we have to accept our own sadism. It may be more comfortable to believe that he and ourselves are good. When *Wuthering Heights* was first published in 1847, the critics complained at the stark brutal quality of Heathcliff. Even Charlotte, Emily's sister, tried to persuade her to temper her characterization of Heathcliff for propriety's sake, but Emily refused. She was not going to moderate the way she saw things. The public wanted an illusion and not the real psychopath whom Emily portrayed. The uncompromising way in which revered values and standards are swept aside by the psychopath shocks us today just as it did our Victorian forebears.

The other reaction is to deny our sadism by projecting it back on to the criminal psychopath. Frequently criminals feel that they are being victimized, and their perception is accurate. They are particularly suitable scapegoats on to whom we can project our own sadism, but to relate with neither disbelief nor condemnation is extremely difficult. The two sets of reactions could be clearly seen in the debate as to whether Myra Hindley should be given parole or not. The same split can be seen in the response aroused by the psychopath who goes into a psychiatric hospital, where he is met with disbelief, and in prison, where he meets condemnation.

Both disbelief and condemnation are products of the same emotional neglect: the failure to accept the psychopath *as he is*. The foundation stone of any treatment is to respond with neither disbelief nor condemnation. To be present to the psychopath as he is becomes the *sine qua non* for successful treatment. The psychopath does stir our sadism and tries to induce our disbelief or provoke our condemnation. When we come to terms with this in him and in ourselves we have laid a basis for a fruitful analysis. Of course, it must not remain in the mental sphere, but be demonstrated actively in the treatment situation. Only then do we reach the unconscious phantasies wherein his difficulties lie.

Commentary

I think the origin of psychopathy lies in an experience of sadness so intense that it is not experienced consciously but dispersed through the personality in the form of ruthlessness and despair. The merging of Heathcliff with Catherine is indicative of a merged state of affairs between himself and his mother. This merging protects him from the subjective experience of loss. When old Earnshaw found the gypsy brat he was an abandoned child who had lost his mother. The lost mother is displaced on to Catherine and the determination to own Wuthering Heights and Thrushcross Grange are his concrete manner of trying to reunite with her. He lost his mother when she was a physical extension of him. Subjectivity only occurs in the state of separateness. The loss, the horror, is not experienced by Heathcliff himself until the end, but is experienced by all those around him. They do not only feel horror but actually die. This represents a savage rupture from his mother when he was still a suckling.

CHAPTER SEVEN

The origins of rage and aggression

"Paradoxical as it may sound, I must maintain that the sense of guilt was present before the misdeed, that it did not arise from it, but conversely—the misdeed arose from the sense of guilt. These people might justly be described as criminals from a sense of guilt"

(Freud, 1916, p. 332)

I t is a mistake to think that psychoanalysis has one theory. Psychoanalysis is a clinical methodology that encompasses a wide range of theories. Nowhere is this more evident than when psychoanalysts start to discuss the cause of aggression. At its most simple there are two theories. The first states that aggression arises when a human being's basic needs are frustrated. This theory is based upon the homeostatic theory of motivation. This states that the organism has a built-in tendency to equilibrium, to homeostasis; when inner tension arises, the organism is programmed to reduce that tension through incorporating food, water, or finding an object that will satisfy a sexual need. Aggression arises when one of these needs is frustrated. Aggression is therefore a reaction to frustration.

The other theory states that aggression is a basic instinct in man. Those who hold the latter theory say that man is a savage creature by nature, but those who follow the former state that man is essentially benign and only becomes savage when frustrated of his basic biological needs. I believe that both theories are wrong. The homeostatic theory is wrong because it fails to account adequately for certain areas of human experience like a person's love of beauty, the individual who dies for his country, and emotional and mental satisfactions in favour of which an individual will be prepared to sacrifice pleasures associated with the homeostatic theory. Although there must be few analysts today who hold the homeostatic theory, many hold what is in fact one of its consequences: that aggression arises through frustration of a basic biological need. Some would extend this to include frustration of emotional needs. The theory that man is innately aggressive does not give sufficient account of the transformations of instinct that have progressively taken place in the evolution of mankind. I want, therefore, to put to you another theory, and to do this I will start from a piece of experience and its interpretation.

In the early 1970s I worked as a psychotherapist at Grendon Prison near Aylesbury in England. Grendon is a psychiatric prison and group therapy was the treatment of choice. Some of you may have read the book on Grendon Prison by Tony Parker: *The Frying Pan*. I was also associated at this time with an organization whose goal was the social rehabilitation of prisoners. It was the philosophy of this organization that rehabilitation started from the day that a man first went to prison. For this purpose then I went one day to interview a man who had just been remanded in custody at Wandsworth Prison. This young man had entered the house next door to where he lived where he found the ten-year-old girl, Isabella. He pulled her by the hair around the top landing and then dragged her screaming down the stairs. When he got her to the bottom floor he raped her and then killed her by bashing her head against a wall.

> I was shown by the warder into the interview room and I sat on a wooden upright chair with the prisoner opposite me and a bare wooden table between us. He spoke in an affectionate manner towards me; he was nervous and looked very young. I cannot remember his age but he did not look over twenty-one. He looked bewildered, as if he

had been catapulted into this world from another planet. After explaining to him the purpose of my visit and asking him for the date of his trial and he giving me some details about his legal representation, I set about asking him about his crime. He had known Isabella quite well, I gathered. The problem arose when it came to the day of the crime. He remembered that he had gone on his bicycle down to the greengrocer. He had come back and he had seen Isabella in the garden and he had gone to play with her and then there had been an accident. I pressed him to tell me exactly what had happened-"We were playing along the stairs, she screamed."

"What made her scream?"

"She was hurt."

"Can you remember what happened?"

"It wouldn't have happened if her mother had been there. She should have come back. Young children should not be left on their own. You never know what might happen to them."

He then wandered off as if in a dream. He started to talk of Isabella's mother, Josephine:

"We used to be together, you see."

"You mean you were having an affair?" He smiled with embarrassment and guilt. I pressed him to talk but he remained silent. I tried to talk of other things. At one moment he murmured,

"Isabella saw us."

"Is that what made you attack her?"

"Hair. Oh heavens—stairs." He then murmured, "Accident—Oh no!"

He was now only semi-talking to me. I had the impression that some visual images were flashing across the memory screen and he was giving his reaction to them. At this point in the conversation a very strange thing happened to me: I fell asleep, or at least I would have done had I not struggled with all my might against it. It was in the morning. I was sitting on a hard wooden upright chair. He commented, "What—sleepy?" and he smiled again with embarrassment. It was as if an anaesthetic slug had been fired into me. I struggled on with the interview but all my energy was directed towards keeping awake. The interview came to an end. I returned for a second interview about a week later. Again when we talked of his crime he went into his "memory screen" mode and I was overcome with sleepiness.

A week after the second interview he went on trial at the Old Bailey, was found guilty, and sentenced to twenty-five years in prison. A few days later a prison warder opened up his cell in the morning and found that he had hanged himself.

I will give you my reconstruction of these events. The facts were that he had committed the crime of which he was accused. When I was interviewing him I do not think that he was consciously suppressing knowledge or lying to me. I think a part of his mind had blanked out his crime and just the odd flashes came back to him but not what he had done himself. Some of you may have seen the film *The Boston Strangler* some years ago. After the police had caught him the film showed a scene where the psychiatrist was questioning him in interview after interview. After a time momentary flashes came back to him. It was similar with the man I am telling you about. My conjecture is that subsequent to the trial a memory of what he had done came back to him and he hanged himself.

In a psychoanalytic treatment the analyst represents a part of the patient's mind which I have termed the *embryo mind*. Speaking generally, we know the mind's enormous potential. The human race has been blessed with Plato, Michelangelo, Shakespeare, Mozart, Kant, Karl Marx, Einstein, and hosts of others too numerous to name. We all know the heights of which the mind is capable. It is my experience as a psychoanalyst that many minds have a latent potential capable of considerable creative emotional work. This is the emotional correlate of what Vygotsky named the *proximal zone*. He meant by this that part of the mind capable of further cognitive development. The *embryo mind* is the *proximal zone* but applied to the emotional sphere of the mind. It is the *embryo mind* that the analyst represents. The phenomenon of the analyst as external representation of this inner capacity of mind is called the *transference*. My mind was knocked for six when I was interviewing this violent prisoner. On the basis of *transference* it leads me to infer that his *embryo mind* was being violently smothered by a part of the mind that is known in psychoanalytic discourse as the *archaic superego*.

I have found a model of the mind where different parts are in relation to other parts of the mind indispensable for understanding the emotional phenomena I encounter in clinical work. So, my own personal experience of being slugged by an anaesthetic dart in itself leads to the inference that his *embryo mind* is being violently attacked. This inference receives confirming evidence in view of the fact that the memory of what he has done to Isabella has been almost entirely obliterated. This paralleled the fact that my mind was not entirely knocked out—a small part remained struggling.

Let us look now at the triple constellation that we have got:

One: A savage tyrant part of the mind—the *archaic superego*—is attacking the part of the mind with all the creative potential—the *embryo mind*—with the result that events of great importance are wiped out.

Two: The young man attacks with great brutality a ten-year-old girl.

Three: In an interview with the young man an analyst's mind is nearly knocked unconscious.

Number Two is an infamous public event; Number Three is a personal private event passing between two people; Number One, however, is an entirely private inner drama. Now I want to trace things in the following manner.

I hope that the following hypothesis will carry some conviction for you: that the prisoner blotted out the memory of what had been done because he was so appallingly guilty. As you can imagine it was a crime that was reported in all the media and sent ripples of shocked outrage through the public community. The world at large experienced the horror that the criminal himself could not experience. It is a phenomenon often observed in clinical psychoanalysis that what is not experienced by the agent himself is projected outwards and experienced in the wider community. The only person who had no conscious horror of the event was the man who perpetrated it. My hypothesis is that to allow himself to know what he had done caused an insupportable guilt. It was guilt, therefore, that led him to blot out the memory of what he had done. If my conclusion is correct, that anaesthetizing my mind was the external correlate of this blotting out of the memory of his crime, then the source of the attack on my mind was the very same guilt. I want now to take a further step that you may be unwilling to take: that the emotional origin of that savage attack upon Isabella was also guilt.

Guilt is a feeling consequent upon an action. Guilt only makes sense if it was within the field of possibility for me not to do the action that produces the guilt. What I am saying, then, is that in the prisoner there was a guilt that led to the killing of Isabella; that there was enormous guilt about the slaughter going on in his own mind. When he killed Isabella he had entirely surrendered himself into the power of that part of his mind which Melanie Klein first named the *archaic superego*.

The guilt about the inner situation is so great that it impels him to dramatize it in the outer world. When the inner drama is cata-pulted into the outer world the man is captured and put into prison. Punishment is society's revenge against the perpetrator of the crime, but it is also the medicine of healing. This, paradoxically, is, I believe, the driving motive behind the crime. This is illustrated most clearly in Dostoyevsky's *Crime and Punishment*. The novel opens with Raskolnikov brutally axing the old woman to death. The main portion of the book describes Raskolnikov's doubt: shall I or shan't I confess? He finally does confess and is sent off to hard labour in Siberia. The reader understands, however, that through the relationship with Sonia the punishment is the first step towards recovering a sane mind. With my prisoner, the moment when recovery might have started he killed himself.

I am saying then that guilt is the instigator of violent outbursts of the sort I have tried to describe. In such outbursts aggression, which is a natural endowment of human beings, is used destruc-tively rather than constructively. I have tried to draw a sketch of the activity in the mind that produces this guilt. To go into how these activities in the mind originated would take us into another area of inquiry. What I am stating is that it is guilt, a guilt that is not conscious, which accounts for these sudden outbursts of violent rage.

Now I want to return to where I started. These violent outbursts of murderous rage neither occur because a biological need has become frustrated nor because aggression is innate in man. The problem is in whose service the aggression is being employed. It is when it is employed against the potential capacities of the mind that guilt arises. A person does not feel guilt unless there was an alternative activity open to him. The origin of violence lies in guilt. This means an inner decision. That the origin of violence is to be found in the ego rather than an instinctual urge means that it is a personal construction in which it is possible to find meaning. In this there is some hope because the possibility of constructing things differently is always there. The more we understand guilt and the way it comes about in the mind the more chance we have of arriving at measures which are prophylactic against the eruption of violence in our society. It is to this I believe that we should address ourselves.

CHAPTER EIGHT

The psychotherapy of a mentally handicapped patient

"... from this crude simulacrum of a human being one looked for no more than an animal's response. But again she was surprised. The child, leaving the nurse's side, moved into motion as if sucking-in a long tube of paste, her whole face was gradually caught up in an expression that seemed unquestionably human—the look of a greedy old woman, mischievous without the light of humour, shameless and sly. She gave a little cry like a bird's imitation of human laughter. In one movement she dropped to a squatting position, stretched both her hands to seize the one which Stepan held out to her, pulled it to her face and fastened her teeth in the flesh below his thumb"

(Hutchinson, 1983, p. 74)

T his paper is a resumé of the treatment of a man, aged thirty-three at the beginning of treatment, whose IQ was said to be fifty-nine. I had reason to believe that it was higher than this.

The account covers a period of two years, during which time I saw him regularly once a week. At the end of two years, he told me he did not wish to come any more. I do not know whether the treatment was a success or a failure. My purpose in presenting this treatment is to stimulate further discussion on this subject, challenge the assumption that psychotherapy requires a normal or above-normal IQ to be successful, and to investigate the aetiology of mental retardation. This two-year period of treatment was extremely enlightening and opened many avenues of thought, which are presented here only in the most embryonic form. So I start with the background to the case and some of the reasons why I decided to take him into treatment, then a summary of the course of the treatment, and finally a discussion of some theoretical issues of psychological interest.

Background to the case

As leader of a team working in a small psychotherapy unit in central London, I was asked to act as consultant with a particular "trainee", whom I shall call Harry Smith.

I was told that Harry threw violent tantrums and the staff did not know how to deal with them. Also, the staff told me, in some distress, that they felt that all the progress that they were making with Harry became sabotaged at home. I offered to conduct a family interview to try to assess the situation further, so, together with the social worker assigned to Harry Smith by the local area team, I saw for an extended interview Mr and Mrs Smith and their son Harry, who at the time was aged thirty-three. A younger sister, married with children and living south of the river, was not available to attend the interview.

The family was working class, living in a council flat, and the father and mother both worked and Harry went daily to the day centre. Mr Smith was a sheet metal worker and Mrs Smith had a cleaning job. Mr Smith and Harry were both clean, smart, and well dressed. Mother's appearance was more bedraggled. In the course of the interview some important facts emerged. Although mother and father lived under the same roof they led completely separate lives. Father had his own bed-sitting room with his own television, armchairs, and his own personal possessions around him; he lived as though he were a lodger within the flat. Mother and Harry each had their own bedrooms, but spent most of their time together in the sitting room. Communication with father from mother was minimal. It emerged further that, for the first ten years of Harry's life, Mr Smith had been drinking very heavily and was, therefore, not able to take any interest in his son. When Harry was ten years old, through the help of an appropriate organization, father gave up drink and had been sober ever since; but, at the interview mother expressed bitter resentment that father had not been available to take an interest in Harry during the formative years of his life. Father blamed the day centre for Harry's difficulties; he said that the day centre neither provided an educative programme nor paid an appropriate working wage.

What emerged, however, was that neither mother nor father (and Harry as I was subsequently to learn) was clear what were the mental capacities of their son. At one moment father was praising his son and telling us how capable he was and that he should be given a decent job, and the next moment he was pouring scorn on him and saying that he was useless. I had the impression that father had never come to terms with the massive disappointment of having a mentally handicapped son. Mother's attitude was less easy to determine. She appeared to be dejected and also distressed on behalf of her son but I did not feel there was affection for him. We ended the interview saying that we would try to work out a treatment plan and then get in touch with the family again.

Reasons for taking the patient into therapy

Over the course of the next two weeks, I decided to take Harry into individual treatment. I would like to enumerate the reasons for this decision. Shortly after the family interview, the social worker and myself had a joint interview with Harry on his own. Stimulated by enormous anxiety, Harry hounded us with questions like:

"Tell me, is my father a bad man?"

"Am I not able to work?"

"Am I bad?"

"Tell me, should I listen to my father?"

These questions came pouring out one after another and no sooner had the social worker started to attempt to answer one when it was followed up with another. It was clear that the social worker's attempts to answer all these questions were useless and counterproductive. In the course of the interview Harry said, "Everyone keeps telling me different things."

The process was quite clear: he hounded people with questions, they answered the questions and he then felt persecuted at having so many different opinions floating around in his head. He had had many different social workers, but I thought it likely that they had probably also colluded with his defensive mode of communicating. I thought it would be worth while to try and reach the anxiety that underlay it and perhaps, with luck, alleviate it.

Also in the family interview there was a significant moment when mother and father were discussing his mental capacities. Father said, "He can count money and knows perfectly well what change he should get in the shop."

Mother quickly turned on father viciously and said, "Yes, that was because when he was a young boy his uncle took an interest in him and used to take him to the betting shop every Saturday afternoon and showed him how to count the money out for his bets and what he could expect to receive if a bet was won."

That was a vital piece of information because it suggested that if someone took an interest in him then he was able to learn. I suspected that he had a large *proximal zone.* This is the term used by Vygotsky (1962) to denote a mental area capable of further cognitive development. I thought it likely that he had not had sustained interest from outside the family. On reading his case notes, I was struck by the fact that for twenty-five years he had had a veritable procession of social workers, very few of whom were assigned to him for a period of more than nine months. Also, their contacts with him were irregular and spasmodic. I received the notion that a regular sustained interest, even in my drab consulting room rather than in the exciting atmosphere of a betting shop, just *might* have a similar effect on his cognitive processes, even though he was now in his early thirties.

Finally, I had a sense that behind the tantrums, the compulsive questioning, and frantic frustration was a screaming communication: that he was beating the air with frustration, trying to induce someone to listen to him. For these reasons I decided to take him into once-a-week individual therapy.

I subsequently felt that the therapy might have been more effective if I had seen him more often, and perhaps, by not suggesting this at the outset, I was colluding somewhat with the view that the journey, and indeed the whole endeavour, would be too much for him. I later explored the possibility of increasing the number of sessions, but this then was experienced as an intolerable demand and it revived powerful resistances to parental demands.

Anxiety in those in charge of the patient

When I had made an inner decision that I wanted to treat Harry in individual psychotherapy, first I asked him if he would like to come and see me once a week and I would try to help him with his problems, and he immediately accepted my invitation. I thought it likely that in the course of the therapy he might get worse, so I had a meeting with the staff of the day centre and asked them how they would feel about my taking Harry into treatment, and my suggestion was received with a great bound of enthusiasm. I told the staff that he might well get worse and asked them if they were prepared for that and explained that it might cause them even greater difficulties than they were having at the moment. Despite this warning they were still keen that I take him into treatment.

Attempts were made to treat, concurrently, his parents in marital therapy, but these failed, partly through lack of resources and partly due to unwillingness on the part of the mother. I think the outcome of the therapy might have been better had this endeavour succeeded.

I was asked if I would see Harry at the day centre, and I explained that he would have to come to the unit where I work. There then ensued a prolonged discussion between the staff, the social worker, and the parents as to how he was to get to me and back. Finally the social worker valiantly agreed to bring him for an early morning appointment, stay in the waiting-room during the session and then take him back at the end of it. This she did for two months until I was able to change the time to an afternoon, whereupon his mother was able to bring him. The significance of these circumstances will emerge presently.

The course of the therapy

The beginning of the therapy

Harry is about 5ft 9in tall, with black hair which is slightly wavy, always well brushed, and light brown eyes. He was always clean and neatly dressed, wearing a sports jacket, well-pressed jeans, with a shirt, tie, and pullover. Frequently, during the course of a session, he would take off his jacket, usually at the moment when the therapy was becoming stressful; he would usually accompany such a gesture with a comment like, "Cor, I'll have to have a cup of coffee when I get out of here."

He was careful of his personal appearance and, in the course of therapy, often needed to prove to me that he was a clean and well-dressed man. He always spoke, at the beginning of the therapy, in a rapid but faltering way and even when he was not talking to me he would punctuate the silence with mumbling undertones; he would do the same when I was talking. I had, as it were, actively to clear a space for myself when I wished to talk, his capacity to listen being extremely small.

He used to come into a session and start with a particular question that he wanted me to resolve for him. I am quite unable to give you the full content of a session at this early stage because I was inundated with a mass of different questions, problems, difficulties that appeared disjointed, and it was not possible to follow any one line of inquiry with him. It was like listening to a schizophrenic's flight of ideas. He might start a session something like this:

> Now you tell me, now you sort it out for me. Why did that girl say she would report me to the police, I didn't do anything, I just touched her. Why if a coloured man can do it, but look at me I am a good clean-dressed man, I know I didn't do anything because I was with her just like I am with my sister.

The portion like this would be just part of a torrent that would go on and on or, on another occasion, he would start like this:

> My dad says that I shouldn't work on the machines, Mr James (the name I shall give to the administrator of the centre) says I should work on the machines, Charlotte says I am a healthy working-class man,

Roger says I shouldn't be at the centre, I went to the Labour Exchange, there's a million out of work in Britain at the moment.

His voice would get louder and louder and then he would start shouting:

. . . and I only get 30 bob a week, that's not a working man's wage.

At the very beginning I tried mistakenly to intervene on this point or that, but to no avail, so I just sat and looked at him and he constantly pounded me with questions, and I sat and watched him, but gave no answer. He would look at me with a puzzled expression and I had the sense that in a session, bit by bit as time went on, these moments of awareness of my presence grew. But as time went on his preoccupations began to centre around particular themes. Clearly he was saying to me that different people had different pictures of his capacities. Initially these people were numerous, and he would name many different people that said different things and each one in contradiction with the other. Corresponding with his growing awareness of myself, the number of these people became smaller and smaller until it narrowed down to about four and, as they were saying different things, who was lying? The very clear preoccupation was with how intelligent he was, and he asked me repeatedly to tell him. As I actually did not know any more than he did I investigated the matter with him. Using my hand on the wall of the consulting- room, I marked out the different positions that people placed him in. I must abbreviate here and say there were two positions that were the focus of his anxieties. His father thought of him as through the roof at the top of the wall, and Mr James right on the ground, then the usual question—him asking me where *I* thought he was. I did not tell him but got him to estimate roughly where he was, and the top of the mantelpiece became average, the place of average intelligence, and he placed himself just a little below that. Then, in later sessions when he would go back to the father–Mr James duality and ask me again what I thought, I would remind him of where he had placed himself.

He then became very preoccupied as to why his father placed him "through the roof", as he put it. In one session he became so incensed with the notion that his father was lying and why he was lying that I tried to illustrate for him what I thought was the reason for his father's overestimation of him. I asked him whether he had a dog and he hadn't, whether he had a cat and he hadn't, and then I asked him if he had any pet. He told me that he had a budgerigar. So I said to him:

"Let us pretend that your budgerigar escapes."

He rapidly interjected and told me that in fact it had once escaped. I asked him what colour it was and he told me it was blue, and I said to him:

"Let us pretend you come in here and there are six budgerigars of different colours."

and I asked him if they were all as good as each other and he said "Yes". Then I said to him:

"If your blue budgerigar was among them would you think it was much better than the other five?"

and he said, "Yes", and I then explained to him that because he was his father's own son his father evaluated his intelligence much more highly. This calmed him down, but I noticed that he quite often came back to that illustration and I felt that it caused him some anxiety. This was, of course, because there was the implication in it that his father loved him.

The pound note

Then something very gratifying happened. It was about four months after his therapy had started and, as far as I knew, his mother was still accompanying him, as the waiting-room was two floors below and I did not see her. He came into a session and he was waving a pound note. I asked him what it was about and he told me it was to pay his fares for the journey to see me and then the return home.

"Did you come on your own then Harry?" I asked him, and he told me that he had come on his own and what was more he had come on his own for the previous two sessions. So he was quite able to make the journey to me and back and the notion that he would be unable to do it was an illusion. I then acknowledged with him that he was more intelligent than people took him for. I then pointed out to him very firmly that he must be pulling the wool over people's eyes. He agreed with this and wondered why it was. In the same context we got to the fact that he clowned a great deal so that people laughed at him and thought him more of a fool than he was. I interpreted that he felt there was something wrong with him and that he was extremely anxious lest people did laugh at him for that, so he exaggerated the process and was thus able, within himself, to say that he was really perfectly all right but what caused him pain and anxiety was a sense that there was something wrong. We came back to these points more than once, but it was clear that he was taking in the interpretations and that they were becoming integrated in his personality.

Anxiety about the "pictures"

As I have said earlier, a central anxiety was the different pictures that people had of him and which one was right. Gradually the pressure grew and grew for me to give him a picture, and his anxiety became intense. I should say that he never sat down in the chair for more than a quarter of a session; he would walk about the consulting room, he would illustrate points that he was making to me, sometimes he would go out into the corridor and come back and explain some incident and I myself used to walk around quite a lot of the time. I felt more comfortable responding to him in this way, but then every so often I would return to my chair and make a gesture to him and he would return and sit for a while. His anxiety, then, reached a stage of extreme intensity at the time when he was pressuring me to give him a picture. I had steadily agreed that what we were trying really to discover was who Harry was and not what others thought of him. However, this in no way curbed his pressure on me to give him a picture. I pointed out to him that it was these different pictures that caused him so much anxiety and, therefore, why did he want a further one from me? During these sessions he screamed at the top of his voice; several times people came to the door to ask if everything was all right and whether I needed any help. Although he put enormous pressure on me to give him a picture of himself I did not do so. I am very glad I didn't because I think that bearing his anxiety was probably crucial. Then in a session when he was screaming at me I said:

> "You must need these pictures to protect yourself from something very painful."

Then he mumbled something, which he had mumbled before, that he was thirty-three years of age and was that nothing; and I suddenly saw in a flash what it was and I said to him:

> "Harry, the fact that you feel they have been thirty-three years of emptiness, waste and nothingness is so painful that it is better to have people's pictures of you than to face this ghastly nothingness."

Then more quietly, but still in a loud voice, he said to me:

> "Well, if you won't give me a picture what do I come here for?"

and I stood up and placed myself alongside him and I said:

> "Harry, it is like this. There is in front of us thirty-three years of waste, nothing and emptiness; it is like sitting in a train; opposite we have a man with a wounded and diseased face and it is so horrific that you have to hold pictures up in front of you because it is more than you can bear, but the reason you come to see me is that perhaps there is just a possibility that if you have me beside you [at this point I held his arm] then you can look at it."

From that moment his anxiety dropped dramatically. The sessions became quite different; he was able to sit much more peaceably, he spoke in a more measured tone of voice and he was able to listen to me in a way that was appreciably very different. This change was noticed by several people and was mentioned to me.

Symbolic failure

I have had to be selective; there are many things that I have had to leave out. There was another aspect that was crucial to the therapy. I knew that he was handicapped in intelligence but what this meant, what failure there was in his mental processes, I did not know. There were certain things, however, that I had begun to notice.

He had an enormous fear of ambulances, police cars, violence, and the subject of death. After the interpretation about the pictures it was possible to take each of these matters and examine them with him. Ten years earlier, when he was aged twenty-three, his mother was admitted to Friern Barnet (a large psychiatric hospital in north London), followed shortly afterwards by Harry. He had a terror of hospitals and ambulances. His fear of police cars I put down to the fact that he had violent fantasies for which he expected punishment. It was difficult to interpret because, as with certain borderline patients, he would take any observation of mine concretely. He could take interpretations in other areas but not in this one of his aggressive fantasies. He had similar anxieties surrounding the subject of sex. He could not refer to any bodily organs that had a sexual significance: the penis, the vagina, breasts, and so on. On one occasion, in order to describe to me how a boy put his hand up a girl's jumper, he described it by mime. However, as the therapy progressed, it became evident that his sexual desires increased and also his aggression towards those in his environment. I noticed that staff at the day centre began to become apprehensive that he might hit one of them.

I tried to bring staff of the day centre into an understanding of the treatment and some of Harry's difficulties. The staff were very willing to help, but to communicate what I had learnt in a thera-peutic encounter, through rational explanations, was only mini-mally successful. On reflection, it might have been helpful if the staff could have participated concurrently in some modified kind of training group.

I knew that what was so persecuting to him about the "pictures" was that people's words actually lodged inside him, and particu-larly the words of his father. He came to understand that the ther-apeutic task was not to get rid of the people but rather to seek out the reason why the words lodged inside him and persecuted him. This seemed to help him. So much I understood but there was something else which I could not put my finger on. Then, in one session, he spoke of the extreme anxiety he experienced when two people, on seeing a police car passing by, joked to him that it was coming to pick him up. He was unable to tune in to the fact that it was a joke but thought they meant it, and it sent him almost berserk. I had noticed this business about jokes before and was not quite sure what it meant. I was inclined to think that he was so sensitive to aggression towards him that he only experienced the latent factor within the joke. I was basing this on the notion that there is some ingredient of aggression in all jokes. This failure to differentiate between a joke and a serious statement is a well-known characteristic of subnormal patients and has been noted by many different authors (e.g., Pearson, 1942). But he could see that there was something that I did not understand so he came back to the next session and right at the beginning told me he wanted to show me something. He looked at my desk and asked me if he could have some papers, so I gave him a pile of plain white writing sheets. He then pointed to different objects in the room and made me understand that each one stood for a different member of staff at the centre and he named them—Roger, Charlotte, Mr James, Barry, and so on—and as he named each member of staff he took a sheet of white paper and placed the white paper on top of each piece of furniture, explaining as he did so that the white sheets represented the white coats that the staff wore at the centre. He was showing me in a vivid way the staff members with their white coats on and then he turned to me and said:

"Now, when they've got their white coats on I think I am at Friern Barnet."

I said to him:

"You mean because the staff wore white coats at Friern Barnet when you see the white coats on the staff at the centre   then there is no difference between them; you cannot distinguish them?"

And he said "Yes". To clarify it I said:

"So if you came in here one day to see me and I had a white coat on it would be the same?"

And he said:

"Well, I would be very worried."

And then he added:

"You know that time you lay back in your chair, pretending to be dead. I was terribly worried because I thought you were dead."

I then made some whistling sound and gave an expression of compre-hension, so he brought his face right up to mine and said:

"Now do you understand!"

He did not add these words, but the implication was unavoidable: *You low IQ'd idiot!*

This was a great move forward because from then on when he asked me whether I thought there was anything wrong with him I was able to say to him that we both knew that there was something wrong: that he could not differentiate between fantasy and reality. It later became evident that the same thing was true of television programmes, when they were on the subject of violence, death, police cars, or ambulances. To experience so much of his human environment in such a concrete way was a source of severe anxiety for him. What is more, this source was not realized by those around him. Once we had located the dysfunction within the therapy it was a considerable help. When the source of the difficulty is isolated and diagnosed this in itself assists psychic forces to start their work of healing. I will return to this topic in the theoretical part of the paper, but there was another piece of material from a subsequent session with is closely related to the dysfunction I have been talking about.

When I was discussing with him why it was that, although he had been quite capable of coming to see me on his own, yet for some time he had allowed someone to accompany him, he said that if he did not have someone with him he might be mugged. I agreed that this was a possibility but that he seemed more anxious about it than many people who walk around London on their own. He said to me:

"Yes, that's true, but you see if they killed me that would kill my mother."

He was *not* saying that if he was killed that it would kill his mother because she would be so upset emotionally, but that a killing of him would actually be also a killing of his mother. He and mother were in a state of primary identification.

Interpretation of secondary gain

Throughout the course of the therapy he had complained bitterly about his father who, he said, took no interest in him. Also he frequently said, after he had been speaking:

"Now, you tell me the answer; you're the doctor and I'm the patient."

On several occasions I had made transference interpretations with a negative content and he had refused them. He held me very idealized and I felt that I was his idealized mother in the transference. The negative feelings towards his mother had not been dealt with. For most of the therapy I had, from the point of view of the transference, left his negative aspect on one side, though I realized it was crucial. He clearly functioned by splitting: making father all bad and mother all good. Generations of professional workers had colluded with this viewpoint. I knew that when he said I was the doctor and he was the patient it was his way of keeping me idealized and protecting me thereby from his negative affect.

When I did interpret his need to keep me as a doctor who was always right, me right up there and him right down on the floor, the result was dramatic. He became extremely depressed, he no longer wanted to come and see me, his mother started bringing him again and he stopped going to the day centre. In the sessions he cried heart-rending sobs that came from deep down. Mother came to me in distress; he had been sobbing like that at home and the pain of it was more than she could bear. Harry began to experience me as useless and hopeless—like his father—and, at the same time, he began to experience his father as caring for him. Then he said:

"But, if my Dad does care for me then someone has been lying."

He was quite unable to pursue that line of thought as it led to mother. He then began to fall back upon the notion that he had a "nervous disability". I interpreted that he was afraid of being better because he feared he would lose his mother's love. I explained that parents get used to their children in a particular mode and told him of a man, born blind, who had an operation at the age of twenty-four which enabled him to see. He was glad he could see but he was then afraid he would lose his mother's love.

"But he didn't, did he?"

I pointed out how anxious he was about this. He then went on to say that his father wanted him to have a job and all his mother wanted was for him to be happy. Then he asked me if I would see his mother and father, and I tried to join mother and father up for him by pointing out that being happy and having a job were complementary. I spoke of the satisfaction from a job well done and he saw this quite clearly. It is difficult to convey the power of that session. It was clear that he was seeing his world very differently and I was able to speak to him and he understood me as someone with a normal IQ. Towards the end of the session he looked at me and said:

"I don't know whether to laugh or cry."

Quite literally his pathology seemed to fall away in front of my eyes. But then he said:

"I am capable of more than everyone thinks I am but there's tomorrow and Sunday and Monday."

I interpreted that it was all right to know his capabilities but there were so many difficulties to fight through if he were to put them into effect and, in particular, he needed my support not just on Fridays but through the week, and he agreed. But at the end of the session he told me that he did not want to come any more, and that was the last session I had with him.

There were some follow-up interviews, both with family and with some members of staff at the day centre, and the following information was obtained:

1. He was now unwilling to do any work task at the centre.
2. He stayed at home, but reported to his social worker from time to time and continued to wonder whether he should continue treatment again.
3. It was confirmed that Harry was able to conduct a conversation that would have been quite impossible before the therapy began. He was less pressured by inner anxiety.
4. He was more decisive and had a greater sense of autonomy in relation to life's choices.

It seems that his capacities on his own and with life's tasks (e.g., making telephone calls, shopping for himself) had increased, but his willingness to submit to the will of others, especially in relation to manual work, had decreased.

Theoretical aspects of the case

Symbolic dysfunction

I want to turn back to the episode of the white coats and see if it is possible to gain any understanding through it. Unfortunately, the psychoanalytic literature on the subject of subnormality is sparse indeed. I think, however, three authors help to throw some light on this particular aspect of the topic: Clark (1933), Segal (1957), and Mannoni (1972). Pierce Clark was a psychoanalyst practising in America before the Second World War and his book, *The Nature and Treatment of Amentia*, is the only detailed treatment of subnormality from a psychoanalytic stance that I know. He makes two points that are interconnected. First, in the patient of subnormal intelligence there is a libidinal regression to foetal life where pleasure is centred on "stomach satisfaction". The individual is enveloped in primary narcissism and, in its most extreme forms, the subnormal patient frequently adopts foetal postures. This notion of a regression to the foetal stage of development has not received much serious attention from analysts. When Ferenczi (1968) elaborated the idea in his book *Thalassa*, he was considered, even by Freud, as somewhat fanciful. Yet Pierce Clark has found the idea clinically relevant in cases of subnormality. I have experienced what seems to be a foetal transference with physically handicapped patients and I think it likely that it occurs in cases of mental handicap. Why there should be a fixation at the foetal stage of development Pierce Clark does not postulate. I suggest that the patient feels that he has been damaged in the womb and this may have a basis in reality. This causes the patient to have a regression back to the foetal stage of development. It may be that the studies of Sontag and his colleagues at the Fells Institute in America on foetal trauma may have their relevance here.

Pierce Clark's second point is that although the patient is organically separate from mother, yet his ego is united to hers and his unconscious perception is that he and she are one flesh. This would help to explain why Harry felt that an attack on him would kill his mother and he experienced this in a concrete way. Pierce Clark does not elaborate the fact that this identification of the ego in primary narcissism alters the perception of external reality in some of its aspects.

I want next to mention the work of Maud Mannoni (1972). With regard to this case her work has the disadvantage that she was treating children and not adults and, in general, I think her observations tend to become distorted by ideological and political issues. She attacks the problem from the angle of the mother's pathology, which is crucial for any understanding of the retarded child. During pregnancy every mother has a fantasy child, the child of her dreams, to which she is going to give birth. This fantasy child will supplement the deficiencies of her own childhood and help her to work out her castration complex. When an abnormal child erupts on the scene, on the other hand, her own sense of castration is now lived out in the abnormal child. The child then unconsciously gets positive reinforcement to live within the mother's fantasy. This was verified in the case of Harry, though he also lived within father's fantasy; his perception of the world was via these parental fantasies rather than direct contact. When he began to see me directly, and not through the eyes of his mother or father, he entered a depressive episode. So, although Maud Mannoni approaches it from a different angle, her conclusion is the same as Pierce Clark's: the ego of the subnormal patient is not separate from the mother.

Some knowledge of symbol formation is necessary if we are to unravel the problem of the white coats, and I must refer you to the standard literature, in particular Ernest Jones's classic paper (1916). Because with Harry we are trying to understand the cause of a perceptual failure, I want to quote a similar example to the one of the white coats in a paper by Hanna Segal (1957):

> To give a very elementary example from two patients. One—whom I will call A—was a schizophrenic in a mental hospital. He was once asked by his doctor why it was that since his illness he had stopped playing the violin. He replied with some violence: "Why? Do you expect me to masturbate in public?"
>
> Another patient, B, dreamt one night that he and a young girl were playing a violin duet. He had associations to fiddling, masturbating etc, from which emerged clearly that the violin represented his genitals and playing the violin represented a masturbation fantasy of a relationship with the girl . . . We might say that the main difference between them is that for A the symbolic meaning of the violin was conscious, for B unconscious. I do not think, however, that this

was the most important difference between the two patients. In the case of B, the fact that the meaning of the dream became completely conscious had in no way prevented him from using his violin. In A, on the other hand, there were many symbols operating in his unconscious in the same way in which the violin was used on the conscious level. [p. 391]

Now, the disturbance in Harry was similar to the one in patient A: when he saw the white coats at the day centre they *were* the white coats at Frien Barnet. It is difficult to exaggerate the crippling effect this perceptual failure had upon Harry as it extended to many other areas of his life. Hanna Segal traces the perceptual failure to disturbances in differentiation between ego and object. She says: "Disturbances in differentiation between ego and object lead to disturbances in differentiation between the symbol and the object symbolised" (p. 392)

She, therefore, attributes this merging of discrete events in the perceptual field to a psychic union between ego and primary object and then traces this to a regression to the oral stage of development, thereby differing from Pierce Clark. What we have then is clinical evidence that this particular type of perceptual failure seems to correlate with an identification of ego with primary object, without knowing why.

On this latter point all three authors are in agreement: that there is an identification between the ego and the primary love abject. But this does not help us to understand what is specific in the aetiology of subnormality because this same psychological phenomenon is encountered in patients who are psychopathic, psychotic, and borderline and all these groups can be highly intelligent. It is impossible not to be struck by similarities between aspects of Harry's behaviour and those of some borderline patients, but what I wish to concentrate on here is some theoretical explanation of what led to a disturbance of intelligence.

Intelligence and psychotic disturbance

In the subnormal patient there is an active force blocking the development of intelligence. This means that intelligence presents itself as a threat to the organism. To understand what this threat is we need to get some insight into the role of intelligence and its relations to instinct. The current psychological approaches to cognition do not help us much. The reason seems to be that the underlying assumptions behind most cognitive theories are fixist. Although *The Origin of the Species* was published 120 years ago, for the majority of cognitive theories Charles Darwin might not have existed. Theories like those of Piaget, Vygotsky, and Bruner are developmental and not evolutionary, but the thinking of Freud was profoundly rooted in an evolutionary perspective. On the relations between intelligence and instinct the most enlightened thinker I know is Henri Bergson. I will summarize briefly those points of his which are relevant to our purpose.

Bergson (1919) defines life as "the tendency to act on matter". Instinct and intelligence are two different modes of this activity. Instinct is that mode by which the organism effects itself into a fixed instrument and always acts upon the environment through it. So, for instance, the scolia, which is a type of wasp, attacks the larva of the rose beetle, stinging it at one point only, but at this point the motor ganglia are concentrated and those ganglia alone. This paralyses the larva without killing it. The wasp lays its eggs in it and when they hatch they have fresh meat to feed upon. If the sting is a thousandth of a millimetre out then other ganglia would be affected and the larva would die and putrefy. The wasp does this from instinct. It is limited to the use of its own sting and a particular object, the rose beetle, to achieve its goal. If its sting becomes damaged it cannot fashion another instrument and if there are no rose beetles one year it cannot transfer to caterpillars. Through instinct the organism is encased in a fixed relation to a particular object.

Intelligence is another mode by which life tends to act on matter. In this case the organism does not fashion itself into a fixed instrument but rather fashions an instrument from the environment, outside of itself, and acts on matter through it. The organism can fashion more than one type of instrument and this gives it the capacity to move from one object to another. Intelligence, whose function is to abstract similarities from discrete phenomena, allows us to move from one object to another. Symbol formation, which is a more primitive method of movement from one object to another, tied as it is to perceptual cues, is yet dependent on intelligence to abstract those attributes that are similar in different phenomena.

Now, if there is a regression to the foetal stage in development, as Pierce Clark suggests, then to move to a new relation to mother as a result of birth is something powerfully resisted. The hatred of reality and new objects necessarily implies a violent detestation of intelligence. The patient desires to stay in a fixed relation to mother and does not want the emergence of intelligence. The vital question is whether psychotherapy can overcome some of these powerful resistances and thereby lessen the hatred of intelligence and give it space to develop. Very shortly after the incident with Harry, when I held his arm and spoke of the abyss, he came in for a session and at the very beginning said to me, "You know my trouble is education."

He went on to say something about his schooling and I interpreted that he felt healthier now and desired more education. As this seemed to be correct it led to a delicate technical problem: if I tried to organize some education for him then I was treating him as if he was unable to initiate anything himself, and yet if I did nothing would he be able to bring about the desired goal? There is another important problem. Piaget has shown that intelligence develops in stages that are quite rigidly circumscribed but does this mean that if it has not developed when it should that the loss is irretrievable, that each of Piaget's stages are like so many *critical periods*, such as the ethologists describe? I do not know the answer to these questions, but I have a suspicion that when I gave Harry the analogy of the man born blind I may have been nearer the mark than I had supposed. I am not now thinking of the *secondary gain* which a blind person loses on the recovery of sight, though this was extremely important in Harry's case, but the fact that when a person, blind from birth, has an operation enabling him to see yet he does not see. In his book *Eye and Brain*, Gregory (1966) gives an interesting case history of a man, born blind, who, at the age of fifty-two, had a corneal graft which enabled him to see, but in fact he was able to see initially only those objects which he had first touched, and I will quote an instance:

> We showed him a simple lathe (a tool he had wished he could use) and he was very excited. We showed it him first in a glass case. With the case closed, he was quite unable to say anything about it, except that the nearest part might be a handle . . . but when he was

allowed to touch it, he closed his eyes and placed his hand on it when he immediately said with assurance that it was a handle. He ran his hands eagerly over the rest of the lathe, with his eyes tight shut for a minute or so; then he stood back a little, and opening his eyes and staring at it he said: "Now that I've felt it, I can see!" [Gregory, 1966, p. 197]

My intuition is that psychotherapy can partially or wholly restore the intellectual faculty, but in order to use it effectively it is necessary for the patient to have some skilled individual training. In the case that Gregory quotes the man became severely depressed and three years after the operation he died. Gregory attributes it to the man's intense regret at what he had missed for so large a part of his life. Harry became depressed precisely when his intelligence was less obscured by emotional factors. In the psychotherapy of subnormal patients, I would recommend that educational resources be available should the need arise. A close cooperation between psychotherapist and teacher could be extremely helpful in cases such as Harry's.

Criteria for psychotherapy

There are many myths about psychotherapy and those whom it can help. It is an interesting fact that, even in our so-called enlightened age, mental illness is surrounded by a powerful mythology. The reasons why this should be so is an interesting phenomenon in itself but would take us too far from our subject.

One of the myths is that a good IQ is necessary for psychotherapy to be effective. My one piece of evidence seems to gainsay this. I have not witnessed such a rapid change as I did in Harry in any other patient of mine. There is evidence that very considerable change took place in Harry during the two years of treatment, but before making any generalizations from this one treatment the question of differential diagnosis needs to be considered. Some authors, for example Doll (1953), have emphasized the difference between the subnormal person, clinically defined as feeble-minded, and those patients who are called "pseudo mentally deficient". The pseudo category is thought to be so because of their familial environment, and authors point out that with this group there is no real impairment of intelligence but rather intelligence is blocked by powerful emotional factors. This group is distinguished from the truly mentally deficient patient whose condition is attributable to some impairment of the central nervous system or to some brain damage. I must say I find it very difficult to make this distinction as neatly as some authors do. To take the case of Harry, it would be clearly mistaken to assume that there was no organic disability. Rather, I think the evidence points to the contrary and Harry himself seemed to recognize this when we came to look at some of his reasons for clowning. The clinical picture with Harry would seem to be that there was some organic defect to which was added a huge overlay of fantasy that blocked him. I think one needs to consider the question of stereotyped reactions on the part of parents and other family figures to any child displaying some defect. I think we all know from common experience that people do react in a very stereotyped way to visible defects. The person who is born physically handicapped has first the physical handicap to contend with and then the stereotyped reactions of those whom he or she meets. I am, therefore, not convinced by this distinction between mental deficiency and pseudo mental deficiency. I suspect that the diagnosis is made on the basis of the degree of illusion surrounding the patient. In other words, someone described as pseudo mentally deficient would be a person like Harry, who has only minor organic impairment, but a massive internalized maternal fantasy that he is inadequate, helpless, and unintelligent. The true mentally deficient may have greater organic disability and less internalized maternal fantasy, but it is just a question of degree. I think that it is dangerous to make too many assumptions that may only serve to block psychoanalytic research.[1]

I think the other factor that needs serious consideration are the fundamental questions: "What is intelligence?" "Where is it rooted?" "In what way can it be damaged organically?" "Even if damaged, can psychotherapy help to restore the efficiency of intelligence?" We need to consider some of the rehabilitative work that has been done on people who have suffered strokes and also with people whose brains have been severely damaged through some accident. There is a very strong tendency for people to despair as soon as the word "organic" is mentioned. I have become more and more convinced that *unwarranted* despair on the part of those engaged in helping mental defectives is a far greater handicap to the patient than the organic defect. Neurological growth can be stimulated and it is certainly not static. What remains static are people's expectations that change cannot occur.

I would recommend, therefore, the greater use of psychoanalytic therapy for the mentally retarded, not only to help those individuals who are being thus treated, but also as a research method into an area that still remains largely unknown.

I think there may be another reason that deters us from treating people who are subnormal. It is that we are retarded in some areas of our mental functioning. One of us says, "I am absolutely useless at maths", another says, "I can never understand a word of philosophy", and another, "I can never understand a word of economics", and so on. When we treat a subnormal patient, we are reminded only too poignantly of our own mental retardation. It is only too understandable that we prefer not to be so reminded.

Commentary

I would today understand more his inner realization of his mother's intense attachment to him and how if he were damaged it would destroy his mother. This would also fit with his stopping therapy when his pain was too much for his mother to bear. She could not bear seeing him weeping with deep pain. I would also today emphasize more and put centre stage the merged state between himself and his mother but also how this extended to other people and that such a degree of closeness prevents the person's ability to distinguish between fantasy and reality. This is because fantasy can only be known to be fantasy if there is space between him and the object, whether the object be mother, father, a joke, a television programme: perception requires some distance, which is the basis for reflective intelligence.

I did learn a lot from treating this man. I had been told that psychodynamic psychotherapy only worked with people who had an IQ of 120. The treatment of this man taught me that this was entirely false. I realized that a lot of mythology builds up around psychoanalysis that it is wise to disregard.

Note

1. I later started a workshop for the treatment of the mentally retarded at the Tavistock Clinic. After I left, Valerie Sinason carried on this work and carried it much further and published a book about her researches into mental handicap.

CHAPTER NINE

Countertransference with mentally handicapped patients

"If only Walter had been born a dog and not a human child, how easy it would be to end her sense of responsibility. A vet with a pill or an injection, administered while she protested love and kindness, could free her"

(Cook, 1978, p. 46)

At the time when I was conducting a workshop on the psychotherapy of mentally handicapped people at the Tavistock we were all confronted one day with a very shocking piece of knowledge. It was a piece of knowledge that each of us possessed but it had not come to light until one particular session of the workshop. It was that we all treated mentally handicapped people with contempt and that we did not have this contempt towards "normal" people. I will explain the matter in more detail.

In the workshop we had decided in one term to try to differentiate our psychodynamic technique with the mentally handicapped from that used with "normal" people. Thus, we investigated our manner of interpretation, the nature of the transference in this category of client, and the anxiety attending on change. The question of countertransference also came under review. It was then that the discovery I have alluded to was made. On the level of consciousness we had sympathy towards mentally handicapped people, which had in part instigated the formation of the workshop. We had also come to realize the painful isolation that many mentally handicapped people live in. Therefore, on the level of consciousness, we were passionately devoted to our work with these people, had a self-righteous self-regard, and felt critical towards those colleagues of ours who would only consider people suitable for psychotherapy if they had a university level IQ. Our contempt then had been below the threshold of awareness. This is how the shocking story of our inner attitudes came about.

We first realized that there were certain things that we did with these patients which we did not do with others. For instance, with most clients the procedure was that the receptionist would ring and say that Mr or Mrs So-and-so was in reception and did we want him or her sent up to us. We would say "Yes", and the person would come up in the lift and make their way to our consulting room. However, when the people we were expecting had a mental handicap we would invariably go to the lift to meet them and bring them along to our consulting room. We somehow assumed that it was necessary to do this, but was it? Was our behaviour patronizing? Could they find their own way from the lift to our consulting room? We decided that they could, and when we put it to the test we found that they all could. In an attitude that is patronizing there is some contempt, so we went on to question ourselves as to whether there were any other signs of contempt in our attitudes. Were there any ways, even subtle ones, in which we treated these people with less respect? Then one woman in the workshop bravely admitted that she remembered the week before on a Wednesday morning that she was trying to decide how to dress that morning and considered momentarily whom she would be seeing that day. Remembering that "I was only seeing my mentally handicapped client", she decided to wear a shabby dress. Then someone else said that the previous day he had looked at his watch and saw that it was two o'clock so he must go to his consulting room as he had a client, but then, remembering that the client was a person with a mental handicap, he said to himself that he had time to have a quick word with a colleague because "my client would not mind if I were a few minutes late." Bit by bit each of us came out with similar bits of information. In subtle ways all of us were treating these people with contempt. When some members of the workshop presented a symposium on psychotherapy with people with a mental handicap at the Annual Conference of the British Psychological Society in 1981 in York and one member imparted this piece of information, the members of the audience were shocked. One person who was eminent in the field said that we were contemptuous towards people with a mental handicap because we were all used to treating sophisticated Hampstead intellectuals. We did not research the matter more widely, but observation tells me that this counter-transference exists in many carers of people with mental handicap and not just those members of that Tavistock group. I will tell you of just one incident that illustrates the point.

I was interviewing a mentally handicapped man at a large mental hospital. A secretary put her head through the door and said, "Doctor, would you like a cup of coffee?" I said, "Yes, please", and then she looked at my client and said, "And would you, Len?", and he said, "Yes." When, however, five minutes later the secretary reappeared, she had only one cup of coffee, which was for me, and she had evidently obliterated Len from her mind altogether. When I brought this to his attention he just shrugged his shoulders with depressed resignation. In the rest of what I am going to say I am going to take it as fact that mentally handicapped people are treated with contempt at a level that is below the threshold of awareness. I want to investigate why this is so and what it implies in terms of techniques in therapy.

In the animal kingdom the flock of birds attacks and kills the one that is wounded. It is also so with a pack of wolves and many other species. There is, I believe, also an instinct within human beings to kill off the handicapped member. It is deeply shocking when this actually occurs, as it did in Nazi Germany. It is, however, one of the deepest anxieties of those who are handicapped, either physi-cally or mentally. The fundamental existential question of mentally handicapped people is: "In truth, would you prefer to blot out my existence?" On one occasion I was treating a mentally handicapped girl and evidently at the end of a session as she was leaving I folded my arms. When she returned for the next session the one question on her mind was: why had I folded my arms when she was leaving? Was I relieved to be rid of her? Would I not prefer it if she were wiped off the face of the earth? In that sensitive novel *Walter*, by Peter Cook, he describes how Walter's mother decided to push him over the bridge on to the railway line before an oncoming train but, at the actual moment, she could not bring herself to do it. What the mentally handicapped person is concerned with is not the surface appearance of things but what it is that the therapist feels at the centre of his or her heart. That is why the only matter that the client was concerned about was why I had folded my arms.

Now I want to propose a shocking suggestion. Let us say with that client that I *do* want to get rid of her, that I *do* wish she would take a running jump into the lake. Let us provisionally say that that is exactly what I want. I then need to ask myself what would be the reason for it? Is it that I share the instinctual impulse of the animal kingdom to get rid of the damaged member? I could just say "Yes", but it is not as simple as that. When I told you that all members of our workshop shared an experience of contempt for mentally hand-icapped people it left out the fact that we have all sometimes felt a similar feeling towards a *particular* client. I have had patients who get into a frenzy if I am a minute late. I have had patients who show no external sign of minding at all. What was distinctive about the mentally handicapped patients was that the same feelings were experienced towards the whole group by all of us. It was not that we had not experienced such a feeling towards one particular person rather than another, but that the mentally handicapped person invariably evoked that contempt. What I am getting at is this: is it the mental handicap itself that evokes this reaction, or a psychological concomitant that always accompanies it? If it is the psychological concomitant then what exactly is it? What is it that provokes contempt? Let me try to describe this psychological attitude.

In my home we once had a woman to stay. As she walked through the door she said, "Oh, it's so kind of you to have me. I could easily have gone and stayed at a hotel. I know that it must be an awful trouble to you to have me, when you are all so busy." Then, as we showed her up to her bedroom, she said, "Oh dear, I am afraid it troubles my eyes to have a bed facing the light of the window." We hurriedly said, "Oh, that's all right, we'll move it for you around against the wall." Then she said, "Oh, no, don't trouble, I'll do it. I am sorry, I don't want to be a nuisance." A bit later that day I yawned and she said, "Oh, I can see that I am a burden to you." When my wife moved her chair to accommodate our guest, "Oh, I can see it would be far easier if you did not have me here." When I started to read the newspaper in the sitting room she said, "Oh, I can see I must be boring you."

I think you get the picture of what I am talking about. She focused her attention on every gesture in evidence of her conviction that she was a nuisance and a bother and that we would far prefer to be rid of her. Her focused attention to every gesture of ours and the constant interpretation of it along those lines were exasperating to us and it produced the very desire in us that she kept such a sharp look out for. In other words we all began to wish she would go and the sooner the better, but it was the focused attention that produced this wish in us. To have to be on constant guard against yawning or reading the newspaper is exasperating in the extreme. It is this focused attention generated by a paranoid motivation that is so tiresome and which made us all wish she would disappear for good. I think we have all met people like this, but how should we describe this particular pathology? I want now to examine it more closely.

This paranoid focus comes out of an omnipotent ego-structure. If when I am yawning it is because of this woman guest, if when I read the newspaper it is because of this woman guest, then she feels herself to be very powerful. The thought that I might yawn because I got up too early that morning or that I read the newspaper because there is an interesting item of news I want to know about is an affront to her omnipotence. It actually suggests that she may not be as powerful as she thought. What I am saying is that what I call *paranoid motivation* is generated by the presence in the ego of a powerful god-figure. It is a god-figure who cannot bear to be ignored. I am making the inference that many of the mentally handicapped people whom we were treating were behaving like our unwelcome female guest. It is this paranoid focus that leads to the exasperation and the desire to have done with the person once and for all. What I am proposing is that the contempt that we all felt is generated by the omnipotent introject, which itself fuels the paranoid focusing, and that it is this which generates the contempt and the desire to get rid of the person.

Therefore, what I am saying is that it is not the mental handicap itself that generates this particular countertransference but rather *the emotional tides stirred by the god-figure within*. We might say that this introject tries to arouse the animal reaction. What happens, though, is that the reaction is aroused at a subliminal level and then compensated against at the level of interpersonal interchange, so the mentally handicapped person is neither obliterated nor encouraged to develop, and so remains stuck. The human is different from the animal in that she is offered the opportunity to rise to a level of action higher than the instinctual but the only way of achieving this is through thorough self-scrutiny such as we attempted in the workshop.

What are the reasons for this omnipotent ego-structure present within the mentally handicapped patients who presented themselves to our workshop for psychotherapy? Underlying it is an ego that is disintegrated. The integration of the ego comes about in normal development when the infant makes emotional contact with the personhood of the mother. When the mother remains a functional object in emotional perception, the ego cannot integrate and the mentally handicapped individual's ego stays dysfunctional. The dysfunctional ego is reinforced by society's attitudes. It is rare for mentally handicapped people to have jobs in the workforce. When it comes to offering work to this category of persons the attitudes are as patronizing as were the attitudes of the therapists in the Tavistock workshop. That these people are frequently capable of doing jobs in the workforce is very likely. In emergency situations this has been recognized. During the Second World War mentally handicapped people were given jobs in the army. To feel useful to the community is ego enhancing and diminishes omnipotence. The long-term rehabilitation of the mentally handicapped requires the mentally handicapped to be integrated into the workforce. In the absence of a war, when every hand on deck is needed, a revised system of values is needed that gives recognition to the precise capacities that the mentally handicapped are able to contribute. It is outside the scope of this paper to discuss the ways in which social reorganization could assist the personality development of this category of persons. Clearly a very radical re-evaluation of social goals is necessary. It is my belief that such a re-orientation of values would benefit not only those who are mentally handicapped but also the emotional lives of most of us.

When the members of the Tavistock workshop first became aware of this contempt, the immediate reaction of one member was guilt and this transmitted in varying degrees to others. The problem, however, is that guilt cripples and is ineffective. I believe that it was this contempt that existed below the surface of awareness that created the guilt that then made us overcompensate and so go to meet our mentally handicapped clients at the lift. The particular problem about such a guilt is that it creates an infertile cycle. Contempt is stirred up in the therapist, which fashions guilt, which leads to a patronizing attitude, and the real problem of this is that it leads to a sterile situation in which no change can take place and this, I believe, is the heart of the problem: there is a deep-seated aim within the mentally handicapped person to block development. I want first, however, to examine the thesis that a mentally handicapped person subtly stirs up this contempt about which I have been talking.

The feelings that are below the threshold of consciousness in the therapist are what constitute the countertransference. Those feelings of contempt that I have described were the countertransference of each one of us. At the moment when they become conscious they are available for interpretation and no longer constitute a countertransference. My contention is that this feeling of contempt was stirred up in each one of us by these people through a power derived from the omnipotent introject. If we were in touch with our own mental handicap then we would not be host to these powerful stirrings. This means that the tendencies in us to be contemptuous towards people damaged or less fortunate then ourselves derives from a mentally handicapped enclave in each one of us that is unbearable. The mentally handicapped person then slips into this ecological niche of our own unbearability. There is comfort there because there is no challenge to development. Thus is created the cycle of contempt–guilt–pity and all further development is stifled. We do not desire development in the person we feel sorry for or pity.

Something else we discovered in the workshop was this: many of these clients would be in a hospital, a sheltered workshop, or at home with mother without being able to go to school or a job. The therapy would progress well, even quicker than usual, and the point would come when the client was all poised to move from the sheltered position. This would be on the point of happening when there would be a set-back. The client would stop treatment or would behave in an alarming way that would prevent the new step from happening. This happened again and again in our workshop and the feeling in the therapists was one of despondency. We learned two things: that there was a powerful resistance to a developmental step and that such a step was inseparable from severe psychic pain. It was coming up against such a severe pain barrier that led to this retreat.

In his classic book on this subject, the American psychoanalyst Pierce Clark (1933) believed that these people are fixated at the foetal level of development and when there is a psychological thrust towards birth it is countered by a violent regressive pull back to the womb. This model makes sense of the experience that we all had in the workshop. The therapist, in order to break out of the infertile cycle, has to help the client face an indescribable amount of pain. The first step on this journey is, however, the moment when the therapist recognizes the contempt. With acknowledgment of it there is hope of growth, but without it there is none.

PART IV
PILGRIMAGE

Introduction

"Now just compare this fellow with someone else we know—they are both practical men, but you see what a difference there is: in one case there's a genuine, living ideal inspired by life itself—whereas here there's not even a sense of duty, but simply an official honesty and superficial, practical ability"

(Turgenev, 1977, p. 153)

I did my analytic training within the bosom of the Independent Group of the British Psychoanalytical Society. I was well ensconced within this group and *The Analytic Experience* (1986) was clearly written by someone within the Independent School, but when I reached Australia I found that the thinking in it was not deep enough to be helpful for the types of disturbances I was beginning to meet clinically so I had an infatuation with Kleinian thinking. A colleague in London referred to me at this time as "an independent Kleinian".

I had already been attracted to this outlook and in London I had attended for six years the fortnightly seminars run by Herbert

157

Rosenfeld. I found these enlightening. I began to see some of the more primitive mental processes operating in the personality. I had also had a patient who had led me into these deeper pathways. (See Chapter Two, "The patient makes the analyst".) I thought that my own analysis and the thinking of the Independent School was experientially ignorant of this deeper layer within the mind. This area has been called the psychotic area, the primitive mind, the pre-Oedipal, and so on. I am sure some of my colleagues would immediately point out that this was the same area that Michael Balint called the "area of the basic fault" and that Winnicott also treated this area in the personality. Although Michael Balint did know about this area in that he had the common sense to leave a patient in peace when this area was arrived at and restrained himself from hammering the poor patient with more and more interpretations, yet I believe his understanding was deficient. The reason, as he put it, for this basic fault was a mis-fit between the mother and the baby. I am sure that this was pointing in the right direction, and this was developed further and elaborated with more sophistication by both Bion and Frances Tustin. I think the failure here was truly to believe what had been discovered. Balint was, I believe, too focused on the faults of the Kleinians and Freudians—his energy was too taken up with that so he did not direct his psychic attention sufficiently to what he had adumbrated. As Ernest Jones pointed out in his biography of Freud, many people (Jones quotes Wordsworth as a particular example) had pointed out that the emotional events of childhood structured and gave form to adult character, yet it took a Freud to believe it and make this discovery a lifelong project. Jones says it is the difference between a flirtation and a marriage. So Balint flirted with the idea of the basic fault but failed to believe it, engage with it, and make of it a life's project, and so also with his followers in the Independent Group.

Winnicott, on the other hand, did engage with this area and had great understanding of it, but his definition of psychosis as *an environmental deficiency disease* (1965, p. 256) struck a very discordant note in me. I think he was right in pointing to a deficiency, but it was in the personality as well as in the environment. Many of Winnicott's papers are superb, but his understanding of the primitive level of operation in the personality has not been followed by those in the Independent Group. So, in the 1970s and 1980s, I did not come across any psychoanalysts in the Independent Group whom I felt understood the psychotic area in the personality; thus, I turned to the Kleinians and there I learned something of this primitive area. As I did so and became more influenced by the thinking of this group, so my colleagues in the Independent Group became more and more hostile towards me. I had become a traitor in the camp. On one occasion a colleague was going to include a mention of me in a paper he was presenting about the philosophy of the Independent Group but he was advised against doing so because he "would become the laughing-stock of the Kleinians". The petty-mindedness of such attitudes and its betrayal of truth sickened me.

In his autobiography Bertrand Russell says that although he was associated with many different groupings in his life he was never totally *in* one. He says, for example, that during the First World War he was a pacifist and the Pacifists claimed him as one of their heroes, but that when the Second World War came along he supported the Allied Cause and the Pacifists called him a traitor; but he explains, and to me convincingly, that he had never been a Pacifist with a big "P", but only a pacifist in a given situation. He thought that Britain's reasons for going to war in 1914 were not justified, but that in 1939, on balance, they were. He goes on to say that he was always a man on the edge of the group, never grafted into its centre. I think this general sentiment has been true of myself also. At one time I used to teach Fairbairn as part of the training programme of the British Association of Psychotherapists in London. I taught it for about three years and then one day I heard myself referred to as a "Fairbairnian". I knew it was time to stop teaching Fairbairn. I belonged to the Independent Group as it seemed closest to my own value system. However, if it meant that I had to be anti-Kleinian or anti-Anna Freud, then the group had better dismiss me to its outer perimeter. I think this is where I still am.

So I was in sympathy with the Kleinians for some years, until I began to ferret into the nature of narcissism. The deeper I explored this condition the more I felt that the Kleinians failed in this area. Then, as I began to think that the narcissistic condition lay at the core of psychosis, I became increasingly convinced that the Kleinians had not understood psychosis. It was more deceiving because the Kleinians claim to understand this area of the personality whereas the Independents, on the whole, do not. The Kleinians had never embraced me as one of their own but had always viewed me with a certain wariness. This vigilance, from their point of view, was now justified.

When I had been in Australia for six years I sent a paper to the Bulletin of the British Psychoanalytic Society in which I was particularly attacking the erection of icons within psychoanalytic societies. This is the first of the next group of three papers. Then, in 1995, the Tavistock had a conference to celebrate its seventy-fifth anniversary and they asked me to come and present a paper at it, which I was pleased to do. So the second of these three papers was what I gave on this occasion. I was in London for just a week and then proceeded on to San Francisco. While there I was asked to give a talk to a newly established psychotherapy association in Oakland, so I spoke about my own struggle to achieve independence of mind within the British Psychoanalytic Society. This is the third of the papers presented in this section.

Looking now at this period of my development, I can see something of the "angry young man". I think it is usual when an individual is freeing himself from the chains of discipleship that he shouts and screams against his erstwhile captors. These papers carry that tone of rebellion. But they were important stepping-stones across the wide river as I struggled towards the opposite bank. That is a place I have not yet reached.

CHAPTER TEN

Independence of mind: attachment and the British Society

"Nothing creates such untruth in you as the wish to please"

(Hazzard, 1981, p. 209)

I t is nearly six years[1] since I was working as a psychoanalyst in London. Until shortly before the time of leaving in 1985 I was closely involved in the administrative and emotional life of the Society. I felt with passion about many of the theoretical issues and had participated, along with my wife, in most of the Scientific Meetings for a period of years. Since being in Australia I have no longer shared in the close workings of the Society, but have continued my association through reading the bulletin, visits to London, and conversations with colleagues.

When in London I knew there were certain things wrong with the British Society, but I was too closely involved to be able to see them properly. I could not see the wood for the trees. Since being in Australia I have arrived at certain insights and perspectives that I will try to outline.

One thing I knew for certain: that analysts defend with passion the views and outlook of their own analyst. If they did not defend specifically the view of their own analyst, they defended the particular school to which their analyst belonged and behind this the figures who had become the icons of each particular grouping. So, those who had been trained and analysed within the Kleinian group defended in particular the views of Melanie Klein and, to a lesser extent, the views of some of the senior figures within the Kleinian group. In a similar way members of the Contemporary Freudian Group would defend the approach and outlook of Anna Freud, and finally, although members of the Independent Group tended to eschew erecting icons, yet Winnicott and, to a lesser extent, Balint and Fairbairn had become the icons of that group. There was the sense that analysts were defending the emotional viewpoint of the icons in their School and that if one of them were attacked they would rush to his or her defence.

As the truth is never totally incarnate in any one person, it of necessity means that the truth is not being defended but instead what is being defended is a particular person—a person with his good insights as well as his prejudices. It may be that the analyst has expressed some very important truths and that people may be fearful that those truths will be lost, and so they end up defending both the truth and also untruths. But we analysts know that when an individual defends, without any censorship or inner editorial process, the views of a particular person, he or she is in a paranoid state. I once saw a prisoner strike a man who criticized his mother. We know that it is his own self projected into the maternal image that he is defending and that makes him attack his critic with such venom.

In the British Society we have a situation that is very like that. I have seen Melanie Klein attacked and watched Kleinians smouldering with rage. I have seen Winnicott attacked and the Independents react with the hurt and fury that one associates with a personal insult. I have seen Freudians campaigning in order to defend one of their members who was making a presentation at a Scientific Meeting. There are exceptions to this, and people may wish to qualify or smooth down the harshness of my words, but I defy anyone to deny that the general tenor of what I am saying is true.

There is one conclusion from this that is unavoidable: that none of us is able to tolerate criticism. When an Independent gets up to give a paper, his fellow Independents all go to his defence and the same is so of the Kleinians and the Freudians. I am not saying that any of us likes to be criticized or to have his or her views exposed to scrutiny, but it is a very serious situation when we cannot bear it at all, when we have to dragoon our own group to support us. My preoccupation is this: what has gone wrong in an analysis if at the end of many years I cannot tolerate criticism? If we diagnose the situation, then I think it means that at the end of an analysis most of us end up with a well established narcissistic character structure underneath which is an underdeveloped ego. You certainly could not say that we demonstrate ourselves to be people of robust mental health, people who can tolerate criticism, people who are not overly sensitive.

What is the reason for this situation? I want to approach this from two angles: first from that of the individual's own personal analysis and second from the point of view of the organization. There is a phenomenon very often commented upon, and that is the tendency of analysts to adopt the mannerisms, tones of voice, and gestures of their own analyst. I believe this is connected with the paranoia that I spoke about. It does mean I believe that the analysand has projected himself or herself into his or her own analyst. I remember a colleague telling me jokingly that when he started seeing patients he used to stand by the door and fill himself out in order to be as broad-shouldered as his own analyst had been. We could all multiply examples.

The phenomenon coincided with what I was saying about the individual analyst really defending, in the guise of his or her icon, his own narcissistic self. We project ourselves into our analysts and derive false ego strengths on the basis of omnipotent identification, with an undeveloped ego crushed underneath. When someone is defending the truth, they do so with passion, but not necessarily with that paranoid zeal engendered if they feel that a treasured darling is being injured. The little darling who cannot be hurt is projected into the icon and protected there. Not only is it protected there by the individual, but the individual receives massive support from the group for this manoeuvre.

There is some way of projecting the easily hurt narcissistic self into the icon; this very action establishes or perpetuates the narcissism. I think it happens something like this. When the analyst makes an interpretation or some management decision, it stimulates enormous secret admiration and powerful envy in the infantile ego of the analysand. The ego then projects itself into the envied object and becomes an object to be envied. To be admired becomes the motivational thrust of all activity. To be attacked or to be criticized is met with rage, and rationalizations are summoned to smooth the criticism away.

I have called this process of projection into the icon a *mimetic transference* (Symington, 1996b). The patient gets inside the analyst, right into his attitudes and outlooks, and, usually together with the analyst, he scornfully dismisses the voice of unease that resides in the infantile ego and is frequently voiced through figures in the alien groups. What I refer to as mimetic transference is nothing new: it comes about through a combination of projective and introjective processes. A narcissistic idealized ego is projected into the icon and the icon, duly castrated of many real elements, is introjected into the inner forum of the personality.

When this happens it always occurs at the expense of a part of the self that is got rid of into one of these disturbing voices inhabiting the members of an alien group. When a part of the self is got rid of in this way, the ego is left impoverished. The very process by which an analyst joins with his patient to recommend a supervisor thereby, either tacitly or openly, colludes in the scorn for another. Such a procedure very easily gives rise to this kind of evacuative action. At the end of a training, the individual may be standing in a precarious state with a weak ego unable to make the free and independent choices that one would hope for from a person who had been analysed. The inference here is that the trainee will be less well analysed than the "layman".

When an individual has got rid of parts of him or herself in this way, then the person lives vicariously through the eyes and ears of the icon. In this state the individual necessarily blocks out certain perceptions. He may see minor faults in his icon or in the important figures of the icon's group, but will be blind to major deficits. I think one of the problems about our icons—Melanie Klein, Winnicott, Anna Freud—is that they all had marvellous insights and rare gifts of understanding. It is overwhelmingly tempting to project oneself into this icon and take on board all his or her words and theories and outlooks. It is difficult to tolerate seeing that in each of them, side by side, sometimes right next to an insight that is so good, so inspiring, there lies the most appalling bit of rubbish. It is so much easier to be passive and drink in the lot. We only have to look at Freud to see this. Alongside papers of clinical brilliance and masterful insight, we have the sort of rubbish that he wrote about the primal horde in *Totem and Taboo*. It is not that beside the very good there is sometimes the less good, or the indifferent, but often beside the very good is the very bad. But through this mimetic process we end up defending the lot. We are not prepared to place our theories and outlooks under scientific scrutiny. In the same way the analysand drinks in the good interpretation and the bad, not only the bad interpretations but the whole technical procedure of the analyst. The purpose of the process is to get rid of what is bad and shoddy in one's own work. Instead of the bad being recognized, the bad in one's icon, the bad in one's own work, and the bad in the work of admired colleagues in one's own group is dismissed. The result is that the individual analyst does not sort out the good from the bad in his own work and he has a character structure that is geared to preventing colleagues doing that for him. The problem is that the Society is structured to fit in with this. The critic is so often someone from another group that the colleagues of one's own group all band around one and encourage one not to listen to this prejudiced attack from the member of another group.

I think that all this has led to a very severe impoverishment of psychoanalysis in the British Society but I also suspect in others. Reading the report prepared by Mrs Menzies Lyth,[2] I was struck by the high percentage of patients that are trainees of one sort or another. It is also well known that the patients which we have are often made up of spouses, relatives, and connections of the analysts. This becomes particularly so with senior analysts. It is a bit unlikely that in such a climate the analyst will receive a radical critique. When I was at the Tavistock it was my task, from time to time, to interview people who were applying for jobs. It was often the case that an applicant would be someone who had been working happily at a clinic where the consultant was a psychoanalyst, but that as soon as the consultant left and someone either against analysis or not supportive of analysis took his place, the person was unable to tolerate any hostility or criticism and had to come and find refuge under the skirt of "Mummy Tavistock". These were

166 BECOMING A PERSON THROUGH PSYCHOANALYSIS

people who had been analysed. You would not say that this demon-strated a robust mental constitution. What I am saying here is that what is true of each of the three groups in the British Society is also true of the members of the Society as a whole. Where is that ancient spirit of Socrates, who rejoiced and was in his element when he was in dispute?

Now, this seems to be a very common situation with all people who are analysed, a situation that obtains probably in all analytic societies. I want to come to this wider issue shortly, but in the British Society what we have is a conjunction of three such defensive organizations loosely held together for the purpose of protecting its members from narcissistic injury. It seems to be a very real fact that when an analysand is in the midst of this analytic society, then subtle alliances get set up between the analyst and the patient against the other figures in the analytic society and the scope for a patient to hook the analyst into such perverse alliances is very big indeed. I think it is quite frequently the case that when mention is made of an analytic colleague, it is not taken as an internal object in the analysis. It is for this reason that patients outside of the network may get a better analysis and come out of it with a more robust ego. But senior analysts with so few patients outside of the network may get out of practice.

I just want to dwell a little bit further on what I have said about mimesis. This a process whereby the analysand subtly projects his own ego into the admired imago of the analyst and so sees things through what he believes to be his eyes. The point I want to emphasize is that the analysand then inhabits a kind of dream world and the envious part of him or her which is behind the transaction is got rid of, projected. This leads to destructive behaviour that is kept unconscious.

I want now to discuss the organizational aspect of all this. One of its results is that analysts become defensive and paranoid when psychoanalysis is criticized or challenged. So challenges, which are always opportunities for emotional growth, are turned into agents of impoverishment. There is no doubt that we only grow mentally if our positions are challenged. By rising to this stimulus and addressing our minds to it, our own minds grow and develop. It also enriches our thinking when we are able to incorporate the area of correctness in the attack into our own mental constructs. The way things are structured internally in the British Society, with the attitudes that it fosters, defends all of us from meeting such a challenge from our fellows, because we always have a group of sycophants who will support us against the malevolent critic, but the British Society, and, I suspect, most analytic societies in the world, also have gathered themselves into a defensive huddle against the criticisms and attacks of outsiders. I am well aware that many such attacks and critiques have much that is spurious in them, a lot that may be motivated by personal animosity, but none of this explains why we become, as an organization, defensive. When we are attacked we very rarely distinguish truth from falsehood. There seems to me to be no doubt that a psychoanalytic institute needs to be publicly accountable. If we claim to be a scientific discipline, then is there any reason for an analytic institute not to be in the thoroughfare of the scientific marketplace? We would then be open to challenge; there would be a culture in which it was understood that if analyses did not foster the type of personality that is able to meet criticism, confrontation, and challenge, then we are not conducting the sort of psychoanalysis that is any good. If a military establishment produced soldiers who immediately took flight at the sight of the enemy, a Royal Commission might well close down the establishment and create a new one.

I do not know exactly how a private institute could take its place in the marketplace, particularly the scientific and academic marketplace. That is something that could be worked out as long as there was the will and determination to do it. In the meantime there are some adaptations which could be put into effect more quickly and which would already put things on the right path. Most of what we call scientific meetings are closed. This is because what is being presented is a clinical paper and what the analysts want is a clinical discussion. I suggest that it is a misnomer to call such a meeting a scientific event. Such events are clinical meetings. Such meetings are essential in an analytic society, but we are deceiving ourselves if we think that they are scientific meetings. A scientific meeting is one where some aspect of mind can be discussed in conjunction with other thinkers within the social sciences. So our scientific meetings need to be open to a wider scientific community. I would suggest that the scientific committee has, as part of its composition, scientists from other disciplines, especially the social sciences, but also from the natural sciences as well as from literature, history, and philosophy.

There are very many scientific topics of great interest to which psychoanalysts could make a distinctive contribution. I am thinking of topics such as the following: The Nature of Thinking; The Difference between Emotions and Feelings; The Psychological Roots of Moral Action; The Relation between Thought and Language; The Nature of Symbol Formation; The Nature of Imagination; and so on. There have been symposia on psychiatric conditions in which psychiatrists who have not been analysts have participated, but the kind of topics I am suggesting would bring together thinkers from different disciplines who would join together with analysts to try to deepen understanding of the nature of the mind. I have picked the above topics haphazardly out of a big menu of possibilities. However, the reason why I have picked those particular topics as examples is that they have all been thought about and addressed by philosophers, psychologists, sociologists, and historians. They are topics on which and in which psychoanalysts could make a distinctive contribution, but alongside others who would also be making equally significant contributions. In this way we would have the opportunity to enrich our own insights. I am talking about psychoanalysts researching the human mind along with others who share the same object of knowledge in their researches. I believe that this could lead to a very enriching fellowship. It would, however, test us severely. We could not get away with some of the stuff that we produce at the moment at our meetings and in our journals. One of the reasons why we cower in our analytic ghetto is that we know that the quality of what we produce will not stand up to decent and informed criticism. I do not think we are making notable contributions into the nature of the human mind. This is not because we have no members who have made and who are making profound insights into aspects of mental functioning, but it is because this knowledge is being wasted. It is not being used and inserted into the wider scientific community, it is being used rather as cannon fodder for our petty quarrels. I fear that, unless we do something about this lamentable situation, psychoanalysis will go under; it will become an irrelevant. It will be brushed aside as a piece of absurd folklore, and if we continue in the way we are this is what will happen and we shall only have ourselves to blame.

Commentary

Reading this today I shudder at its self-righteousness—as if I do not share nearly all of the exclusive attitudes that I am complaining about. If I were writing it today I would include myself and my tone would be gentler and my attitude more tolerant. I would try to understand more sympathetically why we make the narcissistic identifications that we do.

Notes

1. This paper was written in 1992.
2. Isobel Menzies Lyth had shortly before written a report on the problems of the British Psycho-Analytical Society.

CHAPTER ELEVEN

Migration from the Tavistock: impetus for mental change

> "There are tumults of mind, like the great convulsions of
> nature, all seems anarchy and returning chaos, yet often, in
> those moments of vast disturbance, as in the material strife
> itself, some new principle of order, or some new impulse of
> conduct, develops itself, and controls, and regulates, and
> brings to an harmonious consequence, passions and elements
> which seemed only to threaten despair and subversion"
>
> (Disraeli, 1845, p. 284)

I worked at the Tavistock as a senior staff member in the Adult
Department from 1978 to 1985. I had for two years prior to 1978
given a series of lectures to social workers. So I worked at the
Tavistock for a period of nine years in total. During that time I
acquired a very unfortunate reputation: that I was believed to be
good at public speaking. On the basis of that reputation I was asked
to give a series of thirty lectures on "Psychoanalytic theory" to
mental health professionals from the three departments of the
Tavistock. My credentials at the time were minimal and my acceptance of the offer can be put down mainly to ambition and

grandiosity. Grandiosity forbade me to refuse offers to speak. I remember in one year counting that, in addition to the standard thirty lectures at the Tavistock, I gave a further seventeen in different places, reaching a total of forty-seven lectures in a single year. The inability to say "No" to these ever-increasing requests meant that the reservoir was almost empty. An academic once confided to me that he was living on capital—intellectual capital, that is—and my position was not dissimilar. I knew the reservoir had to be refilled so, with wife and family, we moved camp across the world to New South Wales. On the way we stopped for eight months at a staging post in the south of France in the little village of Seillans, nestling in the hills of Provence. So, in that idyllic spot with our two boys at the local village school, we refilled the reservoir and more.

On the outside it appeared that we were living a totally indulgent life. We painted, we visited art galleries, toured into Italy twice and once across Spain and into Portugal, and I wrote an autobiographical novel. On the inside, however, was a raging furnace and a period of nothing less than "catastrophic change". All my preconceptions were in the balance. I read where my instinct took me, guided always by this turmoil within. The book that had the greatest influence was Duff Cooper's biography of Talleyrand, which still stands on my bookcase as a reminder of those turbulent days. Never once did I touch a book on psychoanalysis and I did not miss my clinical work in the slightest bit. I had a full-time patient on my hands and had no inclination to attend to any others. This violent change continued its turbulent course for another two years until it reached a climax once we were safely—or more truly unsafely—installed in our home in New South Wales. At the end of this time my view of myself, of psychoanalysis, and of the human psyche had changed very profoundly. Although I changed during the course of analysis I changed in a much more radical way in those three years after leaving the Tavistock. Later I shall discuss whether this would have occurred had I stayed at the Tavistock, but I want first to try to describe the nature of that change.

Before Christmas last year we had a letter from Bob Gosling in which he said,

> "I'm nervous about our tendency to think of objects, whether material or psychic, as things or people when it is their function that

matters: it was not my mother's body or genetic make-up that mattered, but her inclination and capacity to do what she did."

The mother or the breast is not the *terminus ad quem* but the *terminus a quo*. This quest that we make into ourselves is not to discover objects, but rather to discover our inner mentality, which determines the way we relate to our objects. When I use the phrase "inner mentality" I think I am probably referring to what Bion called the "psychoanalytic object". In my Tavistock days, when I was treating a patient and had discovered the nature of the transference and learned to bear it, either positive or negative, I thought I had discharged my task. I basked in the role in which the patient had cast me. It never crossed my mind to ask what was the nature of the mental activity that was bringing such a transference about.

An essential tool in my work today is a theory of mental action. I had a patient in Australia who would, in a flash, deposit her hatred into me in a glancing look as she left the consulting room, and when she returned next day she found herself in the presence of an ogre and herself in a state of anxious agitation. My attention now is not upon myself as an ogre, but rather upon her activity that turns me into one and, of course, the reason which prompts it. These inner psychic acts that herald a mentality which in turn affects all the variegated operations of the emotions are now the focus of my attention. Patients come to us because they are mentally disturbed, mentally ill, or mentally perverted and seek transformation.

Empathic understanding does not transform, but fixes us in our own inner predicament. Empathic understanding, of its nature, is an attitude that relates to the object and not its function. It is a static attitude towards a static object. Mentality is life, is movement. Hatred and love are the soul in action. The mind *is* action. We tend to think of the mind as static, but it is a reality that is in movement.

On what new ground did this post-Tavistock turbulence place me that was different from the ground upon which I stood before? It was not a total revolution. Signs of it were already there in my work while I was at the Tavistock. A selection of the lectures that I used to give at the Tavistock were published in a book entitled *The Analytic Experience*. To try to distil the difference between my inner philosophy then and now I turn to some of the statements in the book.

In the very first lecture, which was entitled "Psychoanalysis: a servant of truth", I make the statement "Psychoanalysis is a method of investigating the unconscious mind, and its particular focus is on the inner world" (Symington, 1986, p. 16).

That is not a statement that I would wish to change, but at that time I did not know what it was that is unconscious. I had read Freud on Repression and understood that those things that were antagonistic to our self-representation were banished into the Unconscious. Yet it is a fact of clinical experience that patients are often unaware of creative capacity within themselves, so it is not only bad or painful things that remain unconscious. This aspect of the Unconscious had been explored by Jung, yet it does not tell us what sphere of human activity remains unconscious. I am now convinced that it is the sphere of emotional activity that is unconscious in us. Motor activity is conscious, but we remain unaware of our emotional activity. We are conscious of the ways in which people treat us, but unaware of how we act emotionally towards them.

We do not know our emotional activity directly and therefore can only infer it. There are signs and symbols that point to it. We are all familiar with signs that are contained in dreams. There are others, however, such as the differing ways in which people behave towards us. Then we know that those hateful ways in which our intimates treat us are signs of our own emotional activity that we loathe to know about. This particularly applies to those attitudes that we hate in our parents and siblings. So, also, sexually perverse activities are signs of what we are doing emotionally. With Freud, matters stopped at the sexual, whereas we understand now that the sexual is a sign pointing to the emotional. Bodily symptoms are also signs of what is occurring emotionally.

We are not naturally aware of what cannot be known directly. We can make inferences about this emotional activity by interpreting the signs and through intuition. We are, therefore, naturally unconscious of this sphere of action, but I believe it is a mistake to name it "The Unconscious" since this suggests a place, something static, where painful and unwanted knowledge and memories are dumped. I also believe it obliterates thought, stopping us thinking about the sphere of which we are not conscious.

When I re-read parts of my book, I realize that when I was giving those lectures at the Tavistock I was repeating formulae but there was no attempt on my part to penetrate into the mental reality that lay behind them. Bion made a distinction between thinking where I synthesize the thoughts of others as opposed to generating my own thoughts. I was synthesizing, therefore, the thoughts of others which had been passed down to me within the psychoanalytical tradition, but had not penetrated into them. I had no personal understanding of this sphere referred to as "The Unconscious". This bit of material in my mind had not been worked upon by *alpha function*, to use Bion's formulation.

I want now to introduce another piece of understanding that I did not have then but that I do possess now by mentioning a clinical vignette. In session after session a man repeated to me how guilty he felt about all matters sexual. There is one thing I thought I could be certain of: that he knew he was guilty about sexual matters. However, one day he was in a considerable state of shock and told me he had just become aware of how guilty he was about all things sexual. I realized, therefore, that his previous statements could be understood both as an outpouring of unintegrated bits and also as signals of what he was wanting to achieve. On re-reading my book I can see statements that might lead the reader or listener to believe that I had understood and was aware of what I have been saying about the unseen emotional activity, and yet I had not been aware of what I was saying at the time. Again in the first lecture I say,

> Positivistic thinking has had such a strong influence on our basic assumptions that we tend to identify the real with what we can touch, taste, feel, see or hear. We need to ditch this preconception if we are to think psychologically. [*ibid.*, p. 17]

I see that statement now as a signal searching for understanding but realization not having occurred at the time. So I have this strange experience on re-reading my book of finding pieces of knowledge that I cannot say I truly possessed. I believe it was necessary to leave the Tavistock in order to come into possession of this knowledge.

I want to quote another passage from a lecture entitled "The clinical significance of transference":

A patient described a mother who could never *take* any of his concerns. He was a man with passionate feelings, but his mother would always say to him, "Yes, yes, darling", and quickly change the subject. This quality of his mother's absolutely exasperated him, for it was a manifestation of her inability to bear any of her child's anxiety. He described a mother who seemed unable to cope with any demands from her baby: once she found herself responsible for her baby she just dumped him on to someone else. This for him was the unbearable response. Now I think it likely that his mother really was like this with my patient. Accordingly in the transference he perceived me in the same way. He was sure that I could not bear any demands from him, and he was certain that I would drop him early on in the treatment. [p. 110]

I want to draw your attention to the statement "Now I think it likely that his mother really was like this with my patient". I would today understand that there was an inner mother in him that immediately damped down passionate concerns in him and, although I might interpret his feeling that I could not bear demands from him, I would realize that this was because he was projecting into me this hated inner mother—that he could not bear to know about this part of him that damped down his passionate inner concerns. I would also realize that maybe I was being affected in my responses by this disowned part of him. Today I would not make the statement "Now I think it likely that his mother really *was* like this with my patient", but I want to try to explain why.

The first way of approaching this would be to say that the inner figure affecting me in the transference might also have been affecting his mother in his childhood. You see, the way I saw things then was to say that the external mother *was* like that and there is in it a hint of blame towards the mother. If she had not been like that then my patient would not be suffering his present plight. This is quite subtle, because I do say that I thought it likely that his mother really was like this *with my patient* so there is some room for the possibility that she may not have been like that with everyone else, yet the burden of the statement is that the mother *as a whole object* really was like this. There is no emphasis here upon the possibility that the mother was like this towards her child partly through being stirred by this introject within him.

Today I would be looking to explain the presence of this introject in the patient according to a theory which I tried to outline in a book which I wrote two years ago on narcissism (Symington, 1993). In that book I put forward the thesis that such an introject becomes established in the personality out of guilt. I would, in the analysis, seek out the emotional activity responsible for the guilt and try to win the patient's collaborative efforts against this injurious part of himself. Also, therefore, I would have a conceptualization that saw the patient, the patient's mother, and myself as made up of parts. I realize now that when I was lecturing at the Tavistock I did not emotionally understand the inner world either in myself or in others.

There is another piece of the jigsaw in this constellation, which comes under the title of destructive projective identification and constructive identification. This is a refinement of what I was saying a short while ago about emotional activity. These are two forms of emotional activity. We are most of us familiar with destructive projective identification from the writings of Melanie Klein and her followers, but the constructive, although implied in concepts such as reparation, has had less direct attention. I might resort to a personal example. I mentioned that when we were in France I wrote an autobiographical novel. I introduced a character in it that had come from real life. He was a man whom I had found patronizing, narrow-minded, and, to me, exasperating. However, as the character developed in the book a more sympathetic picture of him began to emerge—a different construction was appearing on the canvas. Had I met him again I believe that a warmer, more genuine encounter might have occurred between us.

The fact, therefore, that we construct our human world has taken a place centre-stage in my theoretical world view. The place that Melanie Klein gave to *phantasy* from earliest infancy is therefore crucial now to my understanding. *Phantasy* means personal emotional construction. I disagree with a lot of Melanie Klein's psychology, but this insight of hers I consider a foundation stone for all human psychology. In an aside, I might put in here that my previous blindness to this can be *partly* accounted for by my psychoanalytic training within the Independent Group in the British Society. One of the sins of the Kleinians is the slavish submission to doctrine in many of the analysts and therapists trained within that school. However, the sin of the Independents has been to fashion an identity on the basis of being against Klein.

Therefore, my impression is that most Independents have not taken into their thinking Klein's concept of *phantasy*. A way of conceptualizing the change in me since leaving the Tavistock would be to say that I have internalized this key concept of Klein and rejected some other aspects of her thinking, and that I have kept some aspects of thinking that are associated with the Independent Tradition while rejecting others. In particular, I reject a theory that suggests we internalize badness from the mother almost on a behavioural stimulus-response model. These two schools of thinking existed in the Tavistock, but they also existed internally within me, side by side, but unsynthesized and unintegrated. I think there is a problem when the situation within is mirrored by the situation in the institution of which one is a part.

I am aware that I may not have drawn clearly the change in emotional perspective that has occurred within me since leaving the Tavistock. I have been trying to give you some pointers. My lectures at the Tavistock were welcomed by quite a number of the audience, and so also my book, and yet these false perspectives and unintegrated features betray, I believe, a very serious defect in psychological perspective. It has made me realize that widespread acceptance of a book should not be taken as a guarantee of truth. I believe that it is the defects and untruths that are responsible for the praise. It is the conjunction of truth next to untruth that elicits praise. It reminds me of a story I once heard about two preachers who gave sermons on successive days at the cathedral in Granada in Spain in the sixteenth century. The first one, whose name eludes me, gave a sermon on the first day and when the people came out of the church they were all talking to each other and saying what a wonderful sermon it was. The next day the sermon was given by Juan de Avila who is the patron of the clergy in Spain. When the people came out of the church after hearing his sermon they were silent, because their inner hearts had been touched.

*   *   *

Now, I am claiming that leaving the Tavistock was an impetus to this inner change. Now, of course, no experimental psychologist would accept a statement such as this as there are too many variables that are unaccounted for. I did not only leave the Tavistock; I left also the various posts I held in the British Psychoanalytical

Society and my close associaton with its scientific life; I also left England, which had been my adopted home for many years. The Tavistock and the Institute of Psychoanalysis are two closely inter-twined organizations with many members of the latter on the senior staff of the former. I have already made reference to the strengths and weaknesses of the Kleinian and the Independent Group in the Institute of Psychoanalysis and these two streams of thinking were strongly represented at the Tavistock, especially in the Adult Department. Unfortunately, the two attitudes I have described also existed at the Tavistock and remained unintegrated. Of one thing I am sure: that it was necessary for me to leave the Tavistock and the British Psychoanalytical Society in order to construct from within. I will try to examine why this was so.

I have mentioned grandiosity in me and also the presence of truths and untruths lying side by side unintegrated. Yet, of course, the latter state of affairs is always so: truths always lie side by side with untruths. There is, one hopes, a slow approximation towards the truth with a purification of untruths in the life process, but truths and untruths always jostle next to each other. I do not there-fore think that leaving the Tavistock can have a special significance in promoting a growth in integration *in itself*. However, I believe that there *is* a significance when the state of unintegration in the individual is mirrored by an unintegration in the institution in which that individual is working. What is the effect of this mirror-ing occurring between the individual and the institution? I believe that it creates a fixation point within the individual so that she fails to integrate and to think. In such a situation she may be a faithful servant of the institution and conserve its functions, but not truly give to the institution something disturbing but growth promoting.

How does grandiosity come into the equation? It takes some strength and other inner resources to give something that may, at first meeting, be received with hostility. In the personality grandios-ity runs parallel to emotional impotence, and here comes my nega-tive judgement upon institutions: that there is a tendency within institutions to require submissive slaves rather than individuals who challenge their in-built conservatism. I think there is another way in which grandiosity plays its part: through identification. Sub-mission does not look grandiose, but the opposite. In fact, however, the grandiosity is projected into the institution. We usually project into a suitable vessel, which is possible when there is this mirroring situation that I have just been describing.

These three elements then lead to a fixation between the individual and the institution: an ideology in the institution and an ideology in the individual, a projection of this part of the individual into the institution and the presence of grandiosity that makes this possible. When these situations are all present together, then I am very doubtful whether the individual can accomplish a radical emotional shift without departing from the institution and placing him or herself at some distance from it.

So, this negative element at the Tavistock was the unintegration of differing schools of thought. At first sight ideological pluralism may sound a good thing, and I believe it is. God forbid that we should ever find ourselves slaves to an all-embracing ideology. I have no quarrel with the pluralism that exists at the Tavistock, but rather the process of splitting whole objects apart from whole objects rather than splitting part objects from part objects. I want to return to what I said earlier: that the staffing of the Adult Department reflected the two schools of analytical thinking from the Institute of Psychoanalysis: Kleinians and Independents. Kleinians, as we know, follow the teaching of Melanie Klein, whereas the Independents today largely establish their identity on the basis of being opposed to Klein. It is a split based on being for or against. What is certain is that the truth can neither lie in the total acceptance of one person's teaching nor in its total repudiation. This whole-object splitting betrays the truth and fosters blind discipleship. My observation was that this was the sort of splitting that characterized the divisions in the Tavistock. The only person about whose inner state I can speak with any authority is myself. When I was at the Tavistock I had within me a mini-Tavistock: a Kleinian and an Independent, but there was no interpenetration between the two. It was a pluralistic society within. Only one critic ever mentioned to me that my book, *The Analytic Experience*, betrayed this inner state of affairs and that she hoped for something more integrated in the future.

What I now think is that from earliest infancy human beings construct our human world. What is real is the product of that construction. Klein's theory of phantasy enshrines this point of view. The untruth in Klein's theory is her espousal of Freud's instinct theory, which, without a theory of transformation at least, goes counter of her theory of phantasy just as also her view that destructiveness lies in human envy is in contradiction to her view that destructiveness is attributable to the presence of the death instinct within. So I accept Klein's theory of phantasy as the foundation for my psychology, but reject her instinct theory. Fairbairn, who has in general been adopted by the Independents, has gone some way to rejecting Freud's instinct theory but, to my mind, has not gone far enough. So, since leaving the Tavistock, I have taken parts from either side and consequently am not acceptable to either party! The split is not now according to a person's teaching but according to a model which tries to be faithful to the personal as opposed to one which is appropriate to human beings as organisms but not as persons.

So, for the reasons that I have tried to outline, I believe that it was necessary for me to leave the Tavistock in order to integrate these unintegrated elements. I have so far tended to mention the less satisfactory elements at the Tavistock, but I want now to say that I also think that I would not have internalized the positive elements either had I not left the Tavistock. To show you the most positive and lasting benefit I have received from being at the Tavistock I must outline in as brief a manner as possible the main "sins" of Australian cultural life. It is a belief that I can become a psychotherapist by piece of cultic magic. There will be a four-day conference for those interested in psychotherapy. An American whizz-kid will arrive, give a series of lectures and seminars and, now that I have attended all of these and touched the hem of his cloak, I am a fully qualified psychotherapist. You will, I hope, forgive the slight exaggeration, but also I hope you will catch the spirit of what I am talking about. The Tavistock taught me that you learn by doing, you learn by struggling, that the mistakes and wrong paths taken in the start of some new project are part of the learning process. The clash of differing points of view are also part of the learning process. After being at the Tavistock for some time this attitude is almost second nature to most of us, and yet I know from grim experience how difficult it is to teach this point of view. Of course, you cannot teach it; you can only do it and learn that way by doing. Yet again I have really only learned the extreme value of this since leaving. I internalized while at the Tavistock, but only achieved awareness after leaving. Awareness comes about through experience of contrast.

I have worked in several institutions in the course of my life and I very crudely divide them into those in which powerful envy is built into the structures of the organization and those in which this is not so. My experience of the Tavistock is that it was, happily, one of the latter. There were, and no doubt are, many envious and destructive forces within the Tavistock, but I thought and still do that they did not permeate the structure of the Institution itself. I think what used to be called the "Boarding House Model" was an expression of this unenvious institution. When I started to do psychotherapy with mentally handicapped patients, Alexis Brook immediately encouraged me to start a workshop to investigate the matter further, which I did. Earlier, Bob Gosling encouraged me to integrate my previous religious education into my later psychoanalytic understanding, and together with him I gave some lectures on "Our adult world" in which I tried to follow his suggestion. It was my experience that creative ideas were encouraged and not crushed. I have, I hope, carried away this ethos into my working life in Australia.

The account that I have been giving you is very personal. I might summarize it by saying that being at the Tavistock was of enormous benefit to me, but that it was also necessary to leave it. I want to stress, however, that this was certainly so for me. Whether it could be so for others might perhaps be a subject worth discussion.

Commentary

It is now twelve years since I gave this talk. I would now modify a number of the things said about both Kleinian theory and also that of the Independents. I would put narcissism centre-stage, and the clinical difficulty of managing to "stand outside of ourselves", and then bring what I have said here about Klein and the Independents into a subordinate relation to that. I would also give some of the statements a bit more elasticity. The point I make at the end, however, I would maintain: that the struggle, the misunderstandings, are part of the work involved in any project that attempts to bring into relation disparate organizations. This has stayed deeply in me and I have the Tavistock to thank for that and, in particular, Bob Gosling, who embodied personally that outlook.

CHAPTER TWELVE

The struggle to achieve independence of mind in the British Psychoanalytical Society

"One of the most difficult matters in all controversy is to
distinguish disputes about words from disputes about facts:
it ought not to be difficult, but in practice it is"

(Bertrand Russell, 1985, p. 124)

There are in the British Psychoanalytical Society three groups:
the Contemporary Freudian Group, the Group of Independent Psychoanalysts, and the Contemporary Kleinians, and
they have been in being since the end of the Second World War. All
committees within the British Psychoanalytical Society have to have
these three groups represented, and the Presidency of the Society
has to rotate through these three groups.

There was a vicious dispute between Anna Freud and Melanie
Klein and their respective followers. Anna Freud believed that in
the analysis of children it was necessary to "educate" the child into
the treatment situation before interpreting its anxieties, whereas
Melanie Klein believed it was necessary to interpret the child's
anxieties from the start of treatment. Melanie Klein believed there
was a rudimentary ego from the start of life, whereas Anna Freud

believed that the ego only developed later in infancy. Melanie Klein believed that the child related to objects from the start, whereas Anna Freud did not. These apparently small differences became the foci of a violent dispute. The place where these disputes become most turbulent is in the matter of training. Just as parents are attached to values that govern how they want their children to be brought up, so also analysts are equally anxious to make certain that their analysands are "reared" according to their own sets of values. Both Anna and Melanie wanted to ensure that their analysands were educated according to a certain set of principles. The Freudians and Kleinians agreed, therefore, to have their own training programmes within the British Psychoanalytical Society. There were, however, some analysts who did not want to commit themselves to either position. They were the Pig in the Middle and so were called The Middle Group, but in more recent times known as the Group of Independent Psychoanalysts. This latter group wanted to be free to find its own path. In its early days it asserted itself against the position of the Classical Freudians and in latter years has taken up a position against the Kleinians. This is the briefest sketch of the present structure[1] of the British Psychoanalytical Society.

I came to psychoanalytic training in my thirties, subsequent to a previous training in philosophy and theology and, wanting to eschew fanaticism, decided to train in the Independent Group. I found it a congenial atmosphere in which to train, I was fortunate enough to have no difficulties during the course of my training, and I had only gratitude to the Institute of Psychoanalysis for the way in which its members encouraged me over the hurdles of training. I became an accepted member of the Independent Group and, I believe, revered in some respect. A couple of papers I wrote, including "The analyst's act of freedom as agent of therapeutic change" (1983) and "Phantasy effects that which it represents" (1985), were slotted into the canon of the Independents' scripture and the former paper was included in Kohon's book, *The British School of Psychoanalysis—The Independent Tradition* (1986), and also given a commentary in Rayner's book, *The Independent Mind in British Psychoanalysis* (1990). I was also at this time working at the Tavistock Clinic in the Adult Department. One of my many duties was to give a year's lecture course on psychoanalytic theory to mental health professionals. These lectures were later published in a book entitled *The Analytic Experience* (Symington, 1986), which was also considered to be faithful to the creed and spirit of the Independent Group and for which I received praise from senior members of the Group.

All this was very gratifying and yet it did stimulate in me an uneasy feeling that I will try to describe. It was that I felt I was being praised when I made any comment that was anti-Klein and, further, that some of the praise and commendation I received was for those juicy little bits of anti-Klein rather than anything creative or individual. I was unhappy about this because, after qualifying as an analyst, I attended fortnightly a group supervision with Herbert Rosenfeld for a period of six years. I learned more about psychoanalysis from Rosenfeld than from any other supervisor, with the exception of Bion, from whom I had just two supervisions, but they were memorable for the light that they shed upon the processes at work in a psychotic patient whom I was treating. So I knew that the Kleinians possessed a treasure that the Independents did not possess. I also understood well one of the reasons why the Independents were antagonistic to Klein. Putting it at its very briefest, it was that there was a moralizing tendency among Kleinians and also a dogmatism that was the antithesis of the Independent's *zeitgeist*.

I was at this time a hundred per cent *in* the psychoanalytic machine. I saw about six patients a day privately, either for analysis or intensive psychotherapy, and I did eight sessions a week at the Tavistock Clinic, where I held various posts of responsibility. Each Monday morning there was a scientific meeting which I attended, as well as numerous clinical presentations and discussions. I was also on three committees of the British Psychoanalytical Society and regularly went to its fortnightly scientific meeting. Psychoanalytic discourse was, as the expression goes, seeping out of my ears. Thomas Aquinas said that too much information inhibits the act of understanding and I entirely agree with this dictum of his. I also acquired a reputation for being a good public speaker. This reputation was a mixed blessing, to put it mildly. Apart from the thirty lectures that I gave each year at the Tavistock to mental health professionals, I used frequently to give a further ten to twenty talks to other professional bodies. On a board above the desk in my office I have on a card the wise words of Bernard of Clairvaux:

If you are wise you will show yourself rather as a reservoir than as a canal. A canal spreads abroad water as it receives it, but a reservoir waits until it is filled before overflowing and thus without loss to itself communicates its superabundant water.

In other words, the reservoir was empty and I needed to do something about refilling it. That was my first task. To cut a long story short, my wife and I decided to emigrate to Australia. My wife is also a psychoanalyst, trained within the Kleinian group of the British Society, and we both wanted to regroup our inner resources, so between England and Australia we planned and executed a staging post: a sabbatical of eight months in Provence. It proved to be a crucible out of which something quite new began to develop.

There are certain psychological or social realities that are quite definite, which have a lasting effect upon individual and cultural attitudes, but which cannot be neatly defined. An example of this, for instance, would be Romanticism. Its expression in the arts and philosophy differentiate it from the spirit that lay behind the Enlightenment but you cannot define it in three neat sentences. The reason why it is so difficult to pin down is that its essence lies in an inner spirit that is quite different from that of the Enlightenment or Classicism, but only graspable indirectly through its manifestations in the arts and philosophy. The change in outlook that is now embodied in what I think and also in the way I practise as an analyst now is as different from the way I thought and practised ten years ago as Romanticism is from the spirit of the Enlightenment. The best way to go about this task of differentiation is to take the key elements of difference and then try to link them, but it is you, the audience, that will have to see what I am talking of through a personal act of insight.

What I have been saying about the inner spirit of a cultural movement is a happy lead into my subject. What I pursue now in my analytical work is to uncover the inner mentality. I am reminded here of how Mike Thompson speaks of Heidegger's notion of truth in his recent book, *The Truth About Freud's Technique* (1994), where he explains that in this view the truth is there to be uncovered, which is different, as he describes, from the correspondence theory of truth. The former is concerned with something inner but the latter with something outer. What I was concerned with when I was practising in England was the relationship between the patient and the analyst, which I saw as paradigmatic of the other relationships of the patient's life. I suppose you could say that I saw the patient coming for treatment because of a *relationship pathology* and, therefore, concentrated my attention on the patient's relationship with me. I did elucidate the patient's phantasies about me, but only to indicate where they were wrong, as if there were fixed images of which I had become the recipient. I believe that in many cases the patient corrected his relationship to me through propelling himself into his imago of me. I will return to this point shortly, but what I want to focus upon here is that my focus was upon the relationship with me, and, regretfully it must be said, with myself centre-stage of the operation. Today I am not concerned centrally with the relationship, but rather the inner mentality that makes the relationship what it is. In other words, I see the relationship as a manifestation of an inner mentality.

Today I try to investigate first the inner mentality and second how that mentality comes about. I will describe to you here two radically different mentalities that existed in the same patient. For the sake of simplicity I will call these two mentalities cooperative and hostile. These two mentalities did not co-exist at the same time. One would be superseded by the other. This patient would for several sessions join me in investigating her problems. She would frequently offer evocative images to describe her difficulties. She was someone very badly affected by me being silent for more than two minutes. She could hold on for a couple of minutes but then . . . We will come to that in a moment. I think that her mentality can best be described as cooperative. Then as she left the session she looked at me with a flash of . . . one of the most difficult things is to describe a look. Some looks are straightforwardly hateful, others loving, others fearful, but there are many looks which do not fit so easily into any category. This look of hers was just like this. The closest I can get to it is "hostile apprehension", but there was also something of murder in it. I felt fearful and was frightened before she came into the next session. I could not have told you what I was frightened of, but somewhere there was an open abyss that was beckoning me into its jaws. The next session, all cooperation had gone. She hated me. Whereas cooperativeness suggests equality, togetherness, goodwill, hostility suggests hate, murder, and subservience. She was now entirely in the grip of this latter mentality. Now, while this mentality was reigning supreme within, she perceived me as an ogre. I had no doubt that this new mentality had been ushered in at the moment of that frightening look which she gave me at the end of the previous session. It seemed clear, then, that a violent inner act was responsible for the hostile state. Return to the state of cooperation was achieved when I was able to put her in touch with her state of mind towards me at the end of the previous session. By getting in touch with the nature of her clinging attachment to me, the sense that she was ripped in two when the session abruptly ended, her rage that it ended at my bidding, and a violent act of hatred towards me that coincided with psychic violence towards herself—getting in touch with all this slowly ushered in the mental state of cooperation. The latter was achieved slowly, the former in a flash. A bomb destroys a building in a moment: rebuilding it takes time.

I give this example to illustrate my present focus of attention: it is upon inner mental states and that which governs their origin, continuity, and decay. My previous orientation completely bypassed this dimension and yet, I must admit, I was bypassing the kernel of what psychoanalysis is: i.e., an investigation of the mind. My previous orientation would have been to interpret the transference phantasy of me as an ogre but omit entirely to investigate the mental activity responsible for its presence.

Another pole in this inner structural reality to which all my research is devoted is *emotional activity*. This is almost synonymous with the term *mentality*, which I have just been using in that it cannot be known directly but only inferred. A very important distinction here is between *emotions* and *feelings*, which are very frequently used interchangeably and this leads to great confusion. An emotion is an activity proceeding from one person to another but is not susceptible *to the senses* by the person from whom the emotion proceeds. The emotion can be known by its subject through knowledge. For instance, if I am boring all of you I will not know it. If all of you start yawning and going to sleep I may begin to suspect it—if I am boring you then you will *feel* bored but I will not feel boring. If you are all yawning and dropping off to sleep I may infer that I am actively boring you. Boring is an inner emotional activity, being bored is the feeling. What I am saying here relies on the distinction between emotion and feeling. The former is the invisible activity, usually of love or hate, of which the feeling is the registration.

This leads to another pole: that self-knowledge is the psychoanalytic task and therefore we have to come to knowledge of our emotional activities as well as our mental states. These two are very closely connected but the difference is that the former is the inner activity from the *perspective* of the interpersonal, whereas the latter is viewed as an entity in itself.

I am investigating, as you can see, the inner psychic activities and also the interpersonal psychic activities. In the clinical example I gave I mentioned that when she flashed me that murderous look it obliterated not only me but also her true self. There are destructive intrapsychic activities and also constructive intrapsychic activities. There is benign splitting and also damaging splitting, and I have been investigating the difference between these two. My present preoccupation is with the agents of these activities within the personality. Who splits, who projects, and who introjects? I am still largely in the dark but remain puzzling over this question.

I hope I may have said enough for you to get some flavour of my thinking and its direction, but where does this place me today in the groupings of the British Psychoanalytical Society? I will speak briefly first of the Freudian Group, because most of my attention will be devoted to the Independent Group and the Kleinian group. My education within analysis has been predominantly fashioned through an interplay between these two groups. You may have noticed that in the field that I am at present investigating I have not once mentioned either instincts or drives. This is not because I do not think they operate in human beings, but because they are not the object of analytic investigation. I have had patients who are hungry, patients driven by a desire for sex, but their emotional significance is what is pertinent for analysts, not the drives themselves. It is a fact that we could not all be present here sitting on these chairs were it not for the fact of gravity, but if someone asked me why you are all sitting here and I answered that it was because there is a force acting between bodies called gravity you would all say that that was irrelevant, that it is a background fact which we take for granted but is not the human answer to the question. If someone said that you had come here to listen to a lecture, that would be more accurate. Freud's metapsychological theory was rooted in the instincts. In his first formulation the sexual instincts had pride of place. Today it is not sex but emotion that is the object of analytic investigation. In fact, it was also the object of investigation for Freud, but because of Freud's loyal discipleship of the Physicalist Tradition he devised a metapsychology based on instincts rather than on emotion. (The analyst who has reversed that is Wilfred Bion.). One of the wedges that drove a division between Anna Freud and Melanie Klein was the former's loyal adherence to her father's metapsychology. In the famous *Controversial Discussions*, Anna Freud said, in discussing Susan Isaacs paper on Phantasy,

> Phantasy as the imaginal corollary of instinct takes the place of the sensorial corollary (pleasure––pain) which, in Freud's view, was the main mental accompaniment of instinctual urges, their satisfaction or frustration. Not that in Mrs. Isaacs' presentation these sensorial accompaniments play no part. But emphasis is shifted from the sensorial to the imaginal experience. When followed up, this cannot fail to influence the theories *concerning the pleasure principle as the sole governing principle within the unconscious.* [King & Steiner, 1991, p. 329, my italics]

Pleasure as the subjective experience of the satisfaction of a drive is therefore an interlocking part of the drive theory. I believe that benign splitting is based upon a categorization according to values as opposed to damaging splitting, which is a categorization according to the pleasure principle. Anna Freud was determined not to let go of the pleasure principle as the sole governing principle within the unconscious. Although there has been considerable development since the days when Anna Freud spoke those words, yet Freud's metapsychology still rules the roost in the Freudian group, whose members have remained faithful to the tradition set by Freud and confirmed by his daughter. I have, therefore, distanced myself from the thinking of the Freudians, whose theory detracts from rather than assists analytic investigation of the mind.

Now I want to turn to Melanie Klein, who revolutionized psychoanalytic thinking about the mind. I am sure that you all know the general outline of her theories. I want to take the foundation stone upon which her discoveries rest: the central place of *phantasy*. *Phantasy* is not a very satisfactory word because it has a *static* ring to it, whereas in fact it refers to an emotional activity according to which I construct my human world. A patient of mine believed that I did not have any personal problems, was free of all pathology. It emerged that he not only believed that this was true of me but also of all eminent figures in the medical profession of which he was a member. He further believed that he was hyper-disturbed and also that all young doctors like himself also were. This was the way in which he constructed part of his human world. This is the operation of *phantasy* in Melanie Klein's language. It seems to me a baseline for all mature psychological thinking that we thus construct our human world. Nearly all the psychoanalytic literature on the subject of reality-testing is based upon a false premise—that reality is as it is rather than a human construction.

I have, therefore, from the point of view of the Independents, committed a very big sin: I have gone into the enemy camp and come away with their flag and held it up as my starting-point for my psychological edifice. I have been called a "crypto-Kleinian", which I think means that I am really a Kleinian but in disguise. Now, in fact, I am very critical of the Kleinians, but I have no doubt that they have a pearl of great price within their system of clinical thinking. Unfortunately, the Independents, rather than be an association of truly independent thinkers, have now fashioned their identity upon being anti-Klein. Creative thinking never comes about on the basis of being against . . . it does not matter who it is against. In the creative fashioning of thought the individual will obviously wish to disagree with one way of thinking or another, but if the impetus and rationale of the thinking is on the basis of being against, then nothing creative can be expected from it. There can certainly be words of wisdom, intuitive insights, imaginative ways of putting things, but the system itself will be dead. The Independents, then, are in a dead end at the moment and I believe they will continue to be so until they turn sympathetically towards the Kleinian thinking rather than shunning it with horror. The Independents, then, do not represent independent thinking. They have become, unfortunately, the anti-Klein club. I will shortly come to what I believe is one of their strengths, but first I must turn to my criticism of the Kleinian group.

Phantasy lies at the heart of Klein's psychology. Words often mislead us and detract us from the meaning of what we are trying to describe. *Phantasy* is such a word because it suggests:

1. that whatever that is being spoken about is not real;
2. that we are referring to something *static*.

In fact, what is being spoken about is real and most definitely not static. As I think you all know, Klein spelt the word with a *ph* rather than an *f*, though Elliott Jacques once told me that he tried to persuade Melanie Klein to use a different term. *Phantasy* refers to something real, but not a reality that we can easily describe. Let us say that I have a deep-seated resentment towards my mother, the breast, and the world, and that I project on to yourselves, my audience, the imago of this mother/breast and I start to speak in a very dull and boring manner. After a time you begin to fall asleep, one by one, and I draw the conclusion that people in San Francisco get up extremely early in the morning and therefore feel inclined to go to sleep early in the evening. So convinced am I of this point of view that I conduct a sociological survey designed to prove it. With a suitably biased sample and questionnaire to my subjects, I come out having proved my point. I go into analysis and describe my researches and tell my analyst the jumping-off point for my research project. My analyst, a shrewd Kleinian, has by now for several years been subjected to my boring monologues. He shows me in a way that I cannot avoid seeing, no easy task, that I am engaged actively in an activity that the English language has called boring. This is an activity, but it is not one which is easy to detect because it cannot be directly seen, heard, or measured, but in fact in this, which I hope is a purely fictitious example, the only way in which it is being registered is your tiredness and feeling bored. I do not feel bored because I am doing the boring. This boring that I am doing is just as real as if you handed me a Black and Decker drill and I started to drill holes in a plank of wood. So, my *phantasy* of a bad breast structures the pattern of this activity. All this is to establish the point that *phantasy* is both *real* and *active* but it also structures my human world. In the somewhat absurd fable I have been spinning, I go off on my tour of America saying that in San Francisco people get up very early in the morning but in Washington people get up later in the morning. The shrewd analyst, however, finds that the origin for this difference lies in the fact that I gave a lecture in San Francisco, whereas in Washington I did not. The point I want to make, however, is that my *phantasy* of a malign breast structures the way I experience my human world. This rather long excursion is to make the point that *phantasy* is the word Melanie Klein used to assert that we human beings *construct* our emotional worlds.

I have taken as central to my psychology this fact that we con-struct our emotional worlds according to deep-seated patterns of which we are not usually conscious. The way I see my parents, my brother, my sister, my wife, my children, the people of San Francisco, communists, capitalists, Jews, Greeks, the working class, history teachers, politicians, men and women, is all determined by my *phantasy* life. So here the analyst of the Independent Group has established as central to his psychology a concept that is at the heart of Kleinian thinking. Now, there are matters both theoretical and technical that are very much part and parcel of most Kleinians' way of working that I reject. It will make sense to you that from what I have been saying about us constructing our world that I accept Melanie Klein's concept of envy—that this is often a determining factor in the way I construct my inner and outer world. However, I reject the death instinct and Freud's instinctual theory generally not because of its truth or falsity, but rather because it is irrelevant to our emotional construction of the world. If you tell me there are destructive forces in human beings I will have no quarrel with you, but the analyst is interested to know how *I* am boring you as in the little fable I have just related and the source of my emotional construction of this world. The introduction of instinct theory at the wrong place has, I believe, done much to muddy the waters and cause confusion. This is one of my main theoretical criticisms of Melanie Klein; the other is a technical one.

What I am going to say now is observable in the Kleinians but is true of psychoanalytic schools universally. It seems to me to be such an important dimension that I must try to explain it in some detail. What I am going to describe is a particular way in which envy functions. I am in analysis and my analyst makes a powerful intervention. At that moment he is powerful and I am very small. I hate being small and insignificant so I project myself *into* the imago of my powerful analyst. I now have his view and orientation to my human world. My own is smothered by this "hostile identification". I am totally unaware of this psychic event. What I am conscious of is believing a particular point of view. I am sure that many of us are attached to a particular school of analytic thinking through this mechanism. Now, the operation of this seems to be particularly prominent in the Kleinian group. One of the things that it gives to Kleinian analysts is *certainty* that their point of view is right. My small insignificance is under threat if I dare let go of that. Therefore, if I am a Kleinian analyst, I stride forth with confidence in my clinical view and it governs the way I pronounce with certainty to my patients. I have read a lot of Kleinian clinical papers where a dream is confidently slotted into "the system", but it seems to me to be frequently very dubious whether the symbols refer to the realities that the analyst purports is the case. This has led to an ossification within Kleinian analysis. I think an illustration of this is the way in which Bion's work has been "appropriated" to the Kleinian corpus and that those elements that do not "fit" declared unorthodox. Melanie Klein was clearly a clinician of genius, and many of her analysands have been some of the most creative people within psychoanalysis: Wilfred Bion, Donald Meltzer, Esther Bick, Hanna Segal, Herbert Rosenfeld, and Elliott Jaques, to mention a few. However, that burst of creativity has certainly died down and we have been left very largely with an unthinking orthodoxy.

Now, on the face of it the Independents look as if they are free of all this. One might say that the key *geist* of the Independents is the cardinal importance of spontaneity and creativity. Dogmatism, fanaticism, and analytic superiority are an abomination to the Independents. They hate these characteristics, which are so prominent in the Kleinian orthodoxy. Therefore, the Independents stress receptivity to the patient, silence, and waiting. "Wait for things to emerge" is a key recommendation of the Independents. "Be attuned to your patient" is stressed by some. Keats's "Negative Capability", which was adopted by Bion, is treasured within the Independent Group. All this I am in total sympathy with, and think that the Independents in the British Society stand for something extremely important within psychoanalysis. Now, I would not wish the criticisms I am about to make in any way to diminish the importance of these values for which the Independents stand guardian.

To be in confusion and not to know can be extremely persecuting to the individual. To be able to bear it and not rush in with a spurious interpretation is a quality to be treasured. However, I have detected within the Independent Group a tendency to *romanticize* not knowing. After all, knowledge is better than ignorance. I have heard presentations from Independents where igonorance of psychotic processes has been *romanticized* into a negative capability. I have heard presentations where, as far as I could see, simply nothing was achieved in the analysis. In particular this seems to be so in those patients in whom there is a strong operation of psychotic processes. The Kleinians clearly have a very considerable understanding in this area. It is an area in which the Independents are weak, if not deficient. I have, I believe, witnessed this deficiency romanticized. This leads me to my central criticism of the Independents.

It is their radical anti-Kleinian stance, and in this we discover all the dogmatism, fanaticism, and arrogant superiority that they believe is the preserve of the Kleinians. It is a negative dogmatism, a negative fanaticism and a denied superiority. The Kleinian doctrine is declared bad in a wholesale manner. The Independents need knowledge of psychotic processes, they need the Kleinian insight into primitive *phantasy* life. This negative rigidity comes about also through the same envy driven "hostile identification" that I have described as being true of the Kleinians. The theory underpinning many papers of the Independent is a crude behaviourism dressed up in psychoanalytic clothing. If my parents were bad to me this is what I internalize and is the source of my bad experience. The notion that I construct this world from earliest infancy is an insight that is often lacking in the Independent literature. It will be seen, for instance, that there is an illusory construction in the transference, but it is assumed that this is a replayed impression from how things actually happened to the patient in his or her childhood. I could quote many instances of this in the Independent literature but will leave it for you to discover it for yourselves.

So, I will leave you with this brief portrait of how things are in the British Psychoanalytical Society. I want you to understand that I have got all I have from it. I owe more than I can say to the education I have received within the British Psychoanalytical Society. I hope that my criticisms are constructive and not destructive, and may lead to deeper searchings into our mental lives.

Commentary

If I were writing this today I would, when talking of the Kleinians, substitute the word *dogmatic* for *certain*. Dogmatism is the product, I believe, of an introject that has not been personally processed or, in Bion's schema, not come under the influence of *alpha function*; certainty, on the other hand, is produced from ingested elements that have been personally worked upon.

Today, also, I would stress the form of relationship established with the superego by both Kleinians and Independents. Kleinians often become embodiments of the superego, whereas the Independents thrust it away. In neither case is the superego transformed, so that rather than functioning as a benign guide in the personality it remains as a persecutor to the subject and to others.

Last, I would arrange my talk so that centre-stage would be narcissism and the way it prevents the establishment of truth and goodness and then place the theories of the Classical Freudians, Kleinians, and Independents in relation to that.

Note

1.   This was written in 1995.

PART V
PAPERS ON NARCISSISM

Introduction

"In some queer way things depend for the knowledge of them upon our personal interest in them. So soon as we depersonalise our attitude to them, they withhold their secret and dissolve away . . ."

(Macmurray, 1935, p. 152)

I n December 1985 my wife and our two boys left England to go to Australia, but we did not go straight there. We took a nine-month sabbatical in Provence in the south of France. This was a time for renewal and reflection and I have described the inner turbulence that occurred when we were there (see Chapter Eleven, "Migration from the Tavistock: impetus for change"). My first book, *The Analytic Experience*, was with the publishers and ready to come out. One day as I was lying in bed I had a strong feeling that the book was extremely narcissistic. I thought I would write to the publisher and cancel its publication. I dallied, and in the end decided to leave it be. However, it was while I was in France for those nine months that the sense of my own narcissism began to hit me. Some colleagues wondered how I managed all that time without seeing patients. I had my hands full with myself and the nine months was not a relaxation but a time of extreme turbulence. As I have said, I think emotional development is made up of two contraries—something that shakes the personality to its foundations and a time of peace for reflection. My life's journey has been made up of these two elements. Here in this book I take only a small slice of that—from the time when I started the analytic training to today—but much greater turbulence had occurred prior to starting this part of my journey. Life's journey has been a determined desire to tackle my own narcissism. What was it that called me, called me deep inside to do this? This I cannot answer.

This awareness of my own narcissism coincided with the realization of the defects of my own analysis. I had projected my ego, that emotional centre, *into* Klauber *and* into the Independent Group of analysts. What began to happen in France was that I was withdrawing myself from that projected position. I was too frail at the time to "go into the desert", so I projected myself into the Kleinian group and was for some years a fellow traveller. It took another ten years for me to become servant to a higher principle, which strengthened me sufficiently so that I no longer needed to seek substitute strength by projecting myself into a group with its ideological system. This projection of the self into a group mentality was, I realize, a central feature of narcissism.

When I arrived in Australia I plunged into the works of Frances Tustin. This is where I was at emotionally and she gave the words that offered form to this experience. I went on one occasion to supervision with her, and I was struck by her unpretentious simplicity. The only fault I detected in her was a tendency to flatter, which embarrassed me.

I started to work on the relationship between psychoanalysis and religion and, as I did so, I began to think that the bridge that connected the two was the condition that is called narcissism. I was struck by the fact that this was a plight that psychoanalysts clearly believed required attention, that it was pathological in some way. It seemed to me that it was the same state of mind that had been addressed by religious teachers and mystics. So, to further my project, I decided to study it as closely as possible. I started by reading some of the classical psychoanalytic texts on the subject, but the more I read the more convinced I became that there was some terrible confusion about the subject, so I abandoned this line of research and decided instead to spend twenty minutes a day engaged in thinking about narcissism. I felt that until I had done this and begun to get some purchase on the subject I could go no further. In order to think I had to put my thoughts into the written word. So, each day, come rain or storm, I opened my word processor and spent twenty minutes a day thinking on the subject.

This procedure created a great deal of interest and enquiry later, so I shall explain how I proceeded. I had certain rules that I made myself obey. The first was that, whatever the circumstances, I would spend this twenty minutes each day. Why twenty minutes? I had once read a book by Sertillanges (1945) on the intellectual life where he said it was possible to lead an intellectual life on the basis of two hours study a day. I could not aspire to this, but I took from this the idea that it needed to be every day without fail. I thought that however tired I might be or however many matters were pressing upon me I could for sure always squeeze in twenty minutes each day. Why not half an hour? I felt that twenty minutes was possible, but that there might be days when half an hour would be just too much. Once that had been decided I did not let myself go on thinking beyond the twenty minutes. Even if my thoughts were flowing I would stop, but I would put a note to myself on the word processor to continue with these thoughts the next day. This was a great help the following day: there was something to look forward to. To decide to press forward with a project the donkey needs a carrot dangling in front of it. As I opened the word processor and there was my note to myself, I would remember the train of thought of the previous day and I would willingly surge forward. Of course, in all writing there are dry periods, and then one just has to press on unrewarded. Why not less than twenty minutes? I thought a shorter time would not give me enough satisfaction and that when the mind was "dry" a shorter time would not give the necessary momentum to get the mental engine going.

Now, this twenty minutes was purely for the generation of my own thoughts. If, in the thinking, something from Freud or Tolstoy or Shakespeare or any thinker came to mind, I would write it and incorporate it into what I was thinking about but I would not go and look it up. The twenty minutes was for *my* thinking, not for browsing into the thoughts of others. Looking up what Freud,

Tolstoy, or Shakespeare actually said was a relaxed pleasure that I could and did enjoy at some other time. I would always do that outside the twenty minutes and it was a fulfilling experience. I read what I had assigned to myself with a renewed spirit of enquiry and interesting new angles came before my mind. It makes a great difference when the reading of an author is driven by an inner personal research—it lights up new pathways that had before been hidden. This point has been made by the philosopher John Macmurray, whom I quoted at the beginning of this chapter.

So, for a year, I did my twenty minutes faithfully every day. As my thinking developed this creature called psychoanalysis radically changed its shape. The ugly duckling had become a swan before my eyes. Externally, what I was doing in the consulting room looked the same, but internally it was completely different. It was arresting and also alarming. I felt isolated from my colleagues and unable to explain the vision that was now before the eye of my mind. I found it difficult to explain the difference to myself. Two men can be entirely different in their mental outlook although they are both called philosophers. You could not have two people more different than Hegel and Kierkegaard, but they are both philosophers. I was a psychoanalyst, along with my many colleagues, but I knew now that the way I thought and my inner orientation to life was very different.

As I described in my book on narcissism (1993), I was one day sitting with some colleagues from the Sydney Institute for Psychoanalysis discussing what programme of lectures we might put on and the thought struck me that I could offer ten lectures on narcissism. I went home feeling that I had been rash to make so impulsive an offer, but when I opened up my word processor I soon found that there was sufficient thinking that could be conveniently divided up into ten lectures. So, a few months later, I found myself in an oblong room surrounded by twenty-four eager colleagues with me outlining each week the contours of narcissism that I had been working out the previous year. These twenty-four seemed satisfied and spread the word, so, a term later, I had a new batch of twenty-four and I gave the lectures again, but now changed as a consequence of having learned more when I gave them the first time.

On a trip to London, I was talking to my friend, Cesare Sacerdoti, who at that time was the owner and managing director of Karnac

Books, and he was trying to encourage me to produce a book for him. I mentioned casually that I had the transcript of these ten lectures on narcissism. His eyes lit up and he said that was just the kind of thing that his readership craved for, so, in a very short time, what had started as an inner emotional travelogue had become a book in the mental health bookstores. Although I had written one book before it and have published seven books since it first appeared, I think it may be my best book. It is clear, simple, and straightforward. *A Pattern of Madness*, which appeared nine years later (2002), is a deeper book but it lacks the joyous surprise of that first discovery.

The four papers that follow are all on the subject of narcissism. Shortly after the book on narcissism had been published, the editor of *Revista Brasileira de Psicanalise* asked me to write a summary of my theory. This is the subject of my first paper—"Narcissism: a reconstructed theory". It was published in Portuguese in 1993 in the Brazilian journal. It is a skeleton of the theory as it appears in the book. Someone with a good head for abstraction will be able to gather the core of the theory from this article, but in order to get some colour into it he or she will need to read the book in order to get the flavour of my position.

The second paper is "Narcissism as trauma preserved", which I gave both in the USA and in London in 1996. It gave an emphasis that had been lacking in the book. It indicated that narcissism was not just the result of a traumatic happening but rather was the trauma in a different form from the original event. I relied on Bion's theory of transformation for this perspective.

The third paper, "The core of narcissism", was given as a lecture at a conference I was giving in Washington in January 1997 at the Object Relations School, organized by David and Jill Scharff. This was then four years later than my book on narcissism and my thinking and clinical experience had developed considerably, and I would today, ten years later, still endorse most of what I say here, although my understanding of envy has changed since then.

The fourth paper, "The corruption of interpretation through narcissism", was given in Portuguese in the city of Porto Alegre in Brazil in 2002. This was the beginning of a clinical theme that has become increasingly important to me: that much of what looks like interpretation is in fact a dictate, an instruction. In this paper I look for the subtle way in which this happens.

CHAPTER THIRTEEN

Narcissism: a reconstructed theory

"Mr. Luzhin was morbidly fond of admiring himself. He had a tremendous respect for his own intelligence and abilities, and sometimes, when alone, he spent hours admiring himself in the looking-glass"

(Dostoyevsky, 1966, p. 322)

Introduction

In a recent book I have sketched the outline for a new theory of narcissism. In that book I give many clinical examples, ideas on how narcissism can be reversed, and the relation of my theory to those of some others. I also make extensive use of Tolstoy's *Anna Karenina* to illustrate some of the central phenomena of narcissism. n this short article all this has been mercilessly cut out and I give here only the skeleton of my theory. What the reader will get from this article is the structure of the theory.

Resolution of contradictions in psychoanalytic theories

Within psychoanalysis there is a strong reluctance to throw out any theory. The result of this is that when a new theory is proposed that is in contradiction to an accepted theory the two are left, one superimposed upon the other. We operate then with a split that leads to obfuscation. There are numerous examples of this, but I shall just give one. Fairbairn radically re-cast Freud's libido theory and in his model he rubbed out the *Id* in Freud's Structural Theory. Many analysts who follow Fairbairn accept his model without rejecting Freud's Structural Model. This means that Fairbairn's theory has not been understood. To make sense of the theory that I am proposing, and if it is to be effective in clinical work, it is necessary to ditch several aspects of received theory. A reader may disagree with my theory, or part of it, and reject it—that is all right, but if you accept it then you will have to do a lot of work in letting go of some theories which are contradicted by what I am putting forward.

An object relations approach to narcissism

I follow the view that emotional and mental life is structured in a relation of the self to objects. This is the view pioneered by Melanie Klein, Fairbairn, Bion, and analysts within the Kleinian School. In this view the infant is object-related from birth, although the object is denuded of wholeness and referred to as a part-object or partial object. This latter is a specific description of the object type and does not detract from the general proposition of this theory that the newborn child is object-related from birth. At one stroke this dispenses with the theory of Primary Narcissism, which posits an objectless state at birth. In the theory we are proposing, then, we reject primary narcissism as being in contradiction to object relations theory. The term narcissism, in the way I use it, is equivalent to what has in the past been called Secondary Narcissism.

I follow Fairbairn, who said that there is no Id. The individual is made up of a structure whose two poles are the ego and objects. What in classical Freudian theory was referred to as the Id becomes, in Fairbairn's theory, split-off parts of the ego. In the treatment of a patient I assume that a sudden impulse that wells up arises from a split-off part of the ego. This was the view of Melanie Klein and most of her followers. Although this is in contradiction to Freud's Structural Theory, yet most Kleinians have failed to reject the Structural Theory. Bion, I believe, did so, but made no formal exegesis of this process of his thinking. In my theory I resolve this contradiction by saying that the ego is in relation to objects in the emotional and mental sphere and that there is no other source of action, such as the Id.

Another way of saying that emotional activity has its source in the ego is to say that it is intentional. All emotional activity towards objects, then, is intentional. Activity whose source is in split-off parts of the ego is also intentional.

This, then, is the ground of my theory, which can be found in object relations theory, if the latter is stripped of contradictions.

Classical definition of narcissism

Narcissism occurs when someone has taken his own self as love-object. This is the classical definition of narcissism. I want here to invoke the *principle of omission*. According to this principle, a more fruitful understanding is achieved through focusing upon what is not stated than what is. Therefore, in this case we wish to focus upon what has *not* happened when someone takes his own self as love-object. It is on this principle that the theory that I wish to propound is founded.

The concept of unconscious choice

What differentiates psychic action that proceeds from the ego as opposed to psychic action that proceeds from the supposed Id is that in the former choice is inferred, whereas in the latter it is absent. I would ask the reader to reflect for a moment upon this. If you do not agree with this proposition then you will need to define for yourself precisely what the difference is. The Id as the repository of the instincts supposes that I am pushed in a certain direction and that the impulses, together with the environmental stimuli, dictate that it could not have been otherwise. The ego, on the other hand, which is a latinized translation of *Das Ich*, "the I", or just "I", is a source of action which went in one direction but could have gone in another. All judgements concerning human motivation assume this. Psychoanalytic investigation into motives also assumes this as a fundamental principle. This principle is a basic assumption in the many examples that Freud gives in the *Interpretation of Dreams* (1900a). It is, however, in contradiction to Freud's metapsychology of the Unconscious. This contradiction remains unresolved in Freud's system of thought.

What we state, then, is quite simple. It is that psychic activity that proceeds from the ego always implies that an alternative pathway could have eventuated and an alternative goal arrived at. Another way of stating this is to say that psychic action is intentional because if when I do A I could have done B, then doing A is intentional. I intended to do A. Much of psychoanalytic experience is the revelation of those intentions of which I was not aware. Unconscious intentionality, unconscious choice, then lies at the heart of psychoanalytic understanding. We often rail against the idea that I choose something unconsciously, but this I believe is because of the guilt that it provokes. We repudiate it because its admission may flood me with guilt. Even split-off parts of the ego choose. This theory of Narcissism implies unconscious choice.

The concept of the lifegiver

So, our position is this: that when it is stated that in narcissism the individual takes his own self as love-object, then it is to be understood that this is an unconscious choice. This means that an alternative goal or object was repudiated. So, when I choose my own self as love-object, then what is the alternative that I have rejected? What is the object that I have turned my back upon?

At the foetal stage, as recent research has shown, the infant turns to the voice of the mother. After birth the infant turns to the breast, at three months to the whole *gestalt* of the mother. The developed adult turns to a sexual object. However, I search for a concept to embrace the voice of the mother, the mother's breast, the mother, and the mature sexual object. The term I have selected is *lifegiver*.

The *lifegiver* has no existence independently of the voice, the breast, the mother, or the sexual mate, yet it is a mental object. It is not the voice, the breast, the mother, or the sexual mate, and yet it has no existence independently of these. One might ask why I have not simply used Lacan's term "the other"? It is because "the other" is external to the self whereas the *lifegiver* is not. Just as the *lifegiver* is not the voice, breast, mother, or sexual mate, and yet cannot exist independently of these, so also the *lifegiver* is not the self and yet cannot exist independently of the self.

In narcissism the self is chosen as love-object and in this choice the *lifegiver* is rejected. The state of psychological health in opposition to narcissism is that state where the *lifegiver* has been chosen. I want therefore to define narcissism thus: *narcissism is that psychological state in which the lifegiver has been rejected.* Herein lies the kernel of narcissism. The choice of the self as compensatory love object is a secondary consequence. The classical definition has failed then to grasp the essence of narcissism.

I have not chosen "the other" as a concept because it is external to the self, but is there a positive reason for choosing the term *lifegiver*? It is that in the very act of being chosen a mental object becomes installed within the psyche and this object is then the source of psychic action. I call it the *lifegiver* because it is a source of autonomous action. Being the source of autonomous action is the characteristic that differentiates animate from inanimate reality, and therefore I have chosen the term *lifegiver*.

The internalization of the lifegiver

I have described above the *lifegiver* as if it were a static object, but such a description entirely fails to conceptualize it. The *lifegiver* comes into being as an object in the very act of being chosen. It does not exist outside of the choice. Just as it has no life independent of the voice of the mother, the breast, the mother, or the sexual mate, so also it has no existence independent of the act of choice. Therefore it has no existence other than that of an internal mental object. It becomes internal in the act of being chosen and has no existence outside of this, and yet it is independent of it.

The question of how early an unconscious choice or repudiation of the *lifegiver* occurs will give rise to much dispute. It is my contention that such a choice occurs at a very early stage of development—certainly in infancy, but possibly even at a foetal stage of development.

It is also necessary to note that a *total* repudiation of the *lifegiver* is not possible. A split occurs and in one part, often hidden, an orientation towards the *lifegiver* remains.

Narcissism as repudiation of the lifegiver

The basis of mental health, then, lies in the acceptance of the *lifegiver*. Narcissism, then, is the refusal of the *lifegiver*. The core of narcissism, then, is a negation. Clinically this is its essence but, lest the reader protest too quickly, I must point out that every psychological trick and device is mustered in order to hide the fact.

On the surface it may look as if the individual is positive and life enhancing, but the reality is not what it looks. The key to understanding the situation is to realize that there is massive guilt in the act of refusal of the *lifegiver*. The individual feels *bad* in relation to his own self. Whereas embracing the *lifegiver* is an act of acceptance of the self, its refusal is a rejection of the self. It is an act of existential self-castration. The individual who has acted thus already has one big problem: that he has no source of psychic action within himself but he has on top of this another: that he is massively guilty for what he has done and, therefore, goes to all possible efforts to hide it from himself and others. It is one of the reasons why, when in analysis this inner situation begins to be revealed, there is frequently a very powerful negative reaction. The patient may leave treatment peremptorily, project envy and hostility violently into the analyst, and thereby put enormous pressure on him or her to act out or project into others who put pressure on the patient to give up the analysis. All this happens to avoid revelation of the guilty secret.

Therefore the person in whom the narcissistic situation is firmly established may appear on the outside to be a typical "nice guy" or "nice woman". This is because the narcissistic individual uses all his or her energy to appear "nice". Psychic energy is mobilized to hide the inner situation. In such a situation personhood is hidden, because truly the birth of the person lies in the acceptance of the *life-giver*. When nearly all the energy is being directed towards hiding the inner situation, then there is very little left over for attention to the other. So we find, for instance, that the person who is intimate with the narcissistic individual finds, over time, that he is bereft of any love or generous impulses coming from him. (In a marriage this may not be noticed because narcissistic persons tend to marry each other. Also there is group support for the narcissistic solution.)

Erotization of the self

What the person in whom narcissistic currents predominate lacks is this inner mental object on which he can rely for the negotiation of the vicissitudes of life. So how does he steer his way through the emotional currents that he meets in the human community, particularly among intimates? He lacks something essential, so he has to enlist people to supply what he lacks. He does not have the emotional motivating principle within, so he has to enlist others to perform the function for him. He functions through getting them to erotize himself. When the self is erotized it supplies partial and temporary energy to the psychic system.

It is here that the classical definition of narcissism finds its place. It is correct that in narcissism the self has been selected as love object, but this is a secondary consequence of the basic repudiation of the *lifegiver*. The self is taken as love object in order to supply psychic energy. If this did not occur, the individual would not be able to function in the human community at all. In someone in whom narcissistic currents predominate, erotization is always at the surface, so there is no source of action from within; action occurs through being "rubbed" and stimulated, as it were, from outside, and this is why it is never long-lasting.

Erotization is never established once and for all. It is always evaporating and therefore the individual has to devote much of his attention to keeping the self erotized. There are two main ways in which this is done: through stroking and through excitement. We shall examine these briefly.

I give a lecture but I do not have in me the source of confidence to know either that it is good, bad, or a mixture. I have, therefore, to get praise for it. I have to be stroked. If I am stroked sufficiently this gives me some motivation to give the lecture again or develop it further. I have to rely on the stroking or praise of the outside person and I put most of my energy, therefore, into making sure that I get it. The lecture I give will be given for that purpose and not primarily to address the subject that is its declared purpose. And as I have said, if the stroke is forthcoming it does not endow me with lasting motivation because I am dependent upon this outer stimulation, and therefore my inner situation is an impoverished one in the extreme.

Excitement is the other stimulant that will inject some temporary life and energy into my system. There is, however, something about excitement that it is extremely important to note. It is that excitement is the sensational reaction to murder. Killing is exciting; sadism is exciting; masochism is exciting. Killing lies, however, at the kernel of sadism and masochism, and is itself the factor that provides excitement. Killing of my own personhood is extremely exciting and gives me a great impetus of psychic energy. This killing of my own personhood is always done in a representative way. For instance, when the analyst is attacked, as in the negative transference, he or she always stands for the individual's own person. What is clear, therefore, is that the self-killing that generates excitement can only occur through murderous attacks on an other in the same psychic act. Therefore, the excitement that the narcissistic person is forced to generate is done through activity, which is extremely damaging, first in the micro-social environment but sometimes also in the macro-social environment.

CHAPTER FOURTEEN

Narcissism as trauma preserved

"The night is darkening round me
The wild winds coldly blow
But a tyrant spell has bound me
And I cannot cannot go"

(Emily Brontë, 1996).

I had noticed in my clinical work the concurrence of trauma and narcissism. I had observed that the most narcissistic people were those who had undergone severe childhood trauma, so I knew that the two were connected. However, one day I realized that narcissism *is* the traumatized state. Let me start by giving you a simple example.

Alphonsus is crossing the road one day and is hit by a car and rushed to hospital. He has broken a leg, ruptured his pelvis, broken his collar bone and some ribs. For a few days he is in a precarious state. While in that state someone comes and asks him if he would like to take out a subscription to the Royal Society for the Preservation of Birds. All Alphonsus can do is moan and cry pitiably, pointing to his chest and leg. The representative from the Royal Society for the Preservation of Birds goes away disappointed that he does not have a new subscriber. In fact, he complains to a colleague that Alphonsus does not seem at all interested in birds, nature, conservation, or the state of the planet and says, "Alphonsus seems to be entirely preoccupied with himself."

I have a feeling that as I tell you this tale, Alphonsus, rather than the representative from the RSPB, will have your sympathy. This is because you believe that in such circumstances he is justified in being preoccupied with himself rather than the outside world. However, let us now shift the focus.

Many years ago a married woman confided in me that her husband was entirely self-centred and that he was utterly devoid of caring and love for her. She told me this with great bitterness. In the way she told it to me, it invited condemnation. But what if that man is like Alphonsus in the hospital? What if he is preoccupied with himself and himself alone because he is the victim of a traumatic event? What if this emotional self-centredness *is itself* the traumatized state? That narcissism is the condition someone is in who has been traumatized? The question then is "Why do I tend to condemn him?" What I want to do in this paper is to try first to establish my thesis that narcissism is a synonym for the emotionally traumatized state. Then I want to look at the reason why this state invites condemnation.

The best way I can approach this subject is to give you a window into my own conflicted state while treating a severely narcissistic man. I had him in analysis while I was living and working in London. Some years after I left England I heard that he had died, and as he lived absolutely outside the professional circles that most analysts and mental health workers inhabit I feel confident in being able to describe him clearly. He was married, had no children, and worked in a library. He was one of the most solitary people I have ever come across. He and his wife had no friends. The only possible exception was the couple who ran a small boarding house in Folkestone, a town on the Kent coast where they went every autumn for a two-week holiday. As they had been going there annually for more than twenty years his wife used to send them a Christmas card and they also received one in return.

The reason he gave for coming to see me was he thought he should have some friends. I think the true reason, however, was that his wife had become ill with multiple sclerosis and he was guilty that he was the cause of it. When I tell you the way he treated her you may be inclined to think that he could have been partly responsible for her developing an illness. He would not on any account allow her to have children. Initially he allowed her to have a cat, but when she began to show it too much affection he drowned it when his wife was out one day. One Christmas he promised her a television set, which until then he had not allowed her to have. In the event he gave her a toy one instead. More than once he promised to take her to a restaurant that she liked and, at the last moment, decided not to go. When his wife turned away from him sexually shortly after he had drowned the cat he spoke with great bitterness of her cold refusal. When I said that her refusal might have been linked to him having drowned the cat he did not speak to me for three weeks. I know from subsequent confirmation by himself that when I said this he believed I was condemning him and that I hated him. My conflicted state was this: I felt like saying to him, "No wonder she's cold towards you. You murder her cat, which she loved, break promises, treat her cruelly . . ."

In other words I was harshly judgemental towards him inside. I also found his sour behaviour towards me well-nigh intolerable, and several times I was tempted to shout at him in the way Nina Coltart describes shouting at her patient in her paper "Slouching towards Bethlehem" (1992) but I did not do so. I did not do so because there was a voice inside that counselled patience.

This patient also instigated an attitude of pity in me. He would speak of the way in which his mother had raised his hopes in childhood and then dashed them to pieces. He described how she would tell him on Christmas Eve that she was going into the local town to buy presents for him and his sister but when she got to the town would become drunk and so the next morning there would be no presents. As he told me this I would want to comfort him. On these occasions the voice would counsel caution. "Be firm with him", the voice would say. The voice cautioned me against consoling him in a sympathetic way. In the one case the voice advised me to feel compassion for the patient and in the other against sentimentality. I suppose you would say that it advised robust resolution. In each case the voice advised against reacting to the surface communication, or against, as Bion would put it, the sensuous level.

Let us look at these two states inside me more closely. I have chosen to say "states" because I wanted as generic a term as possible in order to place them in different categories. When I felt like condemning him and shouting at him there was what is best described as an impulse inside me. I was in an exasperated state; I felt like yelling and screaming. I was a man possessed. In fact, I did not enact this impulse but let us say, for a moment, that I had. Let us say I had said to him: "You treat your wife in the cruellest way; if I point out anything to your discredit you go sour and treat me with all the vengeance that you mete out to your wife. How about having a look at yourself instead of blaming everyone else and stroking yourself in so self-pitying a manner."

In essence I would here be expelling him. I am in a state of arousal and when I enact it I expel him. There are two modes of such an expulsion. In my state of arousal I might be *so* angry that I would shout at him and order him out of my consulting room; alternatively, even without my adding that command, he might be so wounded that he would stamp out and never return. In either of these scenarios there would have been a physical expulsion as well as an emotional one. There is another mode, however, in which there is an emotional expulsion without there being a physical expulsion. In other words, he would remain physically in the consulting room but as an active agent he would be crushed. The act of condemnation crushes his awareness of himself as an acting being.

It is from this perspective that the interpretation born of pity is also crushing because in it there is an inherent labelling of the person as a passive object. If I had said to him, "You have never got over the disappointment of your mother's broken promises to you", there is in it a godlike pronouncement affirming the broken state of his inner life. The voice that counsels me to resist saying this testifies to a creative capacity in him to repair his own damaged state. Before considering in me the state that generated the voice in either case—the voice that counselled patience or respect—I want to examine more closely the notion of someone as an acting being.

Now, you might say to yourselves, "My God, I should think anyone would be angry with a man who behaves as cruelly as that . . .", or, "My God, I should think anyone would be sorry for someone who has been treated as shamefully as that . . .", yet let us try to look at it this way. I am aroused to be severely judgemental by the narrative of his cruelty towards his wife and his vengeful behaviour towards me, or I am moved to be sorry for him. So it is an activity in him that stimulates either harshness or pity in me. What is it in him that stimulates that voice in me that counsels patience or respect for his spirit? Let us say that the state of arousal in me is partly attributable to what Melanie Klein called *projective identification*. What shall we call that process in him that stimulates the voice that counsels patience? I would propose to call it *creative communication*. I think this is such an important process and so neglected, not only in psychoanalysis but more generally in the human sciences, that I want, for the sake of emphasis, to dwell upon it a while.

In my book on narcissism (Symington, 1993, pp. 33–34), I quote a passage from Graham Greene's second autobiographical book, *Ways of Escape*, where he describes the character of Herbert Read, the art critic:

> Certainly my meeting with Herbert Read was an important event in my life. He was the most gentle man I have ever known, but it was a gentleness which had been tested in the worst experiences of his generation. The young officer, who gained the Military Cross and a DSO in action on the Western Front, had carried with him to all that mud and death Robert Bridges's anthology *The Spirit of Man*, Plato's *Republic* and *Don Quixote*. Nothing had changed in him. It was the same man twenty years later who could come into a room full of people and you wouldn't notice his coming—you noticed only that the whole atmosphere of a discussion had quietly altered, that even the relations of one guest with another had changed. No one any longer would be talking for effect, and when you looked round for an explanation there he was—complete honesty born of complete experience had entered the room and unobtrusively taken a chair. [Greene, 1980, p. 39]

This is a supreme example of *creative communication*, but what existed in Herbert Read to an heroic degree exists in all human beings to a greater or lesser extent. The voice that counselled patience in me had been stimulated by the process of *creative communication* in my patient, just as the impulse to condemn or express sorrow was stimulated by *projective identification*.

Projective identification stimulates either something noisy and agitated in me or something sentimental. In either case the creative spirit within him has been smothered. *Creative communication* stimulates peaceableness, strength, gentleness, and the power to think. It is like the "still small voice" referred to in the First Book of Kings (1 Kings 19: 11–12), where the author says that the Lord was not in the earthquake, not in the fire, but in a still small voice. I think this author must have known something about the difference between these two processes and which to trust and which to distrust. The analyst's job is to contain the "earthquake and the fire" and hearken to the "still small voice" in which resides not the Lord but the power to think and transform. It is a "still small voice", but one in which resides strength and creative possibility. I like to call the noisy, the agitated, and the sentimental in me *the shadow*, which, as I am sure you know, is Jung's term for this aspect of my personality. *The shadow* is one aspect of personality, but it suggests that there is another, which I propose to refer to as *the sane*.

Let us define mental health by saying that it exists in direct proportion to the extent to which *creative communication* is active in someone. On this definition we would be saying that Herbert Read was a supreme exemplar of the mentally healthy individual. Therefore, in the clinical example I have given, these two processes— *projective identification* and *creative communication*—are struggling together for . . . for what? For victory. I experience this twofold struggle in myself. I know also that it is the elemental battle going on in my patient. I also know that in him we have just an exemplar of a battle that is deeper and more universally significant than the description of my problems with a particular patient might at first appear to articulate.

It is, I hope, clear that this battle between two processes was going on in my patient *and* in myself. I want first to make a rather mundane point, though I believe an important one, and then go on to one that is profound though, like all emotional realities, difficult to articulate. The first is to dispatch for ever all talk of a patient "putting a feeling into the analyst". When I was sorely tempted to castigate my patient for his cruel behaviour or falsely sympathize with him he was stimulating *the shadow* in me. It was something already in me long before that patient came to see me. I may not have known, and in fact did not know, that it was present in me until I met that patient. What that patient did was to arouse in me something that was dormant, yet "dormant" is not the right word because what we are talking of is a process in me that is active but I am not aware of it. We can say "dormant" as long as it is clear that I am asleep to a process in me that is active. So, *projective identification* is a process whereby a patient (or anyone else for that matter) stimulates *the shadow* in me. All talk that suggests something is put into me that was not there before, which is alien to my nature, is to be banished for ever. So that is the mundane point. Now to the deeper one.

I have spoken so far as if there are two processes—the earthquake-with-fire and the "still small voice", and that I experience a struggle within me between the two, and yet I believe that they are manifestations of one reality. We are talking here, I believe, of something that defies the conceptual capabilities of the mind. Wilfred Bion was referring to this when, after introducing his conceptualization of container and contained, he said,

> I shall therefore close the discussion by assuming there is a central abstraction unknown because unknowable yet revealed in an impure form in statements such as "container or contained" and that it is to the central abstraction alone that the term "psychoanalytical element" can be properly applied . . . [Bion, 1963, p. 7]

I am saying that *projective identification* and *creative communication*, or *the shadow* and *the sane*, are two manifestations of a central abstraction which is unknowable. It is unknowable due to the limitations of the human mind to understand. Kant thought that we understand the world through the prism of certain categories. Implied in this is the knowledge that the human mind is limited in its capabilities. What is not possible for the mind to grasp is that these two are one. It is the philosophical problem of the one and the many that no philosopher has ever solved. It is also, I believe, what Christian theologians were trying to give expression to in their formulation of the Trinity: three persons and yet one God. So I am aware of the duality but cannot grasp the unity. Bion's "reverse perspective" comes in here too. I can see two faces; oh no, I can see a vase. I can know there is one reality but cannot see it; I am limited to seeing it one way or the other. Once, however, I had a clinical example where I caught a glimpse of the unity in the duality. I could not see it but I glimpsed the possibility. I will tell you about it.

This was a woman who had had a psychotic breakdown. She came in one day and said, "All you have taught me is to communicate with the wonderful you. Oh yes, I can speak with *you* but I suppose you think that you are the only one who exists, that you are the only one who is important in my life, that there is no one else in the world outside of the wonderful you."

It was an accurate description of what had been achieved in the analysis. At the beginning she had not been able to communicate with me; now she could, but her capacity to communicate with those outside the consulting room was severely limited. After that session she went to visit a gynaecologist, so the next day she said to me, "Now I have found someone I can really talk to. Now I have found someone who is really sympathetic to women's problems . . ."

Earthquakes and fires were rumbling in me. I was about to point out the way she was pouring scorn on me and the work I had been doing with her, but once again the voice of sanity counselled silence. The earthquake and fires began to subside then I had a creative thought, which I voiced: "So you are letting me know that there has been a good development since you were here yesterday. Yesterday you could not communicate with anyone outside of here but today you can."

I remember well the change of atmosphere that reigned in that room for the next few minutes. A storm had passed, the sun shone through the clouds and peace held sway. So, was her communication a *projective identification* or a *creative communication*? Like the reverse perspective it depends upon the way you look at it. I know it is one process, though I cannot quite grasp that it is so. I believe that *homo sapiens* has a bigger brain capacity than our ancestor *homo erectus*. I suspect that *homo erectus* had a more restricted mental capability than ourselves. It may be that this problem will only be solved when *homo sapiens* has evolved further. If we can avoid wiping ourselves out with a nuclear war or by polluting the planet in some other way, a more developed species may be able grasp what we can only faintly adumbrate with the mental technology available to us at the moment.

You may think that I am wandering off into some transcendent philosophical realm with no relevance to clinical work, yet I believe that insight into these processes is crucial for a successful outcome. You see, I believe that had I "acted out" and condemned my patient for his cruelty, or sympathized with his pitiable plight, I would have crushed *creative communication* in him. You might say that I would have crushed *projective identification* in him, but because the two are one I believe I would have crushed *it*. He would have remained *in* his narcissistic state. What in fact happened was different.

I think I can say that in this battle that occurred in me between earthquake-with-fire and the still small voice it was the latter that won the day. I had evidence later on in the analysis that it also won the day within him. He began to express regret that he had treated his wife cruelly and thought it had been wrong of him to drown the cat. It was now too late to have children. I mentioned at the beginning that his wife developed multiple sclerosis. His reparation towards her was demonstrated in the devotion with which he cared for her in her illness. The sadness he felt at the way he had treated her was extreme. He nursed her with love until she died. Some time later he died himself. I came to believe that the real reason why he had come for analysis was to try to reverse the cruel track in which he was entrammelled.

The narcissistic person is aware of what has been done to him. He is a victim, a wounded animal. He is totally preoccupied with what has happened to him. I have indicated in the account that I have given of him how I was tempted to condemn him. There is also an alternative temptation, which I believe is also to be resisted. It is to be drawn into interpretations that are sympathetic to his plight. He was, in the opening stages of the analysis, very sorry for himself. It was, I believe, extremely important that I did not make any sympathetic noises to console him. There was, I believe, in him a transition from a state where he was sorry for himself, where his mind was full of the misfortunes that had befallen him, to one where he became the autonomous centre of his own activities. *Creative communication* grew to the extent that he was able to communicate to me both the distress he had suffered at the hands of his depressed mother in his childhood years *and* the distress that he experienced at the way he had treated his wife. The point about it is, he became able to communicate these dimensions of his life to me. I grasped and understood the distress he had suffered as a child. I was able to achieve this because he had communicated it to

me. If I carry you back to the imagined incident where Alphonsus
has been hit by a car and the representative from the Royal Society
for the Preservation of Birds returns to see him a week later,
Alphonsus is able to explain to him the accident that has occurred.
"When I am better," he tells him, "I shall be able to take out the
subscription, but I am not in a fit state yet." My patient began to
regret his own cruelty; he began to care for his wife. He became a
creative centre of his own life. I would not want you to have the
impression that there was a total transformation. There were back-
slidings, occasional eruptions of the old manner, but the general
direction had changed and held firm.

Narcissism is that state where I am overwhelmed by what has
been done to me; by the misfortunes that have occurred to me in
my childhood. Self-preoccupation is at its centre, but it is a
restricted view of the self. It is not the whole self, but only one
aspect of the self. This is the part of my diagnosis of narcissism that
I find most difficult to convey. The personality has received a batter-
ing, like the hospitalized individual who has been badly injured by
the car. So where is the inner spirit? The centre that is responsible
for *creative communication*? In the traumatized state the person is a
jelly. There is a discharge of unwanted stimuli, as Freud put it, and
what my patient's wife experienced was just this. What is very
important to realize is that my patient is entirely unaware of the
discharge. You may think that it is obvious that drowning his wife's
cat is going to make her very upset, but this is not so. The patient
is reeling under the impact of what has occurred to him, so he is
completely unaware of his own behaviour. He thought his wife
unreasonable when she became sour and vengeful towards him
after he had drowned the cat. From his point of view he has not
been cruel. "Cruel" is the definition of outsiders; it is not one that
makes any sense to him. He is reeling under the impact of an
assault to his system. The traumatized state and the narcissistic
state are two ways of describing the one reality. The difference
is that what we call the narcissistic state focuses upon the inner
structural system as it is. The term "traumatized state" focuses
upon the aetiology. I want now to look briefly at the inner structure
of narcissism.

The inner state is that of a "jelly". What might have been an
organizing centre is all broken up in bits and held, as it were, in

suspension in the jelly. These bits are responsible for the projection of hated elements into figures in the outside world. These figures in the outside world are then invested with inner parts of the personality, so are real yet delusional. There is also a powerful god that takes up residence in these outer figures. This god may inhabit just one person or may be dispersed through a number of figures. In the absence of an effective organizing centre this god becomes the agent who "drives" the person. He is possessed by this god because part of his personality is in the god. You will realize that the god is like a collage of those parts of the personality that have been projected. The god is hated but, at the same time, the person is tied to the god because it is partly fashioned from her own personality. What I have called the *principle of integrity* means that there is a magnetic attraction to those parts of the personality that have been projected. The reason why the god is hated is twofold. On the one hand the cause of the projection is primitive hatred of an aspect of the self and this hatred remains in place. The second reason is that all human beings hate the object that frustrates their desire for freedom, and this primitive god or gods holds the person captive.

So this is the situation: the person is a jelly living under the direction of a hated god. The god is sensual and punishing and also all-enveloping. This requires some explanation. Although it may not be immediately obvious, the individual is puffed up with omnipotence. This omnipotence may be quite obvious to the outside observer or it may appear that the person is quite the opposite. The person may either act in the persona of the outer god or live in deference to her. In either case there is an opposite to the god: i.e., the worm. In the latter state the person feels he is worthless or useless. The worm is either felt and expressed or is projected. In the latter case it is projected into an outer figure. A typical configuration is the person who is identified with god and the worm is a despised outer person. This despised one may also be a human grouping such as a nation, an age group, or a religious or political institution. Again according to the *principle of integrity*, the narcissistic person is drawn towards the worm that has been projected out into the environment. So here is the structure: a jelly inhabited by small particles, an outer god who directs the organism, a worm that is castigated by the god, and a hatred of all personal deficiencies. When we see this constellation we know that there has been a trauma. The traumatized individual is totally self-absorbed and yet this is what we mean by narcissism. The god, the worm, and the jelly envelop all the surrounding countryside, as it were. The person is therefore totally self-absorbed and this is why I gave the description at the beginning of someone who was lying prostrate in a hospital and quite unable to attend to anything other than himself.

I hope I have given some substance to the claim I made at the beginning of this paper that narcissism *is* the traumatized state. I want now to address the second question: why is it that we tend to condemn the narcissistic person? Why was that woman whom I referred to so bitter towards her husband? I think there are two answers to this question. The first is that the Other becomes encapsulated by a part of the self in the way I have tried to describe. The person becomes the embodiment of the condemning god. The best thing for that woman, for both her and her husband, would have been to speak to her husband and point out to him his neglect of her, but she is captured by this part of her husband's personality and enraged by it. She attacks him at times and at other times she withdraws and says nothing. She has then become a victim, an object, under the control of the narcissistic part of both her husband's and her own personality. The other reason is that all human beings want to be respected for who they are, and in this case the woman is being treated by her husband as an object. She therefore clamours with bitterness.

The analyst's task, however, is to demonstrate to the patient the way in which this narcissistic part of the personality is operating. It is a long task to work out with the patient how the narcissistic system is operating in this particular case. The patient has come because it has become an unsatisfactory way of functioning. As the patient, with the analyst's help, sees clearly its unsatisfactory nature, he or she is able to become the autonomous centre of her own *creative communication*. If this is achieved then the analysis has been successful.

CHAPTER FIFTEEN

Corruption of interpretation through narcissism

"I know how great is the effort needed to convince the proud of the power and excellence of humility, an excellence which makes it soar above all the summits of this world, which sway in their temporal instability, overtopping them with an eminence not arrogated by human pride"

(St Augustine, 1972, p. 5)

That which is most desired and most resisted is an interpretation. It is desired because it is a gateway to freedom; it is resisted because freedom is terrifying. As a free being I become responsible for the passions of my soul. This is agonizing, and I struggle to escape from such a hell. I know with a deadly certainty that I resist interpretations. I only accept an interpretation after a dire struggle. I will try every other avenue rather than the one where I accept freedom and myself. Wilfred Bion (1967, p. 112) says development depends upon a crucial decision: whether to evade frustration or to modify it. For "frustration" I would substitute the word "agony". I believe that what applies to myself is true for all human beings. I have evidence to support this belief from observation of a limited group of people who have come to me for psychoanalysis. This evidence, however, will not convince someone who believes that we are fashioned entirely by our genetic inheritance and our micro and macro-social environment. Those who espouse this view will classify an interpretation as a conditioned stimulus and will therefore disagree with the foundations upon which this paper is based: that an interpretation confronts me with my own freedom. This is the metaphysical presupposition that underpins the clinical problem that I want to put before you (Collingwood, 1969).

A young woman attached herself to me closely so that my voice on my answering machine or one of my books would function as a transitional object that she held on to closely. It reminded me of an occasion when I was walking in Bombay near the Gate of India when a poor urchin child came nuzzling up to me, stroking my hand, pointing to his mouth, and whining in a soft voice, and he would not leave me. Neither food, money, nor gentle encouragement could persuade him to leave me in peace. In that last phrase "leave me in peace" you will detect a note of frustration. A clinging, clawing attachment of that kind troubles my spirit. An analyst would be justified in saying to me: "But why does such an emotional attitude trouble you?"

To answer that I would, I believe, have to say that it stimulates in me an equivalent emotional attitude. That is not something that I like to think about. The image of myself as that urchin child in Bombay is discomforting. I cherish rather a view of myself as a free independent spirit. The discomforting image is the true one: the cherished image is narcissistic if it cloaks the discomforting one. If I want to be a free independent spirit then this is an ego-ideal that I strive for and, to the extent that I know it is unachieved, then to that extent I am in a sane mental state, but when I believe that I have achieved it through a magic trick then I am in a narcissistic state. Narcissistic beliefs cloak truths that are painful to the spirit.

The other thing that I need to tell you about this patient is consistent with her emotional clinging. She hated being dismissed at the end of a session. Staying in the locality, reading my books, listening to my voice on the answering machine, were also reactions to being dismissed. Like the urchin in Bombay she would not be sent away.

So the session came to an end. She got up obediently and went. I was free (or so I thought) and took it into my head to go to the bank and take out some money. Now the bank and our consulting room back on to each other, so a laborious two-minute walk with four 90° turns brought me from our consulting room into the bank. As I walked in, my recently evicted patient was at the counter . . .

The next day I made this interpretation: "Yesterday I summarily dismiss you through the front door. You grind your teeth with frustrated rage and say to yourself 'He may dismiss me through his front door but I will re-enter through the back/bank door'—like a child that has been shut out of her parents' bedroom but, not to be defeated, creeps back in through a back door."

She hated that interpretation, and because it was hated it was expelled. What happens to an interpretation that is expelled? It ceases to be an interpretation, or rather it never achieves the status of an interpretation. It instantly became an instruction: "Thou shalt not go to the bank . . ." and for a couple of years she never returned to that bank—*my* bank. Now you might say that her ability to turn what was an interpretation into an instruction was entirely her doing, yet I believe that she could only do that by finding some purchase within my personality. However, before examining exactly how that element in my personality is used in the process of turning an interpretation into an instruction, I want to examine more closely the difference between the two.

An interpretation is a statement describing someone's emotional motivation. Emotional motivation is inferred directly through intuition, whereas motor activity is perceived through the senses either of touch, smell, hearing and vision individually or through two or more of them. I may say that I can see Mr Smith moving across the room, but I intuit that he does so because he is frightened by the presence of an Alsatian that has just entered the room. In this case the intuition is an inference. I am an outside observer of Mr Smith, but if the situation is different and I turn to him and say: "You are moving across the room in order to get away from me. You are frightened I will smell alcohol on your breath when you had promised me not to drink for the rest of the year . . .", he is confronted with a challenge. He may say, "I have not been drinking. You're just an old puritan kill-joy who can't bear anyone enjoying himself and all you can think is something bad of me", or he may say, "Yes, you're right. I am afraid I have been drinking and I know I told you I wouldn't but I am afraid I have reneged on my promise."

In either case it brings Mr Smith's inner motivational principles from background to foreground, and this is the function of an interpretation. Emotional motivation is intuited directly through the "I–Thou" confrontation. Intuition of this kind is not an inference but a direct apprehension of psychic reality. The "I–Thou" confrontation is the instrument through which emotional motivation is directly intuited. When someone is ashamed or guilty about their inner emotional motivation, then this direct confrontation is avoided. This is why transference interpretations are central to the psychoanalytic endeavour. This intuition is more direct than perception of the world through the senses. I follow here the view of Schopenhauer as opposed to that of Kant.

Kant, following Plato, distinguished between the *phenomenon* and the *noumenon*; the latter being the thing-in-itself that cannot be known. Schopenhauer, however, said that the *noumenon* is the "will", which not only is known, but known directly. By "will" Schopenhauer meant what I refer to as *emotional motivation*, and this is known through an act of intuition. However, this intuition can be obliterated, destroyed, or distorted a split second after it has occurred. I think it likely that the act of intuition itself remains intact but the impressed image can be damaged very shortly afterwards.

I once interviewed a man in prison who a week earlier had raped and killed a twelve-year-old girl. As he spoke to me there were flashes of a happening: "An accident . . . she fell down . . . my bicycle was against the house . . . police were brutal to me . . ."

I believe that what he had done had been obliterated. What had been obliterated had been his own action. In a parallel though less severe way, the intuition into my patient's emotional motivation is instantly destroyed. The incident I have just told you about is of a man who raped and killed a young girl. It is an emotional act embodied in a physical act. That man *did* something. "Emotional motivation" is anodyne language. If we used Anglo-Saxon instead of Latin it would be "I *do* something to you with my inner spirit". Intuition is that direct glimpse into this emotional doing. With an interpretation I put that intuitive glimpse into words. It is Column Six of the horizontal axis and D of the vertical axis of the Grid as devised by Bion. Columns 1, 3, 4, and 5 are psychic steps leading up to the crucial stroke of Column 6. Now back to my patient.

I had seen her hatred at being rudely pushed out of my presence. I had seen her coming back and peeping through the keyhole of my back/bank door. She had seen it, too and, in violent hatred, obliterated it, but we need to invoke here the *principle of conservation*. Just as matter cannot be annihilated but only changed from one form into another, so also with psychic realities. In this case the interpretation is changed into an instruction. For this to be possible certain psychological conditions are necessary. For a statement to become an instruction that has to be obeyed it is necessary that the analyst be adorned in the cloak of god. For this to occur it is also necessary that the patient has, in a momentary act, submitted himself in dependent relation to that god in such a way that the god has been installed as the action station and the instructions are god-given and therefore have all the authority that we associate with the deity.

What I refer to as the *narcissistic constellation* is made up of the following pattern of interrelated events: an inner jelly-like state with no organizing centre, an outer god whose rule determines action, belief that she is a contemptible worm, and the presence of envy, greed, and jealousy, which I call the *liquifiers* because they are responsible for maintaining the psyche in a jelly-like state. Then there is a hatred of these *liquifiers* combined with an intense dependence upon the god. Last, there is a paranoid focus upon one element in the godhead. This is the constellation that is responsible for turning an interpretation into an instruction. It cannot happen without the instrumentality of that constellation. I said at the beginning that an interpretation confronts me with my own freedom. An interpretation is freedom's declaration. In the state of narcissism the psyche is prisoner to the dictates of a god *embodied* in an outer figure. Now, we are talking here of a situation where this god has become incarnate in the analyst. My technical point is this: that this incarnation cannot occur without the analyst allowing it to happen. When I refer to "god" it is always incarnate in an external figure. It is, in fact, an internal figure, but one that is so powerful, so castigating, that the individual has to externalize it to make it bearable. There is a moment of danger in some analyses at the point when the god is being withdrawn from the external figure back into its own internal habitat. The danger then is that the individual may, at that moment, submit to the savagery of so fearful an executioner.

The best example I know in literature of an individual's submission to an outer savage oppressor who represents the inner is that of Anna Tellwright, who is the protagonist in Arnold Bennett's superb novel *Anna of the Five Towns*. In this novel Arnold Bennett charts Anna's slow and painful attempts at freeing herself from Ephraim Tellwright, her tyrannical paranoid father. She tells Willie Price, one of her father's debtors, that she will make sure it is all right for him; in other words that she will see that the debt is written off and forgotten. Now she has to tell her father, who is a cruel miser, what she has guaranteed. She is in a state of inner terror. She gears herself up to the task but, at the last moment, loses her nerve as the narrative recounts:

> Her father, always the favourite of circumstance, had by chance, struck the first blow; ignorant of the battle that awaited him, he had unwittingly won it by putting her in the wrong . . . She knew in a flash that her enterprise was hopeless; she knew that her father's position in regard to her was impregnable, that no moral force, no consciousness of right, would avail to overthrow that authority which she had herself made absolute by a life-long submission; she knew that face to face with her father she was, and always would be, a coward . . . [Bennett, 1969, p. 197]

Later that night Anna steals into her father's office and tears up and burns that offending bill of exchange which is the legal proof of Willie Price's debt. When this is subsequently revealed her father goes berserk, and at last Anna is freed from some element of his power:

> All her life she had been terrorised by the fear of a wrath which had never reached the superlative degree until that day. Now that she had seen and felt the limit of his anger, she became aware that she could endure it; the curse was heavy, and perhaps more irksome than heavy, but she survived; she continued to breathe, eat, drink, and sleep; her father's power stopped short of annihilation . . . [*ibid.*, p. 205]

However, she accepts marriage to a local worthy who, though not such a tyrannical miser as her father, is nevertheless avaricious for

Anna's own estate and it is revealed that in truth she is in love with Willie Price but feels duty bound to marry her fiancé, to whom she is pledged. One sees from this that it is the inner savage god that she is truly trying to liberate herself from. She has partial success but it is not complete. As I said earlier, the moment of great danger when this process is in train is just as the savage god is withdrawn from the outer figure and it is experienced within. In the novel Anna does not commit suicide, yet Willie Price, the one she truly loves, does, as does her father, and her own life becomes a suicide to duty.

When this god is located in an external figure the latter is affected by it. In fact the external figure has to display certain anxious qualities otherwise he/she cannot be host to it. In the story of Anna it is her father's paranoia that is stirred, but what happens when the analyst becomes host to this savage god? The key way in which the analyst allows it to happen is by enacting his agitation rather than containing it. The enactment may be through his paranoia being stirred, but it will certainly be through one element of the *narcissistic constellation* being stirred. Now to return to my patient.

I indicated that I was discomforted by her clinging attachment to me; as if I had found a sticky substance stuck to my skin and was irritably trying to get rid of it. Now I mentioned that intense dependence upon god was one of the elements in the narcissistic constellation, and this is combined with a paranoid focus upon one element in the analyst. The way it works is like this. She hates this clinging attachment and through this primitive hatred expels it into the analyst. It is a principle that when there has been an expulsion of a part of myself into an outer object I am necessarily focused upon that part. So she is focused upon this expelled part of her and she has knowledge that she has expelled it into me. Her silent paranoid focus is upon the tone in me that denotes my distaste of her clinging. Now, when I made the statement to her that she had come in through the back/bank door like a child who'd been thrown out of her parents' bedroom and was peeping back in, it was an interpretation, yet I know I was irritated to find her in the bank. I know that in the statement that I made to her there was a tone in it indicating to her that she should not be using *my* bank. This part of her that had located itself in me now swallowed up the whole statement, turning it from an interpretation into an instruction.

I want to say something here in an aside, as it is a diversion from the main theme of the paper. I have referred to the bank as *my* bank, yet I think you know that this is an analogical way of speaking. It is not, factually, *my* bank. I do not own it, but nevertheless I have come to think of it, however absurdly, as *my* bank. It is the bank I always go to. It is within two minutes of our consulting room. I know all the staff; they know me. Yet, of course, it is absurd. Anyone can enter that bank and my patient has every right to enter it, and yet I feel I have some proprietal rights over it. To this extent I am god and the bank comes within my territory; it is my temple in which people have to take off their shoes and bow. This is I believe the origin of the sacred. My patient had dared to trespass on sacred territory.

It may help here if we refer to Bion's paper on hallucination. He says there that the expelled part swells up and consumes the whole object. Now the expelled part is her submissive clinging to god. God is the agent of the expulsion and its instrument is her hatred. Her focus, however, is upon *my* hatred of her clinging behaviour. The conclusion is inescapable: that her expulsion is only possible because of my hatred of the Bombay child within *me*. A projection of a hated part of the self can only be successful if hatred of that same part can be found in the host object. It is this same god and the instrumental hatred that turns an interpretation into an instruction—an instruction from God-on-High. There is here another unavoidable conclusion: that acceptance of all parts of myself are the prerequisite for interpretative work. In particular, consciousness of our narcissism is the *sine qua non* without which we collude with the narcissism of the patient. We need to remember that *the* defensive manner for the psychotic part of the personality is the stirring up and inhabiting the equivalence in the analyst of that hated part of the self (Bion, 1962, p. 24).

When I referred just now to "god-given" instructions, there was some implication that there could be human instructions motivated by love rather than hatred. What about the instructions as to times of sessions, fee to be paid, and so on? These are the arrangements for the analyst and, to the extent that the patient is narcissistic, they will be experienced as god-given and thereby resented. It is a feature of narcissism to coalesce mental events of a different nature into events of the same kind. The narcissistic patient, therefore, will be predisposed to coalesce all statements from the analyst into the class labelled god-given instructions. All human contracts become god-given instructions. The same principle applies, however: that the human contract only becomes a god-given instruction through the analyst's narcissism. A patient used to pay my monthly account rather late. When I made an interpretation about it he was sniffing in the wind to see whether irritability arising from self-interest was the motivating factor or whether this had been contained and that he was in possession of an interpretation.

It is worth noting here that we very easily make human instructions into god-given ones. Fifty minutes seems to be a suitable timeframe for a session but it is a mistake to cast it in concrete. Michael Fordham, the Jungian analyst, always gave his patients sixty-minute sessions and Herbert Rosenfeld, when seeing a psychotic patient, extended his sessions to an hour and a half. I saw a patient for a period for sessions that lasted an hour and a half. When I was at the Tavistock a patient I saw for analysis one day refused to leave the room at the end of the session. I grew hot under the collar and began to fume inwardly. However, on reflection, I realized that I did not need my room for the next half hour so I left the room and she departed a few minutes later and that became my practice with her and it worked perfectly well. Then circumstances changed and I needed the room on Tuesdays straight after her session. I explained this to her and asked if on Tuesdays she would mind leaving straight after the session and she did so without demur. She had no problem in responding to a human request; she became defiant in the face of god-given instructions.

*   *   *

I want now to reflect a little more on the subjective state of the analyst that enables the patient to transform an interpretation into an instruction. Let us go back to the incident where I meet my patient in the bank. She is quite free to go to that bank, she is free to inhabit my locality and observe me. Yet there is something in me that says she has no right to do this. Now what has happened here? There is no doubt that there is a punishing god inside her that castigates her for her behaviour, but such a god is never inside alone but always *embodied*. It is installed in me. Now, in the case of that particular "bank interpretation" I was aware soon after I had given it that there was a tone in my voice indicating that she should not be using *my* bank. In other words, I delivered it as an instruction or at least it had an instructional undertone. An observer looking through a one-way screen would have said to me, "The way you said that to her did imply that you did not want her to use your bank."

So I enact a god-like position. I am god, in fact. "That is *my* bank. You have no right to be trespassing on my territory." I invest myself with a sacred quality. The essential quality of the sacred is that this piece of territory belongs to god and that no one should enter it unless their head is bowed. Later in this patient's analysis I did interpret this tonal implication of mine and her response to it.

It is clear that my patient has a fearful "god" inside that punishes her clinging to me so tenaciously. Now how is that I find myself "being" that god? A common answer might be: "She projected it into me . . .", but I do not think that is correct. I believe rather that it is like this. She searches out and finds the narcissistic pattern in me. In particular she finds in me the hated part of which I am unconscious. A loved part is conscious; a hated part is unconscious. The search is accomplished through a like-to-like magnetic attraction. The two hated parts fuse and god thunders threatening curses against "her". The attachment of her hated part to mine stimulates god into action. A contract is forged between god and the hated part. The psychotic element in the personality will always "hook into" the narcissistic defences of the analyst. When she has found the narcissistic constellation in me she is able to transform interpretations into instructions. In this way she defends herself against receiving interpretations.

Is the conclusion then that I cannot analyse successfully unless I have resolved all the narcissistic currents in my personality? There are two ways of approaching this problem. Let us call these two ways the particular and the general. I will start with the former.

It is not possible that I can be entirely free of narcissistic currents in my personality. It is probable, therefore, that I shall meet a patient who will "hook into" one of my narcissistic defences. Once this has happened, then the only course open to me is to attempt to resolve that problem in myself. Such a patient therefore challenges me to transform a piece of narcissistic functioning into creative intentional functioning. My willingness to take up such a challenge depends on whether such a desire to transform myself is part of my ego ideal. If it is, then such a patient is an opportunity for which I could be thankful.

If that is the course I decide to follow, then it means that when such a patient "hooks into" my own narcissism, then I have to change mental gear. I start to work on myself instead of working on the patient. Our confidence is that if we succeed in this endeavour it will have a therapeutic effect upon the patient. I examined one aspect of this in a paper I once wrote, but I understand it now as just one illustration of a much wider and deeper process (Symington, 1983). I want now to turn to the other way, which is more general.

I define mental health in this way: "That person is mentally healthy who is able to create for him/herself the emotional capacity to pursue truth, love, courage, integrity and tolerance."

Narcissism is that psychic constellation which prevents such a creation. Envy is an integral part of narcissism and, as Melanie Klein stressed, what envy attacks, strangles, and prevents from coming into being is creativity. What I am stressing here is that truth, love, courage, integrity, and tolerance are personal creations. In fact, they are the creations that make a person mentally healthy. I need to be constantly vigilant against any tendency in myself to make my patient into a clone of myself. You may say that this is an absurd statement, but look at it for a moment this way: why is it that those who have a Kleinian analysis follow the views of Melanie Klein? Those who are analysed by a self-psychologist follow the views of Kohut? Those who are analysed by a Classical Freudian follow the views of Anna Freud? Those who are analysed by a British analyst of the Independent Tradition follow the path of their analyst and so on?

What lies behind all these perspectives is the idea of making the person into something, moulding them according to a particular perspective, and yet this is ultimately a Behaviourist angle on psychic events. To grasp the sense of this one needs to conceptualize that, to the extent to which a narcissistic constellation dominates the action patterns of the personality, exactly to that extent is a person bent to the dictates of god. When god rules, people are bent to a template, however unconscious that may be. Mental health is characterized by personal intentional functioning. Recently, I was treating a young woman who was a fashion designer. One day she was taken with a powerful desire to study psychology. She enrolled herself at evening class at a university. It seemed very "driven", and she knew that I was a psychologist. I made this interpretation to her: "You know that I am a psychologist and believe that I have fallen in love with my own reflection. Only by being a psychologist like me will you gain my love and interest. This I think is how you see things."

This interpretation had an impact upon her and she gave up psychology shortly afterwards. I believe *that* interpretation was the culmination of a process that was largely responsible for liberating her from the slavery to which she was bound. When someone becomes the creative centre of her own emotional activity, a psychoanalytical aim has been achieved. Personal freedom rather than Fate is the governing principle. This was a distinction made by Erich Fromm nearly fifty years ago (Fromm, 1950). Psychotic functioning in the patient "hooks into" equivalent functioning in the analyst. Jung used the term "participation" for this joint defence of analyst and patient. This is how he puts it:

> The emotions of patients are always slightly contagious, and they are very contagious when the contents which the patient projects into the analyst are identical with the analyst's own unconscious contents. They then both fall into the same dark hole of unconsciousnes, and get into the condition of participation. [Jung, 1935, p. 140]

Psychosis has this zoom-camera effect: it zooms down on the area of narcissistic functioning in the analyst and, in doing so, stirs it up in such a way that the patient hibernates under the analyst's narcissistic umbrella.

I believe this is an important issue. We hear a great deal about the crisis in psychoanalysis and about the inward-looking nature of analytic societies and about the failure of analytic institutes to explore the mind. I think *a* factor may be that interpretations are turned into instructions, thereby obliterating all exploration. What I am describing may be quite widespread.

CHAPTER SIXTEEN

The core of narcissism

"Don't take yourselves too seriously. Take life seriously. Take *God* seriously. But don't, please don't, take yourselves *too seriously!*"

(Hume, 1979, p. 26)

In my book on narcissism (Symington, 1993) I said that the core of narcissism lay in an unconscious refusal of life. I referred to this in objectified terms as the *lifegiver*. I have since come to believe that this is too narrow a view. I continue to think that it is a core component but, rather than see it as the cause of narcissism, I see it as one of its manifestations. I see that this emotional act of refusal is something that we shall always come up against in narcissism. It is also true that when narcissism begins to dissolve then one of the cardinal signs of this dissolution is the appearance of acts of emotional generosity. But what enables the act of generosity? Why the refusal? The answer I come up with now is less simple but, I believe, closer to the truth. I see it now that the act of refusal is the natural outcome of a structure of which the key components are the following: god, worm, jelly, addictive dependency, a theory of emotional action, narcissistic objects and a theory of freedom. In addition to this I believe that if we are to get a focus upon narcissism it is necessary to have a different ontological foundation to what exists at present. I am going to start with the jelly, as I have to start somewhere. I am reminded of Bion's comment at the beginning of his book *Elements of Psychoanalysis*:

> In writing this I have to start somewhere and this produces difficulties because the start of a discussion tends to impose an appearance of reality on the idea that the matter discussed has a start. [1963, p. 11]

I want to explain what I mean by that comment. The categories god, worm, jelly, addictive dependency, a theory of emotional action, narcissistic objects, and a theory of freedom are each a hologram that includes all the others. I call this the *principle of inclusion*, which means that in one element all the others are included. There is one diamond with many different facets. From whichever facet you are looking you are seeing the same object.

So we start with the jelly. The narcissistic person may appear stiff upper lip and stalwart, but inside he is a jelly. He has no principle of creative action within him; there is no autonomy within. He is victim to outer events, afraid of hostility, and in a state of panic. A patient said, "When my wife gets angry I am a jelly inside." Another patient said, "I am all broken up inside."

There is a sense of futility and hopelessness. There is a similarity between this state and what Fairbairn called the schizoid state. Fairbairn went to trouble to differentiate the sense of futility from depression (1976, p. 91). This differential diagnosis is even more important when one realizes that depression is nearly always a concomitant of this jelly-like state. Depression is always *about* something and that something is most typically an inner emotional state or an inner mental attitude. One might be able to predict that when there is this jelly-like inner state then there will also be depression. Unconscious knowledge of the jelly-like state is responsible for depression. Elucidation of the jelly within needs to be followed by showing that knowledge of this is what causes depression. Hanna Segal (1981) has shown that it is important that the clinician treating a schizophrenic should be able to see the depression.

When someone's psyche is a gelatinous mass their structural form is moulded by objects in the environment. Actually, this is the way it looks but it is not simply like this, but rather the objects are invested with god-like qualities into whom the psyche is projected, like a jelly into a mould. Then the psyche is made up of a jelly and a hard crustaceous god-like substance. It is important to realize that this substance is not just inner, but rather both outer and inner. An outer person is incorporated, invested with god-like traits, and to that figure the jelly sticks like a piece of plasticine or blu-tack. The figure may be an individual or a body of individuals. In fact it is never a person, but rather an institutionalized body. So, this hard god-like substance may be an analyst, a man, a woman, an American, a Jew, a sick one, a wealthy one, etc. The jelly becomes attached to this substance as to a rock.

Now, the jelly also slops outside its boundaries into frail creatures: babies, animals, insects, plants. These are seen to be more fragile than they are. In the family therapy literature the concept of a mythology is used to describe a false belief that is shared by all the family members. So, for instance, the belief in a family that the youngest daughter is delicate and has to be treated with especial care. So the jelly, as it were, pours out of one member into this "delicate" daughter. This embodiment of the god-like substance in a group and the effusion of the jelly into "frail" creatures may explain, for instance, the myth that men are strong and women weak and needing protection. Whether these wider social phenomena are to be explained in this way is a matter for psychological observation. The jelly is in a state of effusion with frail or inferior creatures.

God, on the other hand, is embodied in "pedestal figures". It may typically be in MPs, Frenchmen, psychoanalysts, priests, doctors, lawyers, policemen, stockbrokers, men . . . One might ask what the prototype of this is for the infant? One might suppose it is the breast dissociated from the personhood of the mother. A breast that feeds, that is hated, is sensual . . . You may be surprised at the use of this last adjective in juxtaposition to god, yet the god we are talking of is sensual in nature. It is a god who will lead, show the way and rescue the individual from the need to make a choice. I had an obsessional patient whose tactics aimed at frustrating me took this particular form. He was coming twice a week.

I had been foolish enough to suggest that he come more often for analysis. Oh, yes, next year he would like to come for a third session, so I offered him Wednesday. Later he told me that the director of a clinic where he was working wanted him to work Wednesdays next year; he was not sure whether he would accept the director's offer. This was duly interpreted. Then . . . would he come Wednesdays or not . . . one week he would . . . next week he would not, etc. I was able to interpret to him that he wanted to exasperate me so I would eventually explode and say, "Well, I must know one way or the other . . ." then he would either come or not come, but he realized that in either case it would not be a choice but rather a reaction to this agitated god who was dancing with madness in front of him. It was free choice that was being avoided. So god and freedom of choice are antinomies.

At the opposite end to god is the worm. Every narcissistic patient believes he is a worm, or a wretch of no value. There are two narcissistic types: the one who swaggers around in an arrogant way and the one who apologizes for himself and is self-deprecatory: god and the worm. Now, it looks as if there is nothing of god in the worm and nothing of the worm in god, yet this is just surface appearance. In the arrogant individual there is always the worm and in the Uriah Heep god is always present. Knowledge of this fact is essential equipment for the analyst. The other component of this god–worm entity is the person's extreme sensibility to hurt.

In *Learning from Experience* Bion (1962, p. 82) says that patients sometimes are not able to solve their problems because they are using the wrong model. This is so not only of patients but analysts also. One reason why we do not solve the problems that are presented clinically through narcissism is that we are working with the wrong model. The false model is the belief that survival is the goal of the human endeavour. The "philosophy" of the narcissistic personality is survival: the "philosophy" of the healthy personality is the achievement of emotional freedom. Where there is a narcissistic current in the personality survival has been achieved but at the cost of losing the privilege of freedom. A Faustian bargain has been contracted where the individual has, for the sake of survival, foresworn his right to be free. It is like someone who has agreed to life imprisonment in order to avoid the death sentence. Narcissism, then, has had its function but it is now a constraint upon a deeper human yearning.

When a narcissistic person comes for analysis it is as if he was saying "Now I have achieved survival but I want something more", and then he turns to Mr Narcissus and says, "You have been a good friend but it is now time to say goodbye." In fact, the struggle in the analysis is precisely to be courageous enough to say "Good-bye". The attachment to Mr Narcissus is enormously strong, and he takes revenge by cajoling or mocking. A patient said to me, "I am very dependent on you. You are like a big breast that I suck upon and cling to with all my might." Hardly had he said this to me when he heard a mocking voice saying, "So you are just a little Mommy's boy . . ." in a very sneering tone. He came to recognize that this was a part of him that held him prisoner, prevented him from coming close to me, from loving, from thinking, from creating his own world—in other words that prevented freedom. So there is in the individual a struggle between self-preservation and the desire for creative freedom.

So, the jelly and god are two sides of one coin and both of them exclude the possibility of creative freedom. Another dimension that is inherent in this constellation is a glue-like attachment to the figure in whom god is embodied. The figure on to whom the attachment is fixed is conceptualized in sensual terms. When awareness of this begins to surface it becomes expressed usually in sexual imagery. So, for instance, a man had vivid "mini-dreams" of my penis penetrating him. At other times it was of him sucking my penis, and this alternated with an image of him sucking on my nipple. Sometimes I was a penis; at other times I was a breast. This symbolized the sensual nature of the attachment. It is an attachment such that the penis or breast is believed to be a part of his own body. One patient would happily talk of his own envy but if *I* did he hated it. This was because something was coming to him not from his own body parts, but from a separate being. When this attachment is disrupted an event occurs because of it. In one case the patient developed an internal cyst; in another the patient had a car crash; in another the spouse had a heart attack. Separation is experienced as a betrayal. This glue-like attachment can be thought of as dependency of a very primitive nature—the way in which the arm is dependent upon the head for its movements. In such cases the patient is dependent upon the analyst for thinking. To be dependent upon another for such an elemental function as thinking is humiliating in the extreme, and the patient envies the analyst intensely. This glue-like attachment and envy are reciprocals of one another.

Envy is a concept that has been developed considerably within psychoanalysis since Melanie Klein wrote her classic book *Envy and Gratitude* (1975). But there is danger of moralism—i.e., that it is only seen and defined from the outside and its inner structure not understood. In primitive envy, such as is being described here, the good qualities are discharged into the analyst and the bad qualities are ingested, so it is a very bad contractual arrangement for the patient. Fairbairn described this as the "internalization of bad objects" but he misunderstood the reasons for it, saying that it was better to have a devil inside but live in a world ruled by God rather than the other way around (Fairbairn, 1976, pp. 59–81). Fairbairn thought the motive was to safeguard the person from depression—i.e. it would be depressing to feel that the world was ruled by badness. This would be the conscious reason that might be given by a patient to a psychotherapist but if this envious activity is seen to be part of the *narcissistic constellation* then it is clear that its function is to maintain an inner and outer *stasis*. The sense of being irredeemably bad is intricately linked to the belief that this is how things are, that it cannot be changed, that conservation of the state of affairs is the only option available.

Envy, however, is not the only agent that is responsible for *liquifying* the personality into a jelly. There are two other agents: greed and jealousy. Greed aims to introject the good but does so with unrestrained violence. The result is that the inner personality is overwhelmed so that the creative centre is again crushed. Jealousy obliterates the third party. The presence of the third party modifies the violence of both the envy and the greed. It may appear that there are here three agents, but in fact we are looking at three facets of one agent. Their joint activity *liquifies* that centre of the personality that is responsible for creative activity. Together they fashion a confusion so that what is inner and what is outer is all muddled up and also *liquifies* the elements in the personality. So, for instance, a sadness, rather than exist as an element in the personality, is dispersed through the personality so it is not recognized as sadness but instead has mutated into depression. So, also, joy has become dispersed through the personality as mania, and so on. Envy, greed, and jealousy are then together *the liquifier*. In order to transform narcissism it is necessary for the therapist to interpret the activity of this *liquifier*.

The *liquifier* receives its power from god. Its power comes from this grandiosity. The grandiosity of god is the source of power but, paradoxically, it is inextricably linked to that glue-like attachment to an embodied god. Such an individual then shows all the signs of being dependent upon others and the very words of others become ingested inside them so that what is being given out is the incorporation of what someone has said to the person recently. A patient of mine fell in love with a woman who lived in the country at some six hours distance from Sydney. He commuted between Sydney and her home town, so sometimes when he came to see me his lady was absent and at others she was present with him. When she was absent he would say things like "I love living in my flat overlooking the beach"; or "I love yachting . . ."; or "I am not a very good businessman . . ."; but when she was present he would say, "I am looking forward to living in a house in the centre of the city . . ."; or "Lucinda loves horseriding. I am happy to take it up and give up yachting . . ."; or "I think I am very good at business."

In this case he changes when Lucinda is present. It was clear to me from his history and other things he had said that he did like his flat overlooking the beach, did like yachting, and was not a very good business man. That was what his self was like. When he fell in love with Lucinda, god became embodied in her and the words that he then spoke were like the words of god installed in him to please her. What I want to draw attention to here is the dependent attachment on another, and that god is implanted in this other.

I want to say the same thing, but from a slightly different angle. It is that a glue-like dependence on another is a core element in the *narcissistic constellation*. From the external point of view it looks as if the person is entirely dependent upon another, uncontaminated by any elements from within. A health worker might say of the person: "He is enormously dependent upon Josephine"; or "She depends entirely on her old boss, Jim, at work"; or "He is devoted to the local Scout Troup. If that packed up he would be a lost soul"; or "She has sacrificed her whole life to parish work. No demand is too great for her. If the parish priest asks something of her she will do it unquestioningly. If you took the parish away her life would collapse." In all these cases it looks as though the *narcissistic person* is entirely devoted just to the external person, group, or organization, but in fact god is always embodied there.

One way of thinking about this aspect is to consider Frances Tustin's formulation of the aetiology of autism. It is that there has been a primitive trauma in which the tiny infant has been prematurely parted from the mother. It is at a stage where, for the infant, mother and child are undifferentiated, so the parting is equivalent to having a limb of one's own ripped off. So the god that is embodied in the external figure or organization means that the latter is part of the self, so the glue-like dependency is upon one's own self.

The *liquifier* and this glue-like dependency are two sides of one coin. Resolution of narcissism requires elucidation and interpretation of both aspects. From the angle of the glue-like dependency are the interpretations concerning the impact of what is done to the patient, particularly by the analyst's absences; from the angle of the *liquifier*, the active reaction to these events.

Another component of this glue-like attachment is paranoia. It will, I believe, help if we understand the structure of paranoia. It is a primitive hatred of all those elements in the personality that obstruct freedom. Now, here is a tricky conundrum. What is it that obstructs freedom? And the answer? Narcissism. The patient (and the analyst also and everyone else in the world) hates those elements inside them that prevent freedom. This is a primitive hatred, and by this I mean it is not consciously known. Violent projection is primitive hatred in action. Once these elements have been projected they are viewed with hatred and suspicion. They are projected into the god-like object. Self-serving motives are viewed with deep suspicion but, as these factors are part of the personality, the patient is stuck to the analyst with glue-like bonding. These elements, which are seen to be present in the other, makes the analyst into an enemy, a spy, someone to be deeply distrusted.

This "primitive hatred is of all those elements in the personality that obstruct freedom". It is not possible to understand narcissism unless one believes that the human goal is the achievement of freedom. Kleinian theory, more than any that went before it, has stressed the centrality of the inner world and that the presence of noxious inner objects obstruct our emotional development. The implication is that our own freedom is obstructed by these bad inner objects. The idea that the achievement of freedom is the central emotional goal for the individual permeates the whole of Bion's work. There have also been certain analysts who have stressed this dimension—for instance, Otto Rank and Erich Fromm. However, in psychoanalytic theory, this has always been seen as subsidiary to the Darwinian view that survival is the human goal. Freud's formulation of the death instinct is couched within the survival framework. The goal of narcissism is self-preservation, which is not the same as survival but it is very close to it and becomes confused with it. With this background theory, narcissism is not seen clearly because it seems to be so closely allied to what is healthy. This is, I believe, the reason why many authors talk of "positive narcissism" or "anti-narcissism", the latter term implying that positive narcissism is a healthy endeavour. However, if you take it that the central human goal is the achievement of freedom, then it becomes clear that narcissism exists in the personality as an obstacle to this goal.

The only way in which the individual can become free is through inner creative emotional acts of which the generation of thoughts or thinking is a core component. This is what the clinician tries to foster in the psychoanalytic encounter. If you think about it, you will realize that what I have said about narcissism at every point thwarts the inner yearning for freedom. A person is only free when he or she is the author of his or her own actions. When I am driven I am a prisoner; when I can be the creator of what happens to me, then I am free. From this perspective it immediately becomes clear that the jelly is pushed around by all the diverse currents of external events, that a person ruled by god (the false god) is unfree, that a glue-like attachment debars the possibility of freedom, and the same goes for paranoia. Also, when someone is in a suspicious, paranoid relation to those around, he or she is captive to those figures, and when I believe that I am bad I do not have the confident base from which to create.

Whether I am free or not is determined by the differential diagnosis of inner acts. There are inner acts that are reactive to outer events and those that are responsive and creative. These two are utterly different in character. They are as different from each other as is the noise emitted by a landslide from Tschaikovsky's *1812*. In the first case, actions occur mechanically under the laws of motion that are familiar to us from our observation of the inanimate world, and in the other there has been a creator who is responsible for the action. In the latter, material has been passed into the psyche and remodelled by a mysterious inner creator. The inner creative act has a quite different social outcome from that which proceeds from reactive activity. I shall give an example designed to demonstrate the different effects of these two sorts of activity.

I arranged to see a man in his mid-thirties for psychotherapy and fixed the starting date nine months ahead. I fixed a lunch hour appointment time, which was possible for him though inconvenient. In the meantime I arranged to see him once in two months. For those few appointments he put considerable pressure on me to see him at eight in the evening. By this time I was certain that his need to bend me to his whims was the issue I needed to tackle. (I had evidence of this also from what he had told me of his control of girlfriends.) So I gave him two appointments, two months apart, at times that were possible for him but somewhat inconvenient. I gave him the times that I had available that were best for him. I did not allow myself to be pressured into giving him an "out of hours" time that I knew I would resent. However, I also did not give him times which were impossible for him. I stress this because I believe I responded to his requests but did not react. If I were right, then, according to my theory, a consonant consequence should have been observable. When he came for the first appointment, which was shortly after the arrangements between us had been made, he was depressed, without female companionship, and degraded by his job. When he came the second time he looked cheerful, had a girlfriend and had a new and better job. In a later session he put these beneficial developments down to his improved emotional state. The latter he linked directly to his relationship with me. He said, "I trusted you and thought it was worth giving psychotherapy a try . . ."

"You trusted me, but when you said you thought it was worth 'giving psychotherapy a try' it indicates that you also trusted something in yourself."

"The most important thing was that although I did not know quite how I was going to manage the times you have given me for psychotherapy next year I just said to myself that I would manage

somehow. I had never trusted in my own resources like that before
..."

This act of trust in me and in his own resources was the creative act that transformed his emotional state, which in turn changed the fortunes of his love life and business career. However, there was subsequently a bad development. He still had to wait six months before starting psychotherapy. He was in a state of frustration and there was undeclared rage towards me for keeping him waiting. How was this manifest? The relationship with the girlfriend broke up. There was no creative inner act here, just undigested rage that blew into his girlfriend's face and she dropped him.

These are the components of what is a unified structure. In order to do clinical work that unity needs to be apprehended. I believe that a lot of intellectual work of an emotional nature needs to be done in order to grasp the unity in this diversity.

PART VI
THE INFLUENCE OF WILFRED BION

Introduction

> "It is as though the solid, respectable mediocrity is a standard jealously preserved, and that a member who soars to fame or drops to notoriety, is breaking the humble tradition . . ."
>
> (Church, 1953, p. 45)

While I was training to be a psychoanalyst and in my early years as a psychoanalyst, I read the writings of many of the well-known analysts. In particular, when I was asked in 1976 to lecture at the Tavistock Clinic to mental health professionals, I read widely the writings of both Freud and his early followers and also of the second and third generation analysts. Of the English school, I read all the works of Melanie Klein, Donald Winnicott, and Michael Balint, and then I alighted upon Wilfred Bion. As soon as I started to read him a musical thrill made my soul shimmer with delight. At last I had found the analyst who really spoke to me. What was it that he had that no other analyst I had come across possessed? I think it was that Wilfred Bion's enquiry was into existence itself, and that he was a contemplative and an utterly simple man.

I have already said in the chapter "The patient makes the analyst" that I went for supervision to Bion when he came to London from California in 1978. I had attended some seminars that he gave to the Kleinian group at the Institute of Psychoanalysis, and also some that he gave at the Tavistock. Then I went twice to him for supervision. I was quite sure, both at his seminars and in those two supervisions, that I was in the presence of greatness. What indicated this to me was his simplicity, which I think is nearly always the sign of genius. In those two supervisions he said very simple things to me, but they were profound and he had the courage to say them.

I was at the time attending a fortnightly group supervision with Herbert Rosenfeld, whose understanding of psychosis was legendary, but I plan here to compare the two men with the purpose of illuminating even more clearly Wilfred Bion's particular qualities. Both men had a profound knowledge of psychosis and it was a knowledge that was born of experience. Both men had been analysed by Melanie Klein. Both men charged very high fees. Psychoanalysis was at the centre of their lives, but I think here the difference stops. For Rosenfeld all truth was subservient to psychoanalysis, but for Bion psychoanalysis was the servant of truth. For Rosenfeld, psychoanalysis was the only way in which the mind could ever be investigated; for Bion it was defective, but the best way that he knew, but perhaps tomorrow a better method might be found. Rosenfeld had a smaller, even a meaner, mind, but Bion had a mind as expansive as the universe. When I encountered Bion I felt I had come home. Only once before on my emotional and intellectual journey had I had a similar experience. It was therefore a great pleasure when, many years later, I collaborated with my wife in the writing of a book on Bion's clinical thinking (Symington & Symington, 1996). As a result of this, I was asked to give lectures on Bion's work from time to time. What follows is first a lecture on the way in which Bion has influenced my clinical understanding. This is only a taste of Bion, but I became a different analyst after absorbing his work.

CHAPTER SEVENTEEN

The influence of Bion on my clinical work[1]

"There are many who set great store upon having seen one or another distinguished world-historical personality face to face. This impression they never forget, it has given to their souls an ideal picture which ennobles their nature; and yet such an instant, however significant, is nothing in comparison with the instant of choice. So when all has become still around one, as solemn as a starlit night, when the soul is alone in the whole world, then there appears before one, not a distinguished man, but the eternal Power itself. The heavens part, as it were, and the I chooses itself—or rather, receives itself. Then has the soul beheld the loftiest sight that mortal eye can see and which never can be forgotten, then the personality receives the accolade of knighthood which ennobles it for an eternity. He does not become another man than he was before, but he becomes himself, consciousness is unified, and he is himself. As an heir, even though he were heir to the treasure of all the world, nevertheless does not possess his property before he has come of age, so even the richest personality before he has come of age, so even the richest personality is nothing before he has chosen himself, and on the other hand even what one might call the poorest

> personality is everything when he has chosen himself; for
> the great thing is not to be this or that but to be oneself, and
> this everyone can be if he wills it.
>
> (Kierkegaard, 1972, p. 181)

B ion was sitting with a friend at a Leicester Conference. All around people were speaking about Bion, Bion this, Bion that. Bion turned to his friend and said, "This fellow Bion must be a very interesting fellow."

I think this remark reveals Bion's scepticism about the personality cult. I hope that this symposium will not be another monument to the cult of personality that imposes such an anti-scientific outlook upon psychoanalytic thinking. If I look at my clinical work and ask myself the question 'By whom have I been influenced?' I would find there a tapestry of interweaving threads that have come from numerous sources. What I am trying to do here is to unthread those strands that come more from Bion than from anywhere else. I do hope thereby to help to identify the particular beliefs and values that underpin Bion's clinical outlook. I have been influenced greatly by Bion but his strands of thought are interweaved with other values and ways of thinking.

In our book on the clinical thinking of Wilfred Bion we quote this sentence from the philosopher Whitehead: "It is a well-founded historical generalisation that the last thing to be discovered in any science is what the science is really about" (Whitehead, 1958, p. 167). We quote it because we believe that Bion discovered what psychoanalysis is as opposed to what it had been believed to be. When an analyst gives an interpretation it is an elucidation of what is—not what should be. Bion gave an interpretation of what psychoanalysis is. Psychoanalysis embodies the observation of surface events and reaches into the depths or heights in an attempt to understand them. So Bion's elucidation of psychoanalysis is both supremely practical and yet is embedded in a metaphysical presupposition that is different from that of Freud and all schools of analytic thinking since then. Initially, it surprised us that academics interested in psychoanalysis have entirely bypassed Bion, until we realized that they are engaged in a system of thought which bears no relation to the phenomenology of psychoanalysis.

A clinical case

A woman called Daphne said: "Johnny Wilson was killed yesterday while out hang gliding." Johnny was her sister's elder son. She said to me, "I think it's dreadful but I don't feel a thing. I know I should feel sad. I know it *is* sad; I know I ought to feel something about it but I don't. Why don't I feel it," she said accusingly. (Why wasn't I doing something about it?)

Why did she not feel sad? What is the difference between *knowing* that an event is sad and *feeling* sad? And why would I just know it but not feel it? Then one of Bion's formulations occurred to me. It is where he talks of the psyche being confronted with the need to decide between evasion of frustration or its modification. Now this led me to the answer, "What has evasion of frustration got to do with your woman friend who was unable to feel sadness?"

But how, I hear you say. Yet even as you speak I think I hear you being tied too closely to the words rather than going towards the experience that the words represent. The fundamental reality for Bion was the personal emotional experience. So the word "frustration" describes a particular type of experience. Frustration is the subset of a more general category, pain, just as an orange belongs to the category fruit. So my thought was: "Daphne cannot feel sadness because it is painful. At some early date there occurred a movement to evade pain rather than modify it."

That is a simple thought. It is what Bion called a definitory hypothesis. This is column one on the vertical axis of the grid. So my definitory hypothesis is that Daphne does not feel sadness because there has been a movement in her to evade pain. I have some evidence to support it. I had frequently noticed that ten minutes before the end of a session she would start to abuse me; I had also experienced considerable discomfort when she punished me with biting words after I had been away on holiday. It suggested that separating from me injected into her an unbearable pain. And here again I have stumbled on another understanding of Bion: "I have pain which I do not suffer; I have guilt which I do not know; I have sadness which I don't experience."

Pain can exist as an abusive outburst, pain can exist as a car accident, or pain can be dreamt, or pain can be felt. Pain can only be felt if, at some point, there has been a movement in my psychological being to modify pain rather than evade it. You might now ask me: "Well, what use is that definitory hypothesis? How is Daphne going to benefit from it?" Well, let us try to sum up what we have collected so far. My realization was that a feeling of sadness is painful whereas *knowledge* that something is sad is not. (Yet even that is not quite right. The knowledge of something sad as the registration of an event that reverberates through the senses is painful.) It was this realization that led me to Bion's formulation that there had been a decision to evade pain rather than modify it. The question is though: what do I now do? Do I tell her "The trouble with you is that you cannot bear pain and you have decided to evade pain rather than face it and modify it"?

You will laugh with sarcasm at the crassness and brutal moralism of such an intervention, but we need to sift out the reason why this would not be a sensible way in which to proceed. This gives me the chance to alight on a theme that is central to both Bion's character and his clinical work. I am talking of freedom.

It was Bion's presupposition that people we interact with exert emotional pressure upon us to follow the trajectory of their own desires. Only when we think and act from our own emotional centre are we free; when we act under the emotional pressure being put upon us we are slaves. Bion had, to a very rare degree, the capacity to be his own person in the face of even extreme pressure. Bob Gosling, one of his analysands, reports this incident:

> . . . a group relations conference in the United States at which he was a member of the staff, a conference in the tradition of the Leicester conferences here. At such events a good deal of confusion and stark experience inevitably emerge as the exploration of groups proceeds. One of the exercises at such a conference has the aim of studying relatedness between groups as it comes about and it usually involves the whole conference at some point falling into a good deal of disarray. On one such occasion the staff had just been evicted from their room, two members were having a fierce argument that looked as if it might escalate into violence at any moment, a whole group of people on the stairs were undecided about whether to go up further or come down again, and several bewildered individuals were drifting around the place as if they were sleep walking. The noise and the turmoil were considerable. In the midst of all this one distraught member came up to Bion in

some urgency and said, "Oh, for God's sake, Dr Bion, what do you think?" It is reported that Bion's reply was "I do not find the circumstances right for thought". [Gosling, 1980, pp. 22–23]

So the problem is this: I have a thought, the *definitory hypothesis*: that the reason Daphne cannot feel sadness at the death of her nephew is because, written deeply in her character, is the evasion of pain. So I say this to her:

"When you tell me about Johnny's death you think there is something odd about the fact that you do not feel sad. There is a sadness that you know about but you are distressed that you do not feel it. It makes me think of the times when you used to abuse me in the last ten minutes before the end of a session. There was anger in you that the session was coming to an end. There was not only anger but sadness also. Your abuse was the anger; your abuse was the sadness. The parting from me caused pain. The abuse was pain screaming. There seems to be a parallel here: the pain about Johnny's death is in the accusation to me. When you said to me 'Why don't I feel it?', it had an accusatory ring—a bit like when you abused me before the session ended. As the pain was in the abuse so also the pain, the sadness, is in the accusation. The accusation is sadness screaming."

I shall go through this interpretation in order to bring out certain points.

When someone is imprisoned within a narcissistic structure one of the key elements in that structure is a persecuting voice. That voice is already saying to Daphne, "You should be feeling." If I echo the inner voice then she will feel shattered and hopeless. I knew from the past that if I said to her, "You feel hurt that I did not remind you that the coming break begins next Thursday . . .", she would draw from it the implication that if she were a mature person she would not feel hurt. Later I would recast this thus: "There is an interaction between us that goes something like this: I forget to say the break starts next Thursday—you get angry—I forget—you get angry. We are on that sort of merry-go-round."

There is no comment here about how she feels; I have substituted the verb "say" for "remind" and brought out the interactive process. This recasting is not to conciliate her, but to reflect the truth more faithfully. I have myself changed radically in my analytic approach in this regard. I was fully in sympathy with those analysts of the English Independent Tradition who have seen the analytic process as one of empathic understanding that is expressed to the patient. In a well-conducted analysis the analyst will feel for the patient. However, I am today very distrustful of the "You feel", or "I think you feel . . ." kind of interpretations. Such interpretations are often incorrect and frequently patronizing, but more important is the question of whether they *do* anything. So, in this case when I forget to remind her, it is part of an interactive process in which she and I are partners. There is no hint of moralism or patronage in the second formulation, which there is in the first.

About twenty years ago my wife and I attended some seminars that Bion held for the Kleinian group at the Institute of Psychoanalysis in London. In one of them he said that the analyst and patient were like a married couple, and interpretations needed to reflect the sort of equal interplay that typified such a partnership. I remembered his words, which means that they must have had emotional signficance for me. Therefore the "merry-go-round" interpretation that I have just given is the fruit of Bion's outlook, digested and thought about over the years.

With a patient like Daphne, the slightest hint of "You should not be feeling . . ." has a persecuting effect, but another factor needs to be noted about this. The fact that it is so persecuting is because there is a harsh tyrant within admonishing her, but the fact that it is hated so much means that she is also in identification with this tyrant. What I refer to here as the "tyrant"—in other words, a crushing force, Bion referred to as the Establishment. Let us try to see what this means. It means she also becomes that Establishment and puts enormous pressure on me to act in a certain way. The fact that I "forget" to remind Daphne that my break starts next Thursday is evidence that I also am acting under the influence of this Establishment. It means that I am host to its influence. It is responsible for my unconscious negligence: I do not remind her that the break starts on Thursday. She has told me in bitterly abusive language that I do not prepare her for the breaks. The prime job that I have to do is well encapsulated in reverie, one of Bion's formulae.

Reverie

Bion gave this image: an infant pouring out anxiety and a mother/breast containing it through reverie. It is important to note that Bion here is not giving a developmental account, but rather an image for an emotional situation. Daphne suddenly says to me: "It's as I always thought. You don't care a bit about me. You're just interested in your holiday." My immediate reaction is to rush to my own defence. The task is to contain it, think about it. In the abuse there is a truth: I don't prepare her sufficiently for breaks in treatment. I *know* that a break is a trauma for her. So what she tells me is true: I need to prepare her better for breaks. However, before I can have access to my knowledge I have to contain her bitterness. She says,"You're *just* interested in your holiday. I believe that this is not correct. I am interested in my holiday. I am interested in the development of her analysis. The bitterness that lies behind the word *just* is to be contained. I need to act on my knowledge and contain her bitterness, which is the manifestation of pain. Emotional containment is the analyst's biggest task. It is symbolized in the image of the anxious baby being held firmly at the breast by its mother.

Bion's incorporation of models

Bion incorporated insights from Melanie Klein into his model of mental functioning. Projective identification was the most important of these. When Daphne said to me, "You're *just* interested in your holiday," I felt angry. The anger that is in her exists in a word spoken in a condemning tone and in me the anger is felt. The anger then undergoes a transformation in this exchange. It exists in one form in her and in another in me. I think it is incorrect to formulate this in a statement like: "Daphne gets rid of her angry feelings into the analyst."

It may seem a nice point to quarrel with this formulation, but I do not believe it is. The anger exists in the form of a word and tone in her. It exists as a feeling in me, the analyst. There is then the possibility of a reaction on my part when there is no further transformation. For instance, I might bite back and say, "I am *not* just interested in my holidays", or "You feel angry because you don't want to let me go." In this case mummy has not contained the poison. The baby has spat out some venom and it has been spat straight back. It has changed from a word-and-tone anger to a feeling of anger, but the transformation has gone no further. The other possibility for action is a transformation where the analyst creates the raw feeling within him into a thought: "A parting like this is always painful, but when I don't prepare you it is worse and gives you a jab of pain." Here the analyst has thought about this feeling of anger welling up inside him and transformed the pain into a different medium.

Bion's theory of transformations is therefore central to his conceptualization of the psychoanalytic process. What I want to show here is how relevant it is to clinical practice. In fact, I now think that we often miss the bulls-eye altogether without a theory of transformations. The little sequence above is a transformation of word-tone to feeling and from feeling to thought. The transformation occurs through containment linked to a desire for emotional development and pursuit of truth. You may think that my statement that without a theory of transformations clinical work is defective is a bit extreme, yet I will try to illustrate it. Let us say that instead of seeing Daphne's statement as a word-tone representation of pain, I believe that it is a feeling that she is repressing I might say to her: "When you hear that I am going away on holiday you feel a pain which you push away." She would rightly reply: "But I don't feel pain at all." The truth of the matter is that there is pain, but it has not reached the level of feeling. Therefore when the therapist says: "You push the feeling away . . ." it is incorrect, because there is no feeling to be pushed away. The necessary transformation has not occurred. An egg is not a chicken. It is not just a matter of language. We are talking here of a misreading of the process. Then again, does it matter? This very question has within it an inherent cynicism. Does the truth matter? If you believe, as Bion did, that the mind is healed by truth, then if we give way to that kind of cynicism we may as well abandon the whole endeavour. So we know that to make statements that are false is to betray our profession and ourselves.

I want to examine what the bad effect is if we misconstrue the process. If the therapist says, "You push the feeling away", there is a hint here that the patient has done something that he should not have done. This installs the therapist as a god who admonishes the patient. This god then has to be placated. The god has pronounced that the patient has "pushed away a feeling" and the patient believes it. Why does the patient believe it? The therapist has tapped into guilt in the patient, but instead of interpreting it and looking for the reason for the presence of guilt it is instead employed so that guilt and badness remain. The patient then relieves herself from this bad inner situation by making herself pleasing to god. So, then, what looks like a transformation is a situation that is unchanged. In another of his seminars at the Institute of Psychoanalysis in London, Bion said that most analysts did not believe that this strange conversation that occurs between analyst and patient was effective. I was very struck by this and in a supervision session I said that I had been very surprised by it, and he reiterated that he thought nevertheless that it was so. I have come to think that he was right, both through speaking intimately to some analysts about their analyses and also through having had patients, who were analysts, coming to see me who have not really believed that this process can work.

What is actually occurring in a scenario like this is that a god in the patient—which is hated—is relocated in the analyst. The problem then is that the patient believes that he is transformed but is not so. It is a problem commonly found in religious people: I am commanded by god to be caring and loving so through a gesture of omnipotence I believe I *am* caring and loving. The analyst has said I should not be pushing feelings away, so through this gestural magic I no longer push feelings away: that is what I believe. My god often gets located in psychoanalysis with a big P or with my position as a doctor, professor, or lawyer. An unchanged paranoid state remains within. Bion was very preoccupied with this state of affairs in his latter years, and he spoke about it almost despairingly in some of the talks he gave in the few years before his death. It is the problem of the patient sniffing out the analyst's attitudes and ways of thinking and injecting himself into that imago through the omnipotent gesture. The patient has then ingested the thoughts without having generated them. This is done through the power of the god in the structure of the personality. I did not learn this directly from Bion, but I was influenced by him to recognize the presence of this god in the personality and its link to paranoia, envy, and inferiority.

Bion had the capacity to avoid standing in the shoes of a god. At the end of one of his Brazilian lectures he said that the analyst's task was to introduce the patient to himself. I want to introduce another clinical vignette to illustrate the way I have been influenced by Bion's thinking. The patient, a librarian, understood that the reason why she always came punctually to sessions—to the second—was that she was thereby magically trying to control a greedy intrusive part. This was conceptualized as a greedy figure within. The patient then went into a constipated silence for two sessions. I made this interpretation:

"When I spoke of that greedy figure within it brought an emotional focus upon it. Then it brought up a great surge within you and you said, 'I loathe that greedy figure'. You located then this demanding greedy figure in me and you felt depleted. This is why you're stuck into a strangled silence."

You may ask where the influence of Bion is in that statement. It is in asking myself the question: "Why is the greedy figure hated?" It is asking myself that question that shows some influence from Bion and not taking it for granted. There is, then, the formulation of Bion's that it is expelled rather than contained.

My experience is that when a part of the self like this is violently disowned, then the personality is impoverished. That greedy part is part of the personality. The personality needs it. When it is disowned and hated the individual lacks a part of the personality that he needs. A greedy part contained is a transformed personality. When the greedy part is contained the individual has within him the wherewithal to stand up to greedy, ambitious and exploitative people in his or her environment.

There remains this question: why is it that if a greedy part or an envious part of the personality is elucidated and pointed out to the patient that a violent hatred is frequently generated? It seems to be an inner philosophy that dictates that the way to deal with something distasteful is to get rid of it. There also seems to be a primordial judgement that a greedy personality within is bad, is evil. The paradox is that if the greedy personality, the envious personality, is contained, it ceases to be damaging to the personality, but if it is expelled it is injurious both to the person and also to others in his or her intimate environment.

I want to say two things about the grid that I have found most useful clinically. The first is by making use of Column Two. Column Two refers to the way in which an insight can be used to block emotional development and the emergence of truth. A patient realizes that she has seen her father through a paranoid lens and this is associated with a development in love towards her husband and a development in trust towards her analyst. Then, in the next session, she is talking about her paranoid attitude towards her father in such a vein as to suggest that this is now a past matter, but in fact it is today being used to hide from herself the fact that she has retreated into the same paranoid state. Whereas on the first day it is the expression of new insight and a changed inner state, on the second it is being used to deceive herself and the analyst into believing that this inner paranoid state is gone forever. I know for certain that, without having come to grasp Bion's concept of Column Two, I should not have realized this with such clarity. It is one of the most valuable things I have learned from him, and I am aware of Column Two not only in the clinical situation but also in situations where group or individual development is being attempted.

The other thing which is equally useful is the use of the grid in the process of evolving an interpretation. The interpretation that makes an impact that leads to emotional change is arrived at in Column Six (Action), but it may take some time before that is arrived at. Let us say that what is noted in one session is that a woman hates being patronized. No judgement is made upon it. It is just noted. The analyst points it out and the patient agrees that this is so. (This is Column Three.) The analyst says that this matter is of emotional significance. (This is Column Four.) There follows an enquiry into why being patronized is so hated and an understanding that it stimulates the hatred of an omnipotent part of the self. (This is Column Five.) At the end of this conversation the analyst notices that there is a withdrawn silence and he says:

"In this conversation I was lecturing you in a patronizing way and this very important person inside you has now said, 'I am not going to tolerate this—I won't speak to him any more.' "

(That is Column Six.) There are several important aspects to this procedure. The first is to recognize that it is the final one that has emotional impact. The other is to realize that we need a lot of build-up before the final interpretation is possible. We need to lay a lot of bricks out before we can build the house and put on the roof. So, often a Column Three Statement is not made because it is felt to lack interpretive judgement. This is correct, but Bion stressed the value of observation. In this instance the Column Three statement is an observation. The "why" of it may be quite unclear. It may take some months or years to clarify, but there is nothing to clarify if the initial observation is not made. This whole procedure is so germane to Bion's insistence on observation rather than omnipotent guess-work. In a supervision I have frequently heard, for instance, a therapist say, "You dare not speak your thought because you fear that I will be condemning of it." I have said to the therapist, "You have evidence that there is a thought which the patient is reluctant to voice", and the therapist agrees. Then I have gone on to ask whether he has evidence that the reluctance is due to the patient's fear of his condemnation and he has agreed that it is just a guess, but often made because he feels that he must deliver what looks like an interpretation. It is not an inspired guess but a ritualized format. But this whole way of proceeding robs the therapist of a voyage of discovery. Why does this patient not want to voice this thought? There is a rich panoply of possibilities and here the therapist has foreclosed on it.

For Bion, psychoanalysis was an investigation into the mind, into mental processes. He wanted to understand how we come to know each other; how we come to know the world we live in; why people fall in love with each other; why we fight wars. He did not think that psychoanalysis was the supreme instrument through which we can investigate these questions about the mind and mankind, but he thought it was the best we had available at the moment.

O

Many clinicians think that Bion had departed this earth and joined the company of romantic mystics when he proposed *O*; yet *O* is an inherent part of his thinking and practical in the extreme. It is the logical outcome of his conceptualization of freedom. *O* is the metaphysical presupposition that makes sense of the rest of what I have said in this talk. When surface observations are abstracted, Bion finds himself with O. What is most abstract is what is most practical because it fits the clinical observations.

Note

1. This paper was given in Melbourne on 30 November 1996. There were two presentations by Joan, my wife, and myself on the work of Bion. This was a half-day symposium organized by the Melbourne Institute of Psychoanalysis.

CHAPTER EIGHTEEN

Bion and trauma transformed[1]

"Chronic mental stress, a state related to processing in numerous brain systems at the level of neocortex, limbic system and hypothalamus, seems to lead to over production of a chemical, calcitonin gene-related peptide, of CGRP, in nerve terminals within the skin. As a result, CGRP excessively coats the surface of Langerhans cells, an immune-related cell whose job it is to capture infectious agents and deliver them to lymphocytes so that the immune system can counteract their presence. If completely coated by CGRP, the Langerhans cells are disabled and can no longer perform their guardian function. The end result is that the body is more vulnerable to infection, now that a major entryway is less well defended. And there are other examples of mind–body interaction: sadness and anxiety can notably alter the regulation of sexual hormones, causing not only changes in sexual drive but also variations in menstrual cycle. Bereavement, again a state dependent on brainwide processing, leads to a depression of the immune system such that individuals are more prone to infection and, whether as a direct result or not, more likely to develop certain types of cancer. One *can* die of a broken heart"

(Damásio, 1994, 119–120)

B ion recommended that an analyst interact with another analyst's paper as he does with a patient. In *Second Thoughts* he says:

> What I have said about the psychoanalytical sessions I consider applies to the *experience* of reading psychoanalytic work. Freud's paper should be read—and "forgotten". Only in this way is it possible to produce the conditions in which, when it is next read, it can stimulate the evolution of further development . . . the best papers have the power to stimulate a *defensive* reading (of what the paper is about) as a substitute for the experiencing the paper itself . . . [1993, p. 156]

So what I am going to say here is a development from Bion's thinking. Those of you who know the works of Bion well may wonder where he makes any reference to trauma. I shall give you one passage to start us off:

> In this paper I propose to deal with the appearance, in the material of a certain class of patient, of references to curiosity, arrogance and stupidity which so dispersed and separated from each other that their relatedness may escape detection. I shall suggest that their appearance should be taken as evidence that he is dealing with a psychological disaster. ['On arrogance', *ibid.*, p. 86]

When we meet an arrogant person strutting around, exploiting others, putting people down, singing his own praises, and controlling others we do not immediately say to ourselves, "He has suffered a trauma." We are more likely to become moralists and say, "He is deliberately putting others down . . ." and "He can only think of himself . . .", or "He spends his life controlling others . . .". But Bion says that here we have signs that there has been a psychological disaster. He does not go into what that disaster may have been. He did not write a paper on trauma, yet he made innuendoes that give us a clue to his thinking. He spoke of the importance of the mother's *reverie* for the mental health of the developing infant. One can suppose therefore that the failure of *reverie* is a trauma for the infant. Once one starts to think in this line it is not difficult to think of other primitive traumata that have been conjectured by analysts such as Esther Bick and Frances Tustin. The former believed that mothers became depressed after birth and therefore were unable to give to their babies in the way that it is necessary for the infant to feel and be held. The latter believed that a primordial trauma occurs when the infant undergoes a premature rupture from its merged tie with the mother. These are "hidden traumata" that affect the baby, but particularly the mother's capacity to give to her baby and to be emotionally receptive. The capacity of *reverie* requires that the mother has some space and be reasonably free from anxiety.

Trauma is more often an absence than a presence. The idea here is that the absence of an emotionally receptive mother is a trauma for the infant and that this is the sort of disaster that may be passed from generation to generation. These traumas follow an individual line but then there are the massive social traumas like wars, epidemics, massacres, and economic collapses that have devastating effects on the human spirit. Mothers caught in these social disasters are focused a hundred per cent for themselves and their babies. When survival is achieved it is often at the cost of the infant's emotional wellbeing. There are also traumas that affect adults, and then these get passed on to their children. A man was tortured in the Sino-Japanese War in the late 1930s, and when he later married he ruled his household with a cruel tyranny that affected his wife and three children very badly. The elder son became schizophrenic, the younger one a severe depressive, and the daughter's love relations were always disastrous. But I do not want to go into an investigation of the nature of the traumata to which all human beings are susceptible, but rather to note that they exist and that Bion saw objectionable human qualities as signs that these had happened.

My own clinical experience accords entirely with Bion's observation and construction. I have found that it is precisely those people who have been through the worst disasters that are ridden with greed, envy, and jealousy. The conclusion I have therefore come to is that envy, greed, and jealousy are the living forms in which the trauma now exists. In order to underline this point I shall try to give a brief sketch of Bion's theory of transformations.

Those of you who have read his book *Transformations* (1991) will remember that he starts off by speaking of a landscape in which there is a lake surrounded by green meadows. An artist with paints of various colours on his palette creates a picture on a square foot of canvas and you look and can see that it represents the lakeland scene. Yet the difference between the two pieces of reality is enormous. In the one case there is six acres of water surrounded by grass and trees and in the other is a small piece of canvas with some coloured paint distributed over it. Yet, says Bion, there is an invariant, or what psychologists usually call *a constant*. I suspect that the invariant lies in the proportions existing between the different elements plus colour. The painting is a transformation of the lakeland scene but we need to go a bit further than that to capture Bion's meaning. The way I have just been speaking suggests that the invariant is the lakeland scene and that the painting is its transformation, but that is not right. The invariant lies in the geometric relations that are manifest in the lakeland scene and in the painting. So there is an invariant and then the differing manifestations of it. The invariant exists in one form—the lakeland scene—and can be transformed into another—the painting on the canvas. So we have the trauma—the baby's agony in the face of an absence of maternal *reverie*, and this absence becomes transformed into greed, envy, and jealousy.

Bion said that the infant, if unable to modify the painful absence, fills the space with bad internal objects. My extension of this is to say that these objects are greed, envy, and jealousy. I need to draw your attention to the fact that this is a little different from what Bion proposed. He suggested, following Melanie Klein, that the envy arose out of the presence of the death instinct. What I am proffering is the idea that envy, together with greed and jealousy, are the trauma in a different form: that they are the absence in a different form. When all the greed, envy, and jealousy are laid bare, there remains nothing but a terrible emptiness.[2] This emptiness is the invariant. The suggestion here that is an amplification of Bion is that unassimilated *beta elements* are patterned in the form of greed, envy and jealousy and are the trauma in a different form—the painting rather than the lakeland scene. The point about these being *beta elements* in patterned form is that they are sitting in the personality like an undigested lump and are propelled out of the personality into the figures or institutions of the surrounding environment.

A woman came to see me. Her mother had died when she was aged eight. She had heard her mother wheezing and coughing with severe asthma prior to dying. An aunt had told her that her mother was going to die. My conjecture was that mother had been so preoccupied with her own condition that she had been unable to give emotionally to her baby. My overwhelming sense was my patient's own distance from these events. Mother's death was an event that had happened to someone else. When an interpretation helped her understand something that had been obscure before she did not attribute this to me but to someone else. I called this envy. However, one could think of it in a different way. It was the trauma transformed. What was expelled was mother's ungivingness. Envy was one part of the form in which her childhood trauma existed. The ungivingness was the invariant. The trauma of an ungiving mother I called envy, but this was my particular transformation of it. It is a transformation based upon my own self-obsessed perspective. As I look at the lakeland scene my vision is distorted because of colour-blindness and my painting is skewed thereby. It is a transformation of trauma through my own traumatized perspective. When I speak of envy it is a me-focused transformation. It arises out of a personal hurt that has been evaded rather than modified. A transformation based upon a modification of the hurt changes envy into respect and reverence.

We all have patients who have been severely traumatized either directly as adults or "indirectly" as children through their parents. The question is, how are these traumata to be transformed? The realization that envy, greed, jealousy, and cruelty are the trauma in transformed mode is the best start, because seeing it in this way will alter the interpretations; and let me say here something extremely obvious. It is my state of mind that is either containing or uncontaining for the patient. A containing state of mind will generate a particular series of interpretations; an uncontaining state of mind will generate another. The words that are spoken are carriers of a state of mind. Whether these words are effective depends upon the state of mind that generates them.

The starting point for the clinician is to be in touch with his own hatred. When the patient does not acknowledge that she has been helped by my interpretation I hate her rejection of me. The realization of this hatred and the containing of it in myself ensures that the hatred exists in this form rather than in the form of expulsion. It is then an *alpha element* rather than a *beta element*. What I am proposing here is problematic because when I expel *beta elements* in a form of hatred (or greed, or envy, or jealousy, or cruelty) I do not know it. That is why Bion said that the only remedy for the analyst's countertransference is to have it analysed. I think this is so important a point that I shall emphasize it by quoting Bion:

> One cannot make use of one's counter-transference in the consulting room; it is a contradiction in terms. To use the term in that way means that one would have to invent a new term to do the work which used to be done by the word "counter-transference", it is one's *unconscious* feelings about the patient, and since it is unconscious there is nothing we can do about it. If the counter-transference *is* operating in the analytic session the analysand is unlucky—and so is the analyst. [1975, p. 88]

So I am not giving here a recommendation, but a description of how it needs to be. If the clinician is expelling *beta elements*, then his communications will be damaging to the patient and it is a situation for which there is no remedy. If the analyst has an enlightenment about what he is doing, then something can be done, but there is no recipe for bringing this about. If the psychoanalyst believes that he has some special endowment in virtue of the fact that an institution has declared him an analyst, then the hope of change is slim.

If the clinician's own hurt, own hatred, is contained, then he will be in a position to deal with the patient's hatred of his own inner contents. The fundamental problem is not the patient's greed, the patient's envy, the patient's jealousy, the patient's cruelty, the patient's childishness, but his or her hatred of it. This violent act of expulsion rids the personality of part of himself. If I cut off my right hand then I shall be ill equipped to write. What is more, if I damage myself in this way I reap a bitter fruit: guilt. The guilt then induces me to do further damage to myself and so my emotional state becomes that of a cripple.

It is very common for the clinician to install himself as a judging god without realizing it. He points out envy and his patient immediately believes that a god is condemning him. So, together with god, he expels the filth from his system . . . or so he believes. This is one scenario, but there is another. This is the clinician who reassures the patient that this envy is all too understandable; the clinician who takes up the position of a benign god. In the first case the clinician installs himself as the external embodiment of a savage god within. In the second case he attempts to override the injunctions of the harsh inner judge by superimposing upon it a benign smiling divinity, but in both cases the savage god that expels all filth from the personality remains actively present. It is this savage, hating god that needs to be analysed. Wilfred Bion said again and again that the analyst's job is to analyse. Only when the presence of this in the personality is recognized is there a possibility of it being analysed. Why has the patient fashioned this harsh god within? What purpose does it serve? What advantages does the patient derive from its presence?

I can tell you the purpose it served in the lady whose mother died of an asthma attack when she was aged eight. This severe god rid her of her sadness. Then why did she come for psychoanalysis? She had to keep at a distance from sadness. If she ever came close to sadness it stoked a furnace within her. So she always had to avoid sadness. But there was sadness all around her, on every side, so she had to keep at a distance from life. Not only did she have to keep at a distance from sadness but from joy also. If she allowed herself to come into contact with joy she had to allow sadness to enter in also. What happens when the joy is over? So she kept isolated from life. She passed through life in a sealed container. She envied all those who participated in life and lived it to the full. The death of the god got rid of the envy, too. To compensate for such desolation she lived a life of sexual rampage accompanied with drugs.

It was important in this analysis that the god was understood also. A god had enabled her to survive, but she came for analysis because she wanted something more than survival.[3] In this lady's case it would be more accurate to call it a goddess. It had enabled her to survive for twenty-two years. Her understanding melted the harshness of god but her sadness kept coming in like an unstoppable wave. When this happened she hated analysis, thought that some other kind of therapy would be preferable. It was a slow transition from a god who banished dark hell to firm arms that took possession of the sadness within her. I have a serious question though—are some tragedies too great for the human spirit to bear? I suspect there are.

You will notice that the envy in this lady was not primary but, rather, consequent upon the expulsion of the sadness. If I lack something then I envy the person whom I believe has it. The envy will not be understood until what I lack has been grasped.[4] It is here where I believe there is either a dichotomy or a development in Bion's thinking. It is here that I require the assistance of the scholar, because only through a close examination of the time schedule of his thinking can this be decided. My rough unacademic surmise is that Bion started with Klein's theory that envy is a manifestation of the death instinct in the personality, then that there is a transition stage in which he sees it both as this and the consequence of a trauma, then moving to a later stage where he saw it entirely as the latter.[5]

Let me try to make a resumé of what has been stated so far: a trauma envelops the personality. Its presence continues to exist in the form of envy, greed, jealousy, a glue-like attachment and a harsh castigating god. The transformation of this debilitating trauma is through analysis of these different elements in the personality, their interrelation and their function. This is the whole story. I could perhaps stop here and say no more. All I shall do is to emphasize certain points that are important for the practising clinician.

The realization that these elements in the personality are not just a consequence of a trauma but *are* the trauma: that it has a traumatizing effect on the personality. Why it has a traumatizing effect on the personality is something that can be revealed through analytic investigation. Curiosity is an essential ingredient for an inquiry of this kind. If you do not want to know why these elements in the personality are traumatizing, then psychoanalysis is not for you. This could be an important diagnosis to make of your own character. It could prevent you from barking up the wrong tree for a whole lifetime. An analyst told me that he had analysed three analysts who came to the conclusion that this was not the right profession for them and they all gave up being analysts with three big sighs of relief. There is no special virtue in being an analyst. It is far better to be a good plumber or accountant than a handicapped analyst.

To know that these elements *are* the trauma leads one to investigate their function. It is to realize that they have a function and then to see how that function is carried out. I stressed their interrelation because one element does not function independently of the others. It is, therefore, necessary for the clinician to have in mind both the whole and the parts. In one session one part is to the fore, in another session it is another. (Bion said that there is a key theme to each session.) The clinician whose focused attention is exclusively upon one element may be demonstrating his own hatred of it and expelling it into the patient.

Hatred is the expulsion by god of these elements in the personality. Their containment transforms them. A supposition would be that envy becomes respect, greed—confidence, jealousy—self-definition, and god becomes personal freedom. These, then, are a pattern of sanity in the personality.

One reason why Bion is a breath of fresh air is that he grasped what is meant by perversion; that this configuration of elements that I have been describing is an attempt on the part of the personality at managing disaster. It is, Bion believes, a solution that does not work, but he notes that the personality is trying to solve the problem. Because he has gone down the wrong path, Bion does not forget that it is a failed attempt. This is why I stress the need to see the function of these elements: what they are trying to solve, and to understand why they fail to do so.

A woman erected me into god. Why did she do this? I did not know, but I was certain that it was damaging her. How did I know this? Because I was always looking down and sneering at her thoughts and imaginings. Her immediate thought was that when I asked her why she wondered whether there was a connection between myself and a man she had recently met, her first thought was that I had asked her this to test her, to see if she got it right. That was her *immediate* thought; a second thought was that I might want to know and understand. She said, though, that the first thought was more attractive because I knew the answer and could deliver it. The second thought required time, struggle, frustration. In both cases there was a problem she was trying to solve, but in the former frustration and pain could be bypassed. God can always perform a miracle. In the second it required her own creative processes or, in Bion's language, *alpha function*. The point I want to stress here, though, is that in the former she was attempting to solve the problem. It is very unfortunate that miracles do occasionally happen, because they reinforce the belief in the pseudo-solution.

I would not want you to believe that I think the analysis of the trauma and its transformation is easy. In the untransformed state, when the elements are being expelled violently the analyst may be the receptacle for this expulsion. I heard of a case where a schizophrenic woman smeared her face with her own faeces and then ran to kiss her therapist. I know that I would not remain calm in that situation. In fact, I know I would become extremely agitated. My reaction would, I believe, have been panic-ridden. This incident did not happen to me but emotional faeces have been thrown violently at me and I have panicked, I have become punitive, I have become frightened. The analysis of trauma requires a great deal of emotional work on the clinician's own self. When the clinician's own projective reactions have been understood it is necessary to interpret his own reactions so that what belongs to the patient and what belongs to the analyst can be separated.

As Bion stressed, no one is ever an analyst. It is not the last station on the railway line. We are forever becoming analysts. In an analysis the process is one of *becoming*. It takes a long time to realize what an analysis is. Yet it is only when we *realize* it—make it real—that the patient's trauma, and our own, becomes transformed.

Notes

1. This paper was given at the Bar-Ilan University in Israel on 8 April 1999.
2. This is best expressed in Emily Brontë's description of Heathcliff's last days in *Wuthering Heights*. See Chapter Six, "The response aroused by the psychopath".
3. This is why the reduction of all human motivation to survival so limits the understanding of social scientists. Civilizations have arisen because human beings wanted something more than survival. When survival is under threat higher aspirations are sacrificed. However, once survival has been established, the desire for what has been sacrificed begins to surface in the personality and in the community.
4. I have just instanced envy here for the sake of simplicity. In another lecture I posit that envy is not a unitary concept. It is rather part of a composite of which the other components are greed and jealousy.
5. I say this because "Notes on a theory of schizophrenia", "Development of schizophrenic thought", and "Differentiation of the psychotic

from the non-psychotic personalities" enshrine the Klein theory but "On arrogance" embodies the other, but they all date from the years 1953–1957, though "On arrogance" and "Differentiation of the psychotic from the non-psychotic personalities" are from 1957.

PART VII

PSYCHOLOGICAL UNDERSTANDING OF PSYCHOANALYTIC CONCEPTS

Introduction

"There is perhaps no great social question so imperfectly understood among us at the present day as that which refers to the line which divides sanity from insanity"

(Trollope, 1869, p. 324)

Two matters came to pre-occupy me more and more. One was the desire to achieve a psychological understanding of some of the most commonly used terms in psychoanalysis, like envy and paranoia. The other was the realization that it was the emotional activity within the personality that governs perception and therefore what we need to focus upon is this activity and not on the perception. The latter is dependent upon the former. Therefore, interpretations that pointed to the patient's idealization of the analyst, for instance, were useless—what needed tracking was the emotional activities that fashioned the idealization. This is just one example. Two papers that illustrate these preoccupations are "Envy: a psychological analysis" which I gave at the British Psychoanalytical Society in London in June 2001 and another called "The structure of paranoia", which I gave there a year later. The two papers are interconnected. I realized after giving the paper on envy that to be fully understandable I needed to complement it with a paper on paranoia.

A third paper is on communication as the organizing concept for psychoanalysis.

CHAPTER NINETEEN

Envy: a psychological analysis

"It is not likely that anybody can truly appreciate the wheat, who cannot also reject the chaff"

(Muller, 1904)

Since the advent of *Envy and Gratitude* in 1957 the word "envy" has flooded the clinical literature within psychoanalysis. It has been particularly profuse within the Kleinian School but this has overflowed into the clinical descriptions both of the Independent Group and that of the Freudians. What I attempt here is a *psychological* analysis of envy because we assume that we all know what we mean by it. I think the meaning that we attribute to it is something like the following: envy is hatred of another for having a treasure I do not possess.[1]

The focus of this definition is upon the other. This, I believe, derives from folk religion and throws no light upon why this entity is damaging to the author of the envy. Is the psychoanalyst's concern the emotional health of the patient or the comfort-zone of those with whom the patient lives out his life? If a psychoanalyst is asked "Why should I not envy another?", I believe the questioner will be given a moralistic answer: "It is harmful to another person to hate him for a treasure that he possesses. Therefore it is bad."

Someone who is satisfied with contract theory might elaborate this further and point out that something that is bad for another is harmful for society and, therefore, ultimately to the person himself and so should be shunned. However, this is dubious and very far from psychoanalysis, which is concerned with the immediate effects of an individual's emotional activities. Let us therefore try to build up a picture of envy as revealed by psychoanalytical investigation.

Idealization: the first stage of envy

Envy is inseparable from idealization. The treasure in the envied one exists in the bosom of someone who is idealized. (The fact that this person is also denigrated we shall come to later.) I believe that this is a clinical fact: that envy and idealization always co-exist. This leads me to my first supposition: idealization is part of the structure of envy. Working on the assumption that this is so, it becomes necessary to look at how idealization occurs. What are the psychological activities that account for it? Let us try first to edge towards a definition of "idealization": it is a perception of the other in which the goodness is exaggerated and the badness minimized. It might be more accurate to define it slightly differently: it is a perception of the other in which the virtues are exaggerated and the vices minimized.

In both of these definitions the focus is upon the moral qualities of the individual or group. But idealization is also used of those who have excelled in scientific endeavour or in the arts. The definition here then would be: it is perception of the other in which excellence is exaggerated and deficits are minimized. This last definition is probably more satisfactory as it can be applied to the field of ethics, aesthetics, or science.

The point to note is that this defines idealization as a deformation of perception. It would be possible to substitute "judgement" for "perception". I have chosen "perception", however, as it conveys immediacy, whereas judgement suggests a time-delay. However, there is always judgement present in perception. One of the faults of faculty psychology is that it creates the false belief that perception, cognition, and motivation are discrete entities. In judgement there is always perception and vice versa. Another way of defining this defective perception is to call it an illusion. From this angle we could define "idealization" thus: an illusion in which excellence is exaggerated and deficits minimized. This has the advantage that it can refer to subject or object.

What I want to address myself to now is not *why* an idealization occurs but *how* it is accomplished.[2] What is the emotional process that fashions this particular illusion? The excellence in the self is projected into the object and the deficits in the object are ingested into the self. The illusory perception is the result. To speak with psychological accuracy, we need to say that the perception records correctly what has emotionally occurred.

It is clear now why envy is damaging to the personality. The envious person has rid himself of what is of worth in him and ingested what is valueless. This way of acting is according to an acquired pattern, but is also maintained through an assembly of minute actions that accumulate and structure the long-term character structure. The analyst's job is to interpret these evacuations of excellence and ingestions of deficit as they occur in the session. The slow erosion of these activities leads to a destablization of the long-term character structure. As these interpretations are made, the patient comes into possession of those elements of worth within him and ceases to ingest the deficits of others. If this is done with constancy, the patient's perception changes. This, I believe, is evidence in favour of my view that perception is the accurate recording of what has emotionally occurred. It is emotional activity that is the governing hand of perception. Therefore, the focus of interpretation needs to be upon the emotional activity and not the resulting perception.[3]

Idealization is the first stage of envy, but also its foundation. I believe I have clinical evidence that if a patient *realizes* this then the rest of the structure of envy crumbles. I now want to consider the remaining structure, which I call the second stage of envy.

Damage to the object: second stage of envy

When the individual has accomplished the first stage of envy he is deprived of self-worth and is full of self-devaluation and self-castigation. He resents this state of affairs. He is not aware of these "invisible" emotional activities that have brought it about, and so blames outer figures for his plight. The subject is now impoverished and the object is enriched. The object comes to be hated. The principles of the process whereby the idealization has come about also apply here. The subject's own activities are obliterated in his mind and those of the object become magnified. The magnification results from the projection and ingestion. So, for instance, a man was aware of his father's authoritarian attitude but not of his own emotional indecision that assisted in its provocation. It is not that the authoritarian attitude was not there, but that it becomes hated through the magnification due to his own emotional activities, which we summarize as "indecision". This attribution of an activity in the subject to a static quality in the object I have called *hypostasization* (see Symington, 2002). The more common way of naming such a procedure in psychoanalytic discourse is to say that the son projects his own authoritarian attitudes into the father. This does not, however, explain how the psychological process works. For instance, the son's emotional indecision is left out of the account; the actual way in which this authoritarianism in the father is generated is not analysed. An account that says the son's authoritarian attitudes are projected into the father is a crude account that bypasses the "how" of the process. It also misses the subtle individual differences in the manner of this generation. Also, if it is interpreted in this way by the analyst it frequently becomes an accusation. This accusation has replaced an interpretation. The heart of psychosis lies in a negative mentation combined with omnipotence. I believe great care is needed by the analyst to avoid slipping into one of the designated roles of this psychotic structure.

So, *hypostasization* may be defined thus: a process whereby emotional activities of the subject become perceived as static qualities in the object. *Hypostasization*, then, is the underlying principle of which idealization is a particular exemplar. It is not only that the projection and ingestion occur but, because these activities are unconscious, only their consequence is perceived. Again, all this needs to be interpreted so that the patient is able to take possession of his own emotional activities and thereby alter them if the desire is there to do so. My experience is that patients often do desire to alter the nature of their emotional activities because they have brought them suffering. Also, if they have been analysed according to "damage to the object" mentality, they frequently have a dim knowledge that their apparent integration is based upon an illusory solution. We shall come to a clinical example of this shortly.

Once this *hypostasization* has occurred then the subject, out of resentment, stirs up the object, controls the object, attacks the object, and so on. It is this stage of the envy that Melanie Klein describes when she talks of expelling faeces into the breast, attacking mother's body, her babies, and so on. This is the reason why paranoia is always part of the picture in any accurate phenomenological description of envy. The projection of faeces and urine, to use Melanie Klein's language, occurs because the inner worthlessness is loathed and is projected by an omnipotent figure in the personality, *not* because of an "envy" whose origin is in "*a constitutional element*" (Klein, 1957, p. 176). The inner worthlessness arises from the presence within of envy, greed, jealousy, and omnipotence, *which is hated*. "I must be utterly contemptible to have all this envy, jealousy, and greed inside me", the person says to himself. Paranoia is the hatred for the inner entity that crushes inner personal creative growth. Expulsion is primitive hatred in action. It also explains why the paranoid person is tied to his object: he cannot be separated from part of himself. The key to understanding the hatred lies in the fact that these inner activities prevent freedom in the subject. This gives meaning to the expulsion into the object. The meaning here is in terms of the subject's need to do it for his own sake and not in order to injure the object. The latter way of seeing things has its origin in a paranoid perception on the part of the analyst.

Focus on the subject rather than object

Melanie Klein does speak very clearly about the way envy strangles the creative and generous impulses in the subject. She also gives considerable emphasis to what is done to the object; how mother's body, babies, and breast are attacked. I believe that this latter focus steals the light away from the activities of the subject and the way in which these are damaging to the subject. It is not that she does not speak about the way the subject's generous impulses are strangled, but that this is frequently overshadowed by her focus on the object's travails.

There is also a philosophical assumption here, which I believe is incorrect and leads to moralism rather than healing. Its origins in nominalism is that subject and object are separate entities, or only can be unified through some social contract theory. I take the view that subject and object share in Being. Therefore, emotional activity that damages Being has consequences for subject and object. Psychoanalysts are familiar with this concept, as it was introduced by Bion under the nomenclature of "O".

There is no doubt that to be the object of sustained resentment for months and years tests emotional endurance to the limit. Being the target of such hostility makes it extremely difficult to analyse the psychological processes that generate it. Yet it may be that the fact that they are not analysed and psychologically understood is the reason why it endures so relentlessly. Bion said that the psychotic patient stirs up the resistance in the analyst. A rephrasing of this would be to say that the second stage of envy smothers from view the first stage. My contention is that it is the analysis of the first stage that disintegrates the envious constellation.

*   *   *

The psychological structure of envy is misperceived if it is viewed in isolation. Melanie Klein associates it with greed and jealousy, noting both the connection and the difference. To these two needs to be added omnipotence, which I prefer to call godhood. We are talking now of an envy where first and second stage is established and kept in being. This means that the action pattern of both the first stage and the second is in constant operation. The individual is ridding herself of her own worth into the object and ingesting[4] the latter's bad qualities into herself and then, in her bitter resentment, ridding herself of these into the object. However, the third party (father) has to be kept out because he represents the eye of awareness which, when fully functional, prevents the emotional activities peculiar to both the first and second stage of envy. Keeping out father is the role of jealousy.

I use almost carelessly the phrase "keeping out father" but who keeps him out? The all-powerful god referred to as "omnipotence" in analytic literature. In a similar way, the emotional activities specific to the first stage of envy are obliterated through this omnipotent agent. God has the power to obliterate. In fact, the reality is obliterated through being split up and expelled, but it is god who does the splitting up and the expelling. When, in the first stage of envy, worth is evacuated and deficits ingested, it is god who is responsible for preventing awareness and, in the social group, for introducing the anodyne word "idealization" to draw a veil over the violent activities under its umbrella. It is a social collusion against awareness. "Omnipotence" also is a poor word, because, although it is a noun, it is not an agent. It is an attribute of god like "kindness" might be an attribute of John Smith, but kindness is not an agent that acts. One might say that John Smith acts with kindness, and therefore it is grammatically adjectival. In a similar way, god acts with omnipotence and his action in the personality is to split, expel, and ingest, which prevents awareness. "Keeping out father" equals keeping out the perspective from the angle of Being.[5]

Envy is accompanied by greed, jealousy, and omnipotence. The omnipotence is incarnate in a figure, figures, or an institutional group. In the analytic situation its typical form is to be located in the analyst and patient. An interpretation about "envy" is seen, I believe, in two divergent yet united ways. On the one hand the patient hears the analyst declaring "This quality in you that I name envy is bad, it should not be in you." This is god making a declaration. For the patient it is rarely an interpretation. The other way in which the patient hears this statement is that it is coming from the bleat of an emotionally wounded child;[6] that when the analyst points out envy he has done so because he is usually persecuted by it. It is the definition of a psychological process from the point of view of the attacked and injured object. All the seven deadly sins, of which envy is one, have been defined in this way, and that is why they are words appropriate to primitive superstition and folk religion and quite unsuitable for a psychological discipline. They are not even moral categories, but, rather, moralistic ones.

I want to make sure that I am properly understood here. I am not saying that envy should not be interpreted—quite the opposite. I am saying that its full psychological structure needs to be understood and interpreted firmly and clearly. To do this successfully each of the elements in the structure need to be kept in mind. So, for instance, when the analyst feels himself under relentless and resentful attack, it is a mistake to point out envy. Once the structure is understood he knows that god in the personality is responsible for it. He knows also that it has been preceded by the activities peculiar to the first stage of envy. He knows also that it is related to jealousy and to greed, both of which are also emotional activities that need to be psychologically described. When they are described in such a way that the patient sees the damaging consequences to himself, it stirs a desire in him to transform the activities so that they enrich his personality rather than damage it. When the psychological processes are described, their damaging nature is obvious to the patient. When a patient says "But heavens, that's mad", then a restructuring is in process. There are a range of inter-locking activities, all of which need to be illuminated. His choice of which activity to highlight will be dictated by what the patient is bringing at any one moment in time, but often needs to be related to the other activities so the whole spectrum can slowly be grasped.

I believe, speaking very generally, that some analysts fall into the trap of speaking of the envy in the patient from the seat of god whereas others, from fear of being moralistic, try to soothe the condemning god away. In both cases the envy and the tyrant god remain active within the personality.

Now, on to greed. Greed determines the intensity of the inges-tion in both the first and second stage of envy. It is responsible for turning something of worth into a deficit. I think the way the inges-tion of a deficit occurs is that what is attempted is the taking in of a good but it is done with such violence that it damages rather than enriches.

*   *   *

In his paper on arrogance Bion says, ". . . that in the personality where life instincts predominate, pride becomes self-respect, where death instincts predominate, pride becomes arrogance" (1957, p. 86). I want to argue here that this is the wrong level of explana-tion. I do not want to enter into the debate on the existence or not of the death instinct but, rather, that all the instincts, whatever they be, are operating at the biological level and that psychology emerges in response to them. This constellation—envy, greed, jeal-ousy, and godhood—are, I believe, the presence of trauma in the personality. I think the definition of envy in terms of something constitutional in the personality or due to the death instinct arises out of a failure to note the presence of pain in the personality. In other words, a definition where a biological process is substituted for a psychological one. The factor that determines whether pride becomes self-respect or arrogance is in whether godhood in the personality is owned or disowned, loved or hated.

I want to put in an aside here about Melanie Klein's theoretical schema. She departed radically from the biological principle when she founded her whole outlook upon *phantasy*, which means the biological and environmental stimuli are fashioned upon an emotional construct; that from earliest infancy we emotionally construct our world out of the inner and outer sensations that we encounter. In this way Melanie Klein laid down her theory upon a psychological bedrock and made a radical break with any stimulus–response model, and I believe that this fundamental vision of Klein's is what makes a theory truly psychological. It was momentous, and I embrace it wholeheartedly and believe that psychoanalytic schools that have not internalized this outlook remain basically tied to a behaviourist model of action and are not truly psychological theories. However, when she slips back into instinct theory and concepts like envy, unprocessed by internal emotional construction, she has betrayed her own basic psychological principle. I do not think this is a great failure on her part, because nearly all new thinkers who discover a new principle do not manage to establish all the ramifications that are implied in their new discovery. It is what Koestler (1978, pp. 216–220) referred to as *snow-blindness*, and Bertrand Russell says, ". . . principles are often acknowledged long before their full consequences are drawn" (1985, p. 20).

This cardinal point in Melanie Klein's formulation I see as so important that I would want to clear away the dross so that it can be seen for being better highlighted. This is why I started with that quote of Max Müller.

I was struck some years ago when noticing that the people in whom envy, jealousy, greed, and godhood were most deeply implanted were those who had suffered catastrophes in infancy or childhood. At first I said to myself that the latter was in some obscure way consequent upon the former. Later, under the influence of Bion's theory of transformations, I came to think that envy, greed, jealousy, and godhood *are* the infantile trauma. Once it is realized how damaging these are to the personality it becomes clear that in them the trauma still lives. It is the psycho–physical trauma that has undergone psychological transformation. The damage to the personality is the *invariant*; the variables are the psycho–physical event in history and the constellation of envy, greed, jealousy, and godhood present here and now. I feel conviction about this that I cannot give adequate account for. I know for myself that this perspective has given me a sympathy at the level of knowledge, even if this is frequently marred at the affective level. I have, I believe, achieved some clinical success with such patients that has been greater than before I had this perspective. When I use the word "perspective" I mean not only the traumatic quality of this envious constellation but also the first and second stage of envy and its relations to its partners: greed, jealousy, and godhood. I see envy therefore *not* as the consequence of a *constitutional element*, but rather an element in a living trauma. When someone becomes aware of the trauma and the pain that goes with it, the envy becomes transformed into moral courage.

*   *   *

Melanie Klein did a great service to psychoanalysis by founding it upon the reality of individual emotional construction starting from earliest infancy. However, the introduction of terms derived from folk religion did her great discoveries a disservice. It is time now for her followers to make a detailed psychological analysis of these discordant anomalies that exist within her psychological schema. Death has the unfortunate consequence of endowing the works of the deceased with a paralysing *imprimatur*. Had Melanie Klein continued to live and defy death she may have developed this first sketch into a more satisfactory explanation where the hidden presence of pain and its psychological management through envy, greed, jealousy, and godhood was more central.

Psychoanalysis is more important than any of the figures who have developed the science and the art. It is my hope that everyone here shares this sentiment. I want to end by quoting from a book that is scarely known today, but which contains a treasury of gems in its slim ninety pages:

. . . I have no objection to people inventing all the words they need. All the fun in talking and speculation comes from seeing whether you can fit words in to fill gaps in your knowledge. But people get into bad habits. They turn words into things; they pretend they're sticks and beat people with them; and when a word has acquired enough status it actually has the power to hurt. [Burney, 1962, p. 36]

Notes

1. Melanie Klein defines envy thus: "envy is the angry feeling that another person possesses and enjoys something desirable . . ." (Klein, 1957). I have changed this definition because unconscious envy does not exist as a feeling. It is unconscious envy with which psychoanalysis is most concerned. Once it does not exist as a feeling then the qualifying word angry does not apply.

2. Melanie Klein's view that it is due to "the universal longing for the pre-natal state" (1957, p. 179) is, I believe, incorrect.

3. I think that the emotional activity that results in the idealized perception is a projection of an unintegrated ego into the other. This other, although frequently symbolized by one person, is always a group-spirit. So, it might be communism symbolized by Marx or by Lenin, Catholicism symbolized by the Pope, or capitalism symbolized by Bill Gates, but in all cases it is a group into which the frail ego is projected. So, what is idealized is the self within a corporate entity. I would today distinguish this from a projection of unbearable object-parts of the psyche into the same groupings. I would further elaborate the fact that when one is happening, so is the other. In view of this I would emphasize that the two processes occur within the same time-frame and not, as this paper implies, sequentially.

4. I use the word "ingest" to emphasize that it is a reactive and not a responsive activity.

5. See Brahman in Muller's *Vedanta Philosophy* (1904).

6. This intuition into the emotional state in the analyst is characteristic of patients in whom psychotic processes are active.

CHAPTER TWENTY

The structure of paranoia

"Another stumbling-block was the insurmountable distrust of the peasants: they could not believe that the master could have any other aim than to squeeze all he could out of them"

(Tolstoy, 1986, p. 364)

When I am paranoid I think my compatriot is out to get me. I distrust him; I believe he plots my downfall, that he envies me. It is not, however, only another individual that I may distrust in this way. It may be the Jews, it may be the Arabs, it may be Englishmen, Roman Catholics, lawyers, accountants, estate agents, freemasons, psychiatrists, politicians, or bankers. It may also apply to phenomena like birth, life, death, or the body. It is a mental orientation and one that has two poles. All the above constitute the object pole; the subject pole is in an emotional state geared to survival and self-protection. I am compelled to be self-orientated and I am in a state that is innately passive though I give all the appearance of being extremely active. After all, I have to be on the watch the whole time in order to defend myself against the missiles flying at me from all sides. When we had a language to describe emotions that has now been smothered beneath psychiatric anodyne nomenclature, what word in the English language would have described paranoia most aptly? Before paranoia had been invented, what word would the English novelists of the last century use that comes closest to what the psychiatrist knows as paranoia? I think it must be *distrust* combined with *suspicion*. I think Francis Thompson, the poet, was talking of paranoia when he said, "Suspicion creates its own cause; distrust begets reason for distrust" (1913, p. 3). This quote is consistent with Winnicott's view that fantasy is primary and reality secondary (1958, p. 153).

How is it and why is it that I see things in this way? In order to answer this question I need to do some unpacking; to look at the elements that go to make up the emotional state which we call paranoia. I will start by looking at the subject-pole.

My preoccupation is with what is being *done* to me, or what *might* be done to me. Although I am one among many, my "I" looms large in my emotional field. In fact, it is so large that it screens out all persons, including my own person. When survival of the organism is first and foremost, development of my own person or that of others is a luxury I cannot afford. I have had two patients, separated in time by many years of clinical practice, who told me that when they were children they each believed that he, in one case, and she, in another, were the only person in the universe —that all the people around them were made of cardboard, figments of the imagination. No one else exists, only me. Now, we need to enlarge upon what I mean when I say that it screens out all persons, including my own person. This is one side of my subjective state.

So, this one side is that I am puffed up and I obliterate everyone else, but the other is that there is a powerful figure that says in the harshest tones, "You don't exist . . .", and the paranoia is a resentful fury towards this powerful figure that proclaims my nonexistence. This also gives us another angle on paranoia—it is directed against verbal statements. I don't say to myself: "Well, this is plainly absurd. I do exist; I won't listen to this flamboyant fool . . ."; no, my focus is upon the fool's stupid words and I believe them. So, then, it is out of this inner certainty that I do not exist that generates the perception that I am the only one in the world who does exist and that no one else does. Now, you will realize that this

"I" is not a person. The "I" that I endow with existence is a mob, a collectivity.

To make sense of this, some reflection is needed to decide what is meant by a person. Let me start with this definition: a person is someone who has actively taken possession of all parts of himself and which is in relation to the other. The human person is a creation. A choice has been made to create out of the disparate fragments a unified pattern. I have been careful when lecturing in recent years to distinguish between a person and a someone; a person being someone who has chosen himself and all that is in him, whereas a someone has things inside of him that he has not chosen, that he has disowned, or split-off, in the language familiar to psychoanalysts. Such a someone is paranoid. There is some aspect of myself that I fear and hate. There is something that terrifies me about it. Am I not right to be terrified of a fickle mob that twists this way and that at the slightest flick of the conjurer's baton? I take up an attitude of violent hatred towards my own insides. Projection out of me and into another is the form that primitive hatred takes. So, ultimately, the fear and distrust is of a quality in myself. The indication that I hate it is that I disown it into another— I emphasize that this is hatred of a primitive kind. So the cure for paranoia is that I have to take possession with tenderness of all that is inside me, be it sadness, joy, envy, disappointment, jealousy, or greed.

When we imagine the very paranoid or distrustful individual our minds tend to focus upon a wolf-like aggression and defensiveness combined with resentful sulkiness. It is outgoing, actively pushing the other person away and, in extreme cases, leading to grievous bodily injury or murder of the other. However, this is one form, but there is another. This is the individual who turns away in disdain, he is above all such contemptible behaviour. In this case not just one element is hated and disowned, but rather the whole paranoid system. It does not look as if he is paranoid, but he is in fact extremely so. We might call these two forms of paranoia the patent and the latent.

Now, can you imagine yourself into the mind of someone who is not a person? What is her nature? If there is not a person there, what is there? Someone knocks on the door and asks "Is anyone there?", and I answer "Yes, me"— yet what is this "me"? You are mistaken if you think I am a person. I may say "I" of myself and say "Yes, this is *me*", yet if you interpret this as designating a person you will be making a very serious mistake. This "*me*" is a group entity. I am a psychoanalyst, don't you know? There were several pathways that led me to this conclusion. I will tell you about one of them.

I realized that Anthony did not differentiate me from other psychoanalysts. He was not talking therefore to me (a person) but to me (a group entity). He was petrified of making any critical remark about any colleague of mine. I *was* them and they *were* me. But why did he perceive me in this way? I think it is that his perception is governed by the state of his own ego. I perceive the world according to the way in which my own self is constituted. That the way in which the ego is constituted effects perception is a point that has been made by Hanna Segal (1957): ". . . disturbances in differentiation between the ego and object lead to disturbances in differentiation between the symbol and the object symbolised . . ."

So I allow the physician to X-ray my soul and he looks at the plate and discovers to my horror that there is a crowd of people with no centre. "I have to tell you", he says, "that I have discovered inside you a very serious condition." He further says, "I have never come across such a case before in my whole professional life. There is no skeleton, so I do not know what holds you up." I go away from the physician's consulting room holding myself very fearfully and looking around for signs of danger. It seems that I am very fragile and have to spend all my energies in protecting myself. There is no leader of this mob inside me to do the job, to stride forth, to make decisions and lead his troops towards an objective.

There is another component to this. You might think that in this pitiable condition I would be modest and, of course, I believe that I am—in fact I parade the fact—but one day I listened outside a door to some colleagues who were talking about me and I was shocked to hear them saying, "God, that fellow Neville, you know, he's so bloody arrogant. He thinks the sun shines out of his arse." So not only am I not a person, but I am just an amorphous collectivity, a random mob of *ne'er-do-wells*. So, I am a rabble but arrogant into the bargain. How come?

Before coming to an explanation that will be familiar to those of us who are psychologically trained in the craft of psychoanalysis, I want to draw attention to a formulation first made by Emile Durk-heim, the sociologist, in his classic book *Suicide: A Study in Sociology* (1951). Who is god or what is god?, asked Durkheim. It is, he said, the group solidified into a compact entity. The group scattered into a myriad elements, like a blob of mercury treated to a blow from a hammer, is not god. A group in this state he named *anomie* (pp. 373ff). The compacted group assumes a god-like characteristic. So when I hear behind a door my colleagues exasperated at my arrogance I should not be surprised, for if I had read my Durkheim I might have concluded, without having to see that dismal X-ray plate, that I was not a person but, rather, a collectivity. It is compacted, like those poor unfortunates in that infamous Black Hole of Calcutta, so I do not feel that I am a random mob. So, these are two elements of paranoia: a collectivity of elements and omnipotence. It would be interesting to speculate how Durkheim came by this insight. After collecting his data, was he inspired through an insight that derived from the state of a part of his own self?

How do we explain psychologically, rather than sociologically, that when in the absence of a person and so being a mere collectiv-ity, I am full of omnipotence? I think that the key to this lies in that primordial emotion of shame. I am ashamed of not being a person, of being merely a collectivity. A critical colleague says to me, "You know what you were saying yesterday about dreams is a carbon copy of what Ella Sharpe says in Chapter Three of her book *Dream Analysis* . . ." I stand up to my full height, spluttering and retorting angrily, "What you are implying is that I just copied it from her while pretending it was something I thought out for myself . . .", and I look shiftily at my threatening opponent. My colleague rightly goes away and says to his mate, "It's no good talking to Neville, he's as paranoid as a startled goose. As soon as I said he had copied his talk on dreams from Ella Sharpe, he started hissing at me as though I were a poultry butcher about to slaughter him . . ." When I am a collectivity that is all I can do. There are two ways of taking in: through a creative act or through ingestion. The subject of the creative act is a person; the subject of ingestion is a collectiv-ity. A collectivity can only take something within after the manner of a tape-recorder. So, in this disastrous state entities are lying around inside me with no coherence. Another sign, then, of this is that what I say today contradicts what I said yesterday, so this same colleague on the warpath says to me: "What you were saying just now that the function of dreams is to synthesize experience is in direct contradiction to what you were saying yesterday—when you said that the function of dreams is to discharge out of the system unwanted accretions of sensations . . ." I become very hot under the collar and say, "I didn't say anything of the sort. You must have misheard me . . ." My colleague was about to contradict this, but he saw the paranoid look in my eye and decided that any further discussion would be a pointless endeavour. I am ashamed at being a collectivity and I do all I can to cover up any signs that betray the fact to my friends and acquaintances.

Also, when my "I", or my ego, is a collectivity I take things in but only temporarily, for the moment. It does not last. Ruskin had noticed this quality:

> You can talk a mob into anything; its feelings may be—usually are—on the whole, generous and right; but it has no foundation for them, no hold of them; you may tease or tickle it into any, at your pleasure; it thinks by infection, for the most part, catching an opinion like a cold, and there is nothing so little that it will not roar itself wild about, when the fit is on;—nothing so great but it will forget in an hour, when the fit is past. [1901, p. 46]

So we note these three manifestations of the ego being a collectivity: that there is no internal coherence, that there are internal inconsistencies and outer elements are not taken into the mind in such a way that they become part of the character structure and endure. This state of the ego is not paranoia itself but, rather, the foundation stone without which the fashioning of the paranoid perception cannot occur.

It is worth noting that the shame indicates that there is knowledge that something is lacking, something is wrong in the foundations of the personality.

Now my *modus operandi* is one that is akin to stealing. What I have inside me is not something that I have bought and made my own. My friend buys a house, decorates it, and transforms it so that the previous owner hardly recognizes it when he comes to visit a year later. My friend is a person. I, however, have a house that I have squatted in—all the contents belong to the owner. They do no belong to me. I have stolen them. This is the way I operate.

Now, one of the problems is this. I am in this scattered state and so I expend all my energy on myself. I must not let anyone see that I am stealing all that I have, that one thing is in contradiction to another, so all my psychic attention is upon myself. I do not know it consciously. I totally disown such an idea—what me (!), this most concerned and thoughtful of people? Now, two consequences flow from this:

1. That, because it is disowned, I believe that everyone else operates according to my own *modus operandi*. Everyone is similarly self-centred; everyone steals as I do. I am shut off from others and therefore the way I act is my only reference point. It is my template. I do not have the experience of making contact with "the other" and compare him with myself. Knowing one thing is always in terms of another. Without access to this possibility of comparison I judge everything according to my own self-enclosed world. I am like those two patients: there are no other people, only me. I see all others through the lens of my own self-enclosed system. I therefore view my fellows with extreme suspicion. They are all out to steal from me, to do me down. I certainly make absolutely sure that none of them ever comes too close to me. Either they will steal from me or they may get a glimpse of my X-ray plate, which I keep as hidden as possible.

2. I am forced to go out of my way to be kind and deferential to people. I have to please them. Why? There are two reasons. I have to give the appearance of concern, that I am a person and therefore one who sees others as persons and treats them so. Then they will not see the X-ray plate. The other is that it keeps others at a distance. If someone comes close it puts a demand upon me, but this I am unable to meet because there is no person inside me able to create or to love.

Perhaps I could put a full stop there. This is the whole story. What follows is an expansion aimed at giving what has been said greater coherence.

*   *   *

I do not think that paranoia can be understood if we base ourselves upon Freud's instinct theory. For Freud, conflict in the personality arises through a clash of opposing instincts. Now all instincts, as assumed by nearly all social scientists and certainly by Freud, are in the service of survival. Yet, as Professor Steve Jones (2002) has stressed, it is a category error to transport this aspect of Darwinian theory into social science. I think the original perpetrator of this misapplication of theory was Herbert Spencer. The conflict within human beings is not between one survival instinct and another but, rather, between survival itself and the desire for civilization. Civilization is evidence of an inner desire for a form of living that transcends survival. Personal development, the arts, science, and religion testify to the desire in human beings for a form of living that surpasses and sometimes eclipses the survival needs of the organism. The conflict in all of us is between survival and the desire for personal fulfilment. In fact, I would go so far as to say that the view that we are creatures governed by the instincts of survival and nothing more is a mental orientation whose source lies in a paranoid perception. There is another link here to what I have been talking about. The thrust for survival, as formulated by Darwin, Huxley, and others, is not concerned with the individual but with the species, the genus, or the race. There is a distinction, first formulated by Weismann, whom Freud quotes (1920g, pp. 45–49), between the disposable soma and the germ plasm, or as Freud puts it, *mortal and immortal parts* (*ibid.*, p. 45). Freud puts it thus: "The germ cells . . . are potentially immortal, in so far as they are able, under certain favourable conditions, to develop into a new individual, or, in other words, to surround themselves with a new soma" (*ibid.*, p. 46).

The transfer of Darwin's theory, which is concerned with survival of the species, into the social sciences, where it has been applied to the individual, is a serious blunder that serves to obscure the true nature of paranoia. If, in the event of a nuclear holocaust, when survival of our species was under threat, I started to clamour that my personal development was being undermined, then my few fellow survivors could be forgiven for giving me a good kick up the backside and telling me that, given the extreme circumstances, more important issues were at stake. However, when after many generations, civilization was again possible, then one of my descendants could treat himself to the project of personal development. This is the fundamental conflict in us human beings: between survival and civilization, not between one instinct of survival versus another. When I refer earlier to the paranoid structure being fundamentally a collectivity, we are witnessing here the state of the human organism entirely under the urge for survival. So this is one dimension of our investigation that is crucial for our understanding of paranoia. Paranoia is at variance with the human desire for civilization, for artistic attainment, for scientific understanding, for religion and personal development. I might say, in an aside, that calling the soma's tendency towards disintegration and death an instinct is a misconception on two counts. In the first its source is not from the germ plasm, and second, as Petocz has pointed out (1999, p. 221), unlike the categorization of all the other instincts in Freud's armamentarium, it is defined by aim rather than by source.

I mentioned earlier that one pathway that led me to think in this direction was the experience of patients not differentiating me from other people in my profession. I was part of a merged, compacted human entity and I judged, as does Hanna Segal in the short passage I quoted, that the self of the patient concerned is compacted or, as Segal puts it, "disturbances between ego and object . . ." (1957), but the disturbance is precisely that the ego and object are merged. Now, the intensity of that merged state determines the degree of merger that exists. The example I gave of me being merged with all other psychoanalysts is a mild state of merger on the graph measuring intensity. However, I have known cases where someone has merged me not only with all psychoanalysts but with all men. I had one case where I was not differentiated, not only from all human beings, but from all living creatures. There was no distinction between me and some ants that he saw on the wall of my consulting room. In this latter case it will not surprise you to learn that his paranoia was so extreme that it entirely dominated his functioning life. What I mean here is that his distrust of me was extreme but again the question is why?

He was in this shattered, broken-up state inside. In the initial interview he said to me that although it might look as if he were functioning all right, viewed from the outside, yet he was a mess of bits inside. Then we need to remember that together with this inner collectivity was extreme omnipotence or god-likeness, but he saw me in the same light. I was a swaggering patrician looking down upon him, this plebeian good-for-nothing. This is another element in a configuration of which paranoia is a part. Not only is there a swaggering plutocrat, but also a contemptible rabble. He hates this haughty aristocrat but he dare not say it because he will otherwise be mowed down with a machine gun as rebels against the tyrants always are. His distrust is extreme.

An analyst said to a patient who had recently visited Nigeria: "I think you identify more with the black natives than with their colonial masters." The patient said nothing, but went off on holiday for three weeks. During the entire holiday this statement of her analyst had been ringing in her ears. She was wildly insulted, and said to her analyst, "So you think I'm just a dirty black native, do you?" What we are looking at in this enquiry is the particular element in the pattern I have been describing that applies to the perception of the other. This arises out of these elements; it cannot occur without them, but it is that element in the configuration that affects the perception of the other that is called paranoia.

The other important factor is that because I disown my collectivity state and believe that I am a coherent unity, a person, I perceive the other as unitary. I see one part for the whole. This is because, under the pressure of shame, I am making myself into a unity when this is not the case, but I perceive the other under the impact of this lens. Therefore, what I encounter in the other is a part, but I see it as a whole "She is a greedy bitch, that's all she is . . ."; "He is driven by envy and nothing else . . ."; "She is so vain that everything she does is for her own self-enhancement . . ."; and so on. That tendency to chase a particular vice like a bloodhound may be motivated by the analyst's paranoia. This kind of perception is like a zoom lens that focuses on one part, blowing it up, so that it obliterates the other elements in the personality. It is the reason I am troubled when a school of analysts attribute all antidevelopmental behaviour to some particular element, be it envy, sexual desire, or the inferiority complex. Other elements are obliterated, and the reason behind it I have explained.

The paranoid mode of perception blows up one element and through this exaggeration obliterates another. All human actions are made up of what arises out of someone's own free choice and that which happens to me over which I have no control—the accidental forces of destiny. The paranoid form of perception attributes deliberate intent to what is impersonal and accidental. That which is determined is attributed to intent. It is paranoid perception that is responsible for animism, as Freud points out in *The Future of an Illusion* (1927c, pp. 15–16). There is a bit of a puzzle here: I have said that the base structure out of which paranoid perception arises is a broken-up state with no inner coherence, so if that is the case then why do I attribute inner deliberateness to my malefactor? I think one has to posit that what I perceive in the other is that which is disowned in myself.

This suggests that there is, in fact, an inner coherence within my own self that I disown. I think the reason why I disown it is easier to understand. It is through the creative activity of my own inner centre that I come into touch with my own psychic activities and this puts me in touch with mental pain. It seems, then, that we are back to that fundamental principle: that the avoidance of mental pain lies at the root of paranoia.

*   *   *

The important question is: how do we tackle this problem clinically? I think the brief answer is twofold: only speak to the paranoid individual in terms that are entirely personal and be constantly aware of the fact that I am not a person but a compacted collectivity in his eyes. Now I want to look at this more closely.

A collectivity does not think; a collectivity makes statements and these are always invested with god-like authority. Thinking, on the other hand, is a creative activity. Thoughts are created in a similar way in which I create when I put up a canvas and start to paint the landscape in front of me. So, if thoughts are created, they can only come from a person. Their source is in the person; the collectivity can only repeat what has been said. What may confuse some people is that the psychiatric textbooks refer to the phenomenon of *concrete thinking*. However, this is a semantic spoof: concrete thinking is not thinking but, rather, the presence within the personality of dictates. The word "concrete" refers to the quality whereby the dictate is invested with god-likeness. I sometimes refer to this phenomenon as "Act of Parliament Statements"—they issue forth from the *Establishment*, as Wilfred Bion called it.

Now, the clinical relevance of this is of supreme consequence. Here am I in the consulting room, but I am not a person. I am a unit in the Establishment and what I say has the most august authority. Now the aim must be for the patient to arrive at an insight into this, but how to achieve it? If I say, "I think you see me as a group and not as a person . . .", the seed will fall on stony ground. The patient will not have a clue what I am talking about and, what is more, he will intuit that I am implying that he should not see me as a group, that he is doing something wrong thereby and no amount of counter-explanations on my part will serve to change this perception. What I am referring to is any statements like: "No, I didn't mean that you should see me as a person. I was saying that this was how you do see me . . .", etc.

Now, insight is also a creation, and therefore can only come from the person. I can repeat what has been said; I can say, "Oh yes, I understand", but for me truly to have an act of understanding then the person inside of me has to be functioning. So, how to assist the patient to have such a personal act of understanding? How to enable him or her to generate a person inside of himself; to bring together those disparate elements, those parts of the rabble and transform them into a coherent whole? My answer is this: *the manifestation of my own person enables the emergence of a person in the other.*

At first sight this sounds like the very opposite of everything that we have learned about psychoanalytic technique. Surely, I hear you say, the very essence of the analyst's mode of relating to his patient is to remain anonymous? To be a unit in the mob? To remain unknown? To hide his own person? This is true in one sense and a disastrous falsehood on the other. It is true in the sense that the psychoanalytic encounter is not the place for speaking about my own life history, about my political views, my artistic interests, details of my home life, or, more importantly than all of these, any discourse whose aim is to supply some need in me other than the emotional development of the patient and myself. If one thinks of one's own needs in terms of one's emotional security, I think many an interpretation that may look as if it is for the patient's benefit is in fact for my own group security. I derive a lot of solace from the comforting nostrums of my psychoanalytic schooling.

I think we all know that there is a very big difference between a statement I make that is the vomit of what I have just been told, or

even told long ago, and one that is the product of personal diges-
tion and re-creation into my own thought. It is the latter that is the
proper discourse for an analyst. Therefore, it is not the outer statement that matters but the source from which it is generated. It is
personally generated statements that slowly, but with persistent
inevitability, undermine the system that sustains the paranoid attitude of mind. That patients intuit the difference emotionally is
certain. Although, for instance, I think very highly of Wilfred Bion
and very lowly of Carl Rogers, I would prefer to go to a therapist
who has internalized the thinking the of Carl Rogers into an inner
creative personal synthesis than to an analyst who has ingested
Bion but not made out of it a personal synthesis.

For some reason the system composed of the collectivity,
omnipotence, and authority cannot accrete to itself personal statements, but can only take into itself depersonalized authoritative
collective dictates. If I speak things that I have imbibed, perhaps
from my analyst, perhaps from my analytic school of thinking,
perhaps from the analytic culture that I inhabit, then I feed and
keep intact the paranoia in my patient. However, if I have thought
them, if my own person has generated a new creation, then, with
defined certitude, the paranoid system slowly but inevitably
collapses. So, one technical imperative is that I speak only what is
personal, and to do this I need to have digested and created an
inner synthesis and this internal work is the prime requisite for the
dissolution of paranoia. The second is that I be aware that I am seen
as a collective entity.

It is a very common error for the analyst to interpret as a
displacement what is in fact an embodied collectivity. So the patient
is talking about John Smith's intrusiveness and I interpret this as
my own, or perhaps his. The error lies in the assumption that I am
a person, John Smith is a person, and the patient is a person. What
is being spoken of is a trait that is embodied in the collectivity. I
look at the crowd in the piazza trying to storm the Prime Minister's
residence and I am in the crowd, John Smith is there, and so is the
patient. There is a mob whose dominant characteristic at that
moment is its driven determination to intrude into the PM's residence. So the interpretation that will more accurately reflect the
situation would be something like: "So intrusiveness has gripped
hold of John Smith, and you, and me, so we are all in its thrall . . .",

or some version of that. The patient will tempt me to speak in dictate form, to speak with god-like authority, to speak from on high, to be a collectivity and not a person. He can then accommodate himself to that and avoid the painful business of creating his own life. As soon as he starts to create he becomes aware of himself, and in this there is always pain. In the paranoid state I discharge noxious elements inside myself into the other. I then become even more paranoid because I have lost part of myself into the other. He has stolen what belongs to me. In the personal state I do not discharge, but, rather, create even what is seemingly noxious into a personal synthesis. In India I have seen faeces from latrines being converted into methane gas. I am impoverished when I discharge any part of myself.

Do I point out envy or greed or jealousy to the patient in this state? The answer is determined by how he will hear me. In the paranoid state he will hear me, the collective authority, saying that this should not be there and this will encourage, if not induce, him to discharge it, to get rid of it. Of course, as we know, it is not annihilated but passes into a different form.

There are two psychoanalytic schools that I am familiar with. In one it is common for the analyst to assume the cloak of this collective authority; in the other the analyst attempts to soothe the vehemence of this archaic superego by speaking in friendly language. In neither case is the power of this authoritative directive, this archaic superego, in any way diminished in its power. As I have said, the analyst needs to aim away in another direction with his personal interpretations, confident that in time the paranoid structure in tandem with this superego will crumble without any further strength to resist.

Patients, of course, try to manouevre the psychoanalyst into the agglomerated impersonal position. So, a man who had had a retinue of analysts and therapists in his life's journey had an appointment with me at ten in the morning. He came first at ten o'clock, then at five past ten, then at ten past ten, then at quarter past, then at twenty past, and then at twenty-five past. I guessed what he was trying to manoeuvre me into, so I said nothing. Eventually he could bear it no longer and he said to me: "I know what you're thinking, I know what you're thinking—you think this coming late of mine is resistance to treatment." Happily, I was able to say quite truthfully, "That is not what I was thinking but what I *was* thinking was that you are trying to put me into uniform." Had I made the comment that he was hoping for, then my reality as a collective entity would have been confirmed and paranoia remained intact.

So there are two angles to this. One is the need for the analyst to resist being compacted into the group and to speak from his own personal understanding; the other is to observe as acutely as possible signs of personal growth in the patient. So, a man led an isolated life, made no decisions, accepted demurely whatever I said or did in one dimension, and contributed his own personal editorship in relation to what I said. He was aware of the first element but not the second. His personal self was overwhelmed by the presence of myself as a powerful collectivity. When I pointed out, ineptly, that he was not aware of his own personal editorship, he became fearful that my collective tyrant would crush him mercilessly. I was able to assist in illuminating this. Shortly after, he had some new subjective experiences. For the first time he felt it would be nice to "come home to someone"; at the same time he was able to tell me that he thought a long break I was taking was too much for him, and concurrent with this was a feeling that his interest in literature was something to be valued and not dismissed as idle indulgence. These were all manifestations that a person was being created inside him. At the same time his paranoia diminished and was most manifest in his relations towards me and his parents.

I believe it is urgent for us analysts to speak in a way that is psychologically accurate; that if we speak in such a manner our patients—and ourselves—will experience relief and healing. I believe many interpretations are based on shorthand formulae that are neat and easy but psychologically faulty. As paranoia is so widespread a condition, I believe it is urgent that we formulate the contours of its condition in as correct a way as possible.

CHAPTER TWENTY-ONE

A theory of communication for psychoanalysis

"... philosophy has been misled by the illusion of an isolated formation of the intellect"

(Dilthey, 1989, p. 264)

When I went into psychoanalysis I knew I had in me some-thing that I wanted to be understood by another. On later reflection I realized that I wanted to understand it myself, and that this was only possible if it were first understood by another. That other person could only provide me with the understanding I was looking for provided that I communicate with him. Through inchoate communication with him I was able to come into communication with myself. This suggests that there was a me not easily accessible to the me that busied around the place in daily life and, further, that I felt a strong need to be in communica-tion with that inaccessible me. In a nutshell, that is how I would sum up the situation when I went into psychoanalysis. You might ask, "Well, why didn't you go to a counsellor or case-worker?" My reply would be that I sensed that the inaccessible me would require the services of someone with a special capacity to reach and communicate with a part of me, perhaps the core of me, that was hidden from view.

Well, that was my position. Since that time I have myself become a psychoanalyst and I think that people who come to see me do so for the same reason. I would today refine and elaborate that basic proposition, but not in a way that invalidates it.

Surely, then, I say to myself, the theory of psychoanalysis must be an explanatory schema describing the nature of human communication but, to my surprise, when I opened the large tomes of psychoanalytic theory, I found nothing about communication but instead arcane language about instincts, affects, cathexes, ego, id, superego, repression, dreams, condensation, displacement, death instinct, and a whole paraphernalia of obscure concepts that seemed to bear no relation to communication. However, in a more reflective mood, I realize that some of the above items are aspects of the very communication that I am talking about but there are other items that are not, are irrelevant to it, and in fact obscure understanding of it. This paper, then, is an attempt to salvage that which is part and parcel of the process of communication and to dispose of those that are not relevant to it. Those that have been disposed of are part of a descriptive mapping of the human animal but not relevant to this specific sphere of human interaction.

Let us start, then, with a catalogue of the processes of communication, and see the place of psychoanalysis within it. I want to start by separating human communication into three modes:

1. Practical communication;
2. Intellectual or speculative communication;
3. Emotional communication.

Under practical communication I intend the disclosure of material facts to another. By material facts I mean when you tell me the time and place of a seminar, the date when William the Conqueror defeated Harold at the Battle of Hastings, the bookshop where I can buy the complete works of Freud, the date of Easter next year, the author of *War and Peace*, where and when tomatoes were first found by Europeans, the distance of the earth from the sun, the number of planets circling the sun, the fact that the planets go in an elliptical orbit, the fact that humans have dreams and that their sleep is made up of two composites: REM and non-REM, and so on.

Intellectual or speculative communication is always related to facts but is distinct from them. So, if we ask the question why William the Conqueror decided to invade Britain, we get from the historians a mixture of fact and speculation or what might be called interpretation. It is the same of all the other facts I have mentioned. If I ask why there is to be a seminar at the university on psycho-analysis, I will get in reply a mixture of fact and speculation; if I ask why this particular bookshop and not others stocks the complete works of Freud, I will again get a mixture of fact and speculation. If I ask why we do not have a fixed date for Easter as we do for Christmas, I will get again a mixture of fact and speculation; why did Tolstoy write *War and Peace* will receive a similar blend of fact and speculation; if I ask why it is that tomatoes discovered in America have been adopted as a food so enthusiastically by Europeans, I will similarly get a mixture of fact and speculation; why the earth is precisely 93,000,000 miles from the sun will receive a similar blend, as I think will be the answer to the question of why the planets describe an elliptical orbit; why humans and all mammals yet not reptiles have REM sleep will also receive an answer that is a mixture of fact and speculation. So, these two forms go into a great deal of human communication.

By emotional communication I mean the disclosure of inner elements in my personality from myself to another. I may tell you that a close friend has just died and that I am feeling sad—a blend of fact and emotion. I may tell you that prior to my friend dying I had promised to send her a book that she wanted but forgot to do so, and that I am feeling guilty for not having done so. I may tell you that I loved this friend; I may tell you that when I first met her I hated her; I may tell you that I had been sexually attracted to her. I am here disclosing to you elements that exist in me and communication of this sort is emotional.

Communication of these elements inside me is not only via a direct expression of my feelings to you. Freud, in *The Interpretation of Dreams* (1971, pp. 152–153), tells of a young girl whose sister had two sons, one of whom had died, and now she had a dream that the other had died and how could this represent a wish, she asks Freud. Freud unravels the fact that when the first boy died a male friend of her sister's, whom she adored, had come to pay his condolences and that he would come again if the other boy died. In this case the young girl was not in contact with her own wish. By communicating the dream to Freud, she entered into communication with the intensity of her own wish. Communication with Freud is the agent that makes possible a communication between her outer self and inner desires. In a similar way, through tracing the reasons for forgetting the word *aliquis* in Virgil's stanza, Freud (1901b, pp. 8–11) brings his interlocutor into touch with his fear that a woman with whom he had had an affair might have missed her period. Through this procedure Freud helps the man to be in communication with a fear within him.

Along the same pattern of principles, Freud was able to translate a symptom, for instance an hysterical paralysis, into a language communicating a conflict of emotions within the person. And, according to the same principles, he was able to show how jokes contain a communication from this hidden part of the personality. Freud, through uncovering the disguise, was able to put the patient in touch with his own unknown self. Repression, which became the cornerstone of Freud's theoretical system, was the psychic mechanism that hid from the person the message seeking understanding. So, repression had within it a force both counteracting communication and yet, at the same time, doing so. Freud's job was to be the translator, so that the patient came into possession of unknown parts of himself. To be in communication with hidden parts of himself was the door that unlocked the sauna of mental health.

Since Freud's day much behaviour that would appear to serve the purpose of satisfying the organism have been understood to be human communications. Joan Symington, in a recent book (2002, pp. 213–226) gives an account of a woman who would rush to the toilet and pour out urine through which she got rid of painful realizations. Later, the patient had a dream and realized that she did not need to go to the toilet during the night. The anxiety was enveloped in the dream rather than in the discharge of urine. A woman would eat chocolate immediately after her analytic session—it seemed to be to dam up a painful realization during the session. Another woman would eat muesli bars just before a session—her hunger for emotional contact being both symbolized and, at the same time, denied. Another patient was extremely tired, due to having had to process painful new emotional understandings. Another patient would masturbate several times after the last session preceding a break in the treatment. After each session a man went to a restaurant and stuffed himself; it emerged that this symbolized the greedy way in which he took in interpretations from the analyst so that they imploded into him and smothered the emotional self, so that he was protected from experiencing pain. So, urinating, eating, sexual activity, and sleeping are all communications of emotional happenings. It is the communicative dimension of these organic functions that is the object of psychoanalytic investigation. These functions have a role in the life of the organism and are in the service of individual and species survival, but this is the object of study for the biologist, not for the psychoanalyst. The psychoanalyst concerns herself with the way in which these functions have become a language of emotional communication. So, in psychoanalysis, a great number of activities that are in the service of survival become part of a communicative language through which the individual is able to come into contact with hidden parts of himself.

The communication between himself and his analyst is the route by which the busy daily part of himself comes into contact with an emotional centre from which he has been out of contact. So, for instance, a man presented himself with a dilemma with two girlfriends—which should he offer to marry? This problem might be approached by a counsellor trying to help him clarify which of the two women seemed to suit him better. The analyst, however, saw it in a different light: that the man was showing a fundamental problem: that he was unable to make emotional choices that were significant in his life. The two women were just one manifestation of the problem. The outer drama pointed to an inner emotional dilemma. This man knew it, but was not aware of it. When the analyst pointed out what he thought was the problem, it rang with an authentic echo for him. Communication to the analyst enabled communication between his practical self and his inner emotional world.

Communication with this inner emotional self and its activities lies at the heart of the psychoanalytic enterprise. An analyst notices that every time he makes a clarifying interpretation the patient scorns the analyst. The analyst takes the view that himself in the role as analyst symbolizes the inner emotional self and that therefore he sees dramatized in the outer forum a noxious activity that is occurring in the inner forum: that the patient's own generative emotional motions are being undermined from within. So, the outer drama is a communication pointing to the inner emotional happening.

An elderly man had difficulty in differentiating himself from his analyst. It emerged that this was an outer manifestation of a problem of differentiating what was truly his own and what had been impressed upon him against his will. The inner dilemma, the intrapsychic, had been transferred to the interpersonal realm. There was an intercommunication between the two such that the outer was the sign and the inner the referent.

This means that there is a connection between the outer and the inner—that the meeting of the inner emotional experience with something similar in another from outside endows my inner one with certainty. It seems that the joining of two emotional elements that echo one another occurs through a bond of sympathy that is articulated through language. The language is the vehicle that carries the one emotional element across to the other. These two find each other drawn together through a joint recognition like two people falling in love with each other. When this happens there is a wedding contract that affirms and establishes what until then had been only half-formed. Wilfred Bion called it a preconception becoming a conception (1962, p. 91). However, he believes that this is a state of expectation mating with a sense impression. I think it is one emotional state that could be called a state of expectation, or inchoate or half-formed emotional state that mates not with a sense impression but with another half-formed emotional state, and the two coming together form what we might call emotional certainty. I think this, then, becomes a new organizing centre in the personality: I become it or it becomes me. That is the person, then, who I am. I think this must be the emotional substrate that lies behind a change of belief or intellectual view. Another way to think of it is to say that the process of communication becomes instrumental in locating an event differently in the mind—moving it perhaps from the periphery to the centre. Freud gives a lucid account of this when he describes how Breuer, Chrobak, and Charcot had a piece of knowledge which was at the periphery, but Freud moved it to the centre.[1]

Looked at in this light it is possible to see that which is part of emotional communication and that which is not. Let us first clear away what is not. Eating, urinating, sexual activity and sleeping are a necessary part of the organism's set up both for its individual survival and species survival. Psychologists have divided these different functions into a set of instincts serving the survival of the individual organism and the survival of the species. But this is not the psychoanalyst's subject of study. He studies these in so far as they have become a language of emotional communication. For psychoanalysis the emotional language is primary, and what needs to be demonstrated is the way in which activities geared to the biological functioning of the organism are taken up into the language of communication. The subject of investigation in psychoanalyis is not how an instinctual activity functions for the survival of the organism, but how it is structured into a language of communication.[2] My emphasis here is to locate precisely the arena of psychoanalytic investigation and differentiate it from that of the biologist's inquiry. It may occasionally happen that when a patient tells me he had to go and eat immediately after a session, he was hungry, and that I need to remind myself that I have had an organism on my couch that needs to survive bodily. However, the usual scenario is that he is communicating his emotional anxiety through this particular language of eating a meal after the session. Therefore, the way we talk about the organic functions and the instincts needs to reflect their subordinate function within psychoanalysis. At present I believe that much psychoanalytic theorizing fails to respect this, and the result is a disjunction between theory and clinical practice.

You may say: "Well, does it matter?" I believe it does. The more we can think clearly about what psychoanalysis is and keep a language and concepts that are consistent with what it is, the more effective will the process be and our logical thinking about it will be consistent. I want to give another clinical example that I hope illustrates the way in which communication is the agent of integration.

A man came to see me who had had ECT, pharmacological treatment, and numerous therapies, more than I could count, a challenge indeed. For me, life without challenge is like a decaying body with no vivifying presence within it, and I therefore engaged in a relationship with this man. I certainly did not "take him into treatment". He had had his basinful of that. I had the view that he had something to teach me and I thought I might have something that I could offer him. He believed the latter, because he had heard of something I had said about compulsive disorders that led him to believe that I might be able to understand some of his inner difficulties. I thought he might have something to teach me because I suspected that there were inner assumptions in me, as there were in his previous therapists, that interfered with my capacity to understand. I thought he might be able to teach me what the inner assumption was that was interfering with the capacity to generate an act of understanding. This set the platform for the communication between us. It was itself, I believe, an emotional basis that structured our communication. In brief, what it generated between us was receptivity. A transformation occurred in which receptivity replaced rejection. This did not happen overnight, but was a valuable piece of territory that was won step by step. Now, this transformation of the emotional communication between us correlated with some internal changes. These internal changes were manifested through dreams and changed responses to him from significant people in his life. Essentially, the dreams were of people important to him in his house: they were inside him rather than being banished from the inner sanctum. His sister and a previous girlfriend both became thoughtful of him in a way that he had not experienced before. These were the changed responses, which, like the dreams, were manifestations of this inner transformation from a rejecting mode to receptivity. I have to ask you to accept from me the fact of these changes, that they really occurred. Now, my supposition is that these changes were generated through the mode of emotional communication that occurred between himself and me; that this was the sign that effected the inner change. Quite why this should be so would require a long exploration. All I want to posit here is that a changed emotional communication led to an inner change: from rejection mode to receptivity, or from disintegration to integration, or from parts split off to parts embraced within.

*   *   *

Freud's structural model is part of the communicative structure. The ego is the inner emotional agent in communication with the id and the superego and the outer figures of the environment. Fairbairn recast Freud's theory so that he replaced the id with split-off parts of the ego. I think this is consistent with an explanatory schema of communication in that a split-off part of the self is in communication, but through gestural language. Let us say that a patient leaves the analytic session and goes to a café where a friendly proprietor gives her the coffee just as she likes it and she feels comforted by this. Let us further say that when she tells the analyst this in the subsequent session it becomes clear that she was in pain through the session and that the experience in the café was a consolation after it; that there was a communication of pain, some hurt at not being consoled, of the session terminating, and that the coffee in the café was the language of this split-off part of herself. It was not primarily hunger and thirst. Or the other case of the man who masturbated three times straight after the session. What is split off is the distress of separation. What is split off is communicated in the "language of the instincts". What needs some refinement here is our conception of the ego.

The ego is the agent of communication. So, when we speak of a split-off part of the ego, we mean that it is in communication but its "language" is via bodily functions. When this language is transformed into verbal communication it is no longer split-off, but has become part of the ego. For this reason Fairbairn's model of split-off parts of the ego replacing Freud's id fits with a communication schema. It is not that there are no instincts, but that their components have been taken up into a system of communication. This view that I am taking is consistent with Bion's theory of dream functioning, which differs from that of Freud. Whereas for Freud they were wish-fulfilments, ultimately of a solipsistic kind, for Bion their function was to synthesize experience. "Synthesize experience" can be thought of as transforming split-off parts of the ego into the ego proper. So the man who masturbated three times no longer did so, but felt the pain of separation and spoke about it in agonizing terms.

So, what are we saying about Freud's theory? I am going to speak rather crudely and inaccurately initially, and then try to refine the issue. Let us think of the human organism's fundamental need to survive. There are certain functions that are "built in" and require no voluntary cooperation from the mind: breathing, heart beating, and so on. Then there are others: eating, drinking, defecating, sexual intercourse, and avoidance of pain, which require mental volition for them to operate. So here the human organism is functioning for its survival. Then we move into the sphere of communication one with another. The organism uses these components (eating, drinking, defecating, and sexual intercourse) as its language of communication. In the course of human evolution there developed verbal language and a transformation occurred from "instinct language" to verbal language. What has been said here also applies to the ego as Freud formulated it. That aspect of it that relates directly to survival—i.e., its management of the id and its relation to reality, needs recasting in terms of human communication for it to fit the level that is the concern of psychoanalysis.

So, I have divided survival of the organism from the process of communication but, of course, the latter is linked into the former. The important question here is: "Is all communication in the service of survival?" I know the answer from many social scientists would be "Yes". I have come to suspect these generalizations. I call them the *missionary spirit* within the social sciences. It is, of course, simpler, more straightforward, if we are able to categorize all human behaviour, including communication, under this single motivating principle, but we may be sacrificing part of the truth in the service of a consoling orderliness.

Let us say that people who approach a psychoanalyst are seeking "fullness of living"; that there is some knowledge in them that their lives are not satisfactory; that a more satisfactory life is possible; that there is an unactualized potential within them; that there is living, and there is *living*. If this is right it would mean that communication serves both survival needs plus the actualization of potential. There is a basic assumption within the Kleinian school that the work of psychoanalysis is the integration of split-off parts of the self; the conversion of the language of instincts into verbal language. The assumption here is that this conversion leads to a fuller life.

Although these two strands, survival needs of the organism and desire for "fullness of life", are intertwined in the most minute way, the focus of psychoanalysis is upon the latter, concentrating, as it does, upon those factors in the personality that strangle and prevent such fullness. Communication between all parts of the ego correlates with "fullness of life". The achievement of communication between parts of the ego is achieved through interpersonal communication; the latter being a necessary ingredient for the achievement of the former. Psychoanalysis is an interpersonal communication whose focus is upon this particular aim. Any diversion from this aim thwarts its achievement. If a bit of theory is in the mind of the analyst, which belongs to survival of the organism rather than "fullness of living", it will thwart the aim. He will have in his hand the wrong tool, not the one that will do the job.

Another place where the two intersect is suicide. Suicide brings the organism's life to an end. People who commit suicide find life to be empty, valueless, devoid of meaning. This is another way of saying that people want meaning, want a fuller life, want the split-off parts integrated. The analyst is therefore always tackling "the suicidal" in the patient: not to prevent his physical death but to promote "fullness of life". If this prevents a physical death through actual suicide it is a lucky bonus.

I believe that if psychoanalysis were to be understood as a particular use and application of communication in the service of human integration it would clear away much confusion.

Notes

1.   "There was some consolation for the bad reception accorded to my contention of a sexual aetiology in the neuroses even by my more intimate circle of friends—for a vacuum rapidly formed itself about my person—in the thought that I was taking up the fight for a new and original idea. But, one day, certain memories gathered in my mind which disturbed this pleasing notion, but which gave me in exchange a valuable insight into the processes of human creative activity and the nature of human knowledge. The idea for which I was being made responsible had by no means originated with me. It had been imparted to me by three people whose opinion had commanded my deepest respect—by Breuer himself, by Charcot, and by Chrobak, the gynaecologist at the University, perhaps the most eminent of all our Vienna physicians. These three men had all communicated to me a piece of knowledge which, strictly speaking, they themselves did not possess. Two of them later denied having done so when I reminded them of the fact; the third (the great Charcot) would probably have done the same if it had been granted me to see him again. But these three identical opinions, which I had heard without understanding, had laid

dormant in my mind for years, until one day they awoke in the form of an apparently original discovery.

One day, when I was a young house-physician, I was walking across the town with Breuer, when a man came up who evidently wanted to speak to him urgently. I fell behind. As soon as Breuer was free, he told me in his friendly, instructive way that this man was the husband of a patient of his and had brought him some news of her. The wife, he added, was behaving in such a peculiar way in society that she had been brought to him for treatment as a nervous case. He concluded: 'These things are always *secrets d'alcolve!*' I asked him in astonishment what he meant, and he answered by explaining the word *alcove* (marriage-bed) to me, for he failed to realise how extraordinary the *matter* of his statement seemed to me.

Some years later, at one of Charcot's evening receptions, I happened to be standing near the great teacher at a moment when he appeared to be telling Brouardel a very interesting story about something that had happened during his day's work. I hardly heard the beginning, but gradually my attention was seized by what he was talking of: a young married couple from a distant country in the East—the woman a severe sufferer, the man either impotent or exceedingly awkward. '*Tachez donc,*' I heard Charcot repeating, '*je vous assure, vous y arriverez.*' Brouardel, who spoke less loudly, must have expressed his astonishment that symptoms like the wife's could have been produced by such circumstances. For Charcot suddenly broke out with great animation: '*Mais, dans des cas pareils c'est toujours la chose génitale, toujours . . . toujours . . . toujours*'; and he crossed his arms over his stomach, hugging himself and jumping up and down on his toes several times in his own characteristically lively way. I know that for a moment I was almost paralysed with amazement and said to myself: "Well, but if he knows that, why does he never say so?" But the impression was soon forgotten; brain anatomy and the experimental induction of hysterical paralyses absorbed all my interest.

A year later, I had begun my medical career in Vienna as a lecturer in nervous diseases, and in everything relating to the aetiology of the neuroses I was still as ignorant and innocent as one could expect of a promising student trained at a university. One day I had a friendly message from Chrobak, asking me to take a woman patient of his to whom he could not give enough time, owing to his new appointment as a University teacher. I arrived at the patient's house before he did and found that she was suffering from attacks of meaningless anxiety, and could only be soothed by the most precise information about where her doctor was at every moment of the day. When Chrobak arrived he took me aside and told me that the patient's anxiety was due to the fact that although she had been married for eighteen years she was still *virgo intacta*. The husband was absolutely impotent. In such cases, he said, there was nothing for a medical man to do but to shield this domestic misfortune with his own reputation, and put up with it if people shrugged their shoulders and said of him: 'He's no good if he can't cure her after so many years.' The sole prescription for such a malady, he added, is familiar enough to us, but we cannot order it. It runs: '*R. Penis normalis dosim repetatur!*' I had never heard of such a prescription, and felt inclined to shake my head over my kind friend's cynicism. I have not of course disclosed the illustrious parentage of this scandalous idea in order to saddle other people with the responsibility for it. I am well aware that it is one thing to give utterance to an idea once or twice in the form of a passing *aperçu*, and quite another to mean it seriously—to take it literally and pursue it in the face of every contradictory detail, and to win it a place among accepted truths. It is the difference between a casual flirtation and a legal marriage with all its duties and difficulties." [Freud, 1914d, pp. 12–15]

2. Superficially, this has a ring of Lacan about it, but it differs in that the language of communication that I am talking of is emotional in content rather than linguistic.

VIII
EPILOGUE

Introduction

The aim of psychoanalysis is the acquisition of self-knowledge. There are many things that we do which we attribute to the intemperate behaviour of others. I give a lecture that is badly received and I say to myself, "The audience obviously have no understanding of the subject". I do not say to myself, "Well, perhaps I did not explain my point clearly", or "Perhaps I delivered it in an arrogant manner". The purpose of psychoanalyis is achieved when I become aware of my own deficits. Also, I may be blind to my own gifts. I may be afraid of my tendency to "big-note" myself; if I become aware that I have a particular gift of imagination I may be afraid of acknowledging it if I fear that I will use this gift to triumph over others.

The aim of going to visit a psychoanalyst is to develop an awareness of who I am. As Bion said, at the end of one of his lectures, the aim of an analysis is to introduce the patient to himself. Once this process has been initiated and installed as part of one's personal inner equipment, then it is time to finish the formal process. But the process is not finished; I still have long years ahead of me and the process of self-analysis continues until the end of life. Freud spent half an hour at the end of each day in this process of self-analysis.

What I have said so far suggests that the formal analysis has plunged down to the unconscious depths and that all that remains for self-analysis is the elaboration of it. I am sure, however, that certain deep panics—*titanic glooms of chasmèd fears* (Thompson, 1913, p. 107)—may remain untouched in analysis. So I have put this paper as an epilogue. At the moment I do not know of any other subterranean panics, but some future event may reveal what I do not know at the moment.

CHAPTER TWENTY-TWO

Self-analysis in flight

"There were these small personal niches and angles to life in the aircraft which, though none of us mentioned them or were particularly conscious of them, were subconsciously recognized as part of the person concerned and not to be trespassed upon. They gave to each of us the home which was our castle. A flying team is effective only when each member is an individual, for most are individualists. They work as a team only if they retain that individuality and freedom of action. Each has a different view of his world in the air"

(Taylor, 1963, p. 206)

Self-analysis of analysts

Freud recommended that analysts follow his example and continue to analyse themselves just as he did. A certain number of analysts have recorded their self-analysis (Beiser, 1985; Calder, 1980; Engel, 1975; Kramer, 1959; McLaughlin, 1993; Sonnenberg, 1991; Ticho, 1967). Engel's self-analysis was instigated by the traumatic death of his identical twin. Calder, who investigated especially his negative Oedipus complex in self-analysis, was prompted to do so by hearing a colleague reporting that he had spoken to a group of analysts who made no serious attempt to analyse their own dreams and decided to experiment and did so with painstaking tenacity for a period of fifteen years. Beiser was stimulated to a period of self-analysis by discovering that a patient had a problem similar to hers. Sonnenberg started a piece of self-analysis when his mother had to have a serious operation. McLaughlin's self-analysis was initiated by a patient he was working with. For Engel and Sonnenberg, analysis was forced upon them and, to a lesser extent, on Beiser and McLaughlin. Calder embarked upon it as a deliberate free act. Kramer, however, emphasized the non-volitional character of her self-analysis and referred to it as auto-analysis: that it occurred even against her will.

The piece of self-analysis I am going to record was similar to Kramer in that when I engaged upon it I was barely conscious that what I was embarking upon was self-analysis. I decided to learn to fly a plane. It was only as I began to fly did I realize that I had engaged in a piece of self-analysis. It was in this way that my experience was like Kramer's. Only one other such circumscribed piece of self-analysis had had equal significance in my life. This piece of self-analysis differed from most of the accounts I have read, which have stressed the quiet peaceful atmosphere of the setting. For instance, Ticho writes of the typical environment for self-analysis: "These situations show similarities to the analytic setting: maximum opportunity for physical and mental relaxation, relative solitude or monotonous background noise, freedom from interference, and agreeable temperature" (p. 310).

The stress is on an atmosphere of peace and tranquillity. McLaughlin, for instance, recommends a sanctuary or place of quiet in which the process can proceed. But my self-analysis took place amidst whirring wings, a fluttering heart, and an indescribable level of tension. The environment of this piece of self-analysis was so different from that described by the above authors that it is being presented deliberately as a contrast. I would want to stress that *some* self-analysis may require a *challenging* environment, if it is to work.

An analysis in flight

At a wedding reception a man engaged me in a conversation about flying. Flying a light aeroplane was a hobby that he loved. That sparked my decision to ring up a flying school and request a test flight. It was a shock when I was beckoned into the cockpit without any preparation, and a frightened mouse settled into the pilot's seat. As we rushed down the runway the instructor said to me, "At sixty-five, pull back the control column"; with heart pounding I did as I was told and we sailed into the air. I can remember little of that first flight except my intense anxiety and surprise that the young instructor got me to handle the plane for most of the time. Back at the flying club I signed up, handed over $2,000 for the first twenty lessons and I was "in". I could have either paid for each lesson individually or paid for the first twenty, which had financial advantages. I deliberately purchased the "package" to make it more difficult for me to back out of it.

For some years I had idled with the idea of learning to fly but never seriously thought I would do it. There was a strange contradiction in my wanting to learn: that I was fearful of flying and that as a passenger I was always extremely nervous when the plane entered turbulence or banked steeply. What I was doing was counter-phobic. Within the first few lessons I realized that I was engaged in a piece of self-analysis.

Initially, I had one lesson a week and during the flight I would say to myself, "This is ridiculous; it's too much. I am going to stop." However, even as I said this to myself there was an edge of doubt and then, as the days of the week passed, I slowly gathered my resolve. Nevertheless, when the next lesson was in progress and I was bumping around in that little plane I might have been in the electric chair or a torture chamber, and yet I loved it. I watched planes with renewed interest and read books about the early aviators and became sensitized to all the metaphors borrowed from aviation provided by my patients: "After that I went into a nose-dive"; "And I spiralled down and down"; "I just flew by the seat of my pants"; "After that I went onto auto-pilot".

As I went on I became determined that I would learn to fly and get my private pilot's licence. All my efforts and energies went into this. There were technical skills that I had to learn with each lesson in the learning programme, but with each new step there were emotional obstacles to overcome.

I was assigned an instructor. Patrick was patient, thoughtful, and obsessional. He was annoyingly punctilious about keeping to the schedule of lessons, but also appallingly unpunctual. I often tore my hair out with frustration. Also, the lessons were often too short and I longed to have a couple of hours just flying with what I had learned so far, but that, it seemed, I was not allowed to do. I developed more sympathy for those patients who are enormously frustrated by sessions that last only fifty minutes. In the early stages I was in such panic that I could not internalize the knowledge that I needed. When the transponder flashed or the plane bucked I was almost sick with anxiety. On one occasion I was close to vomiting. I believe that this inner panic was hidden from Patrick. He was aware that I was learning rather slowly but did not know the reason. What he certainly did not know was that there was an analysis going on. In the intervening week between lessons I had to learn more bookwork but, at the same time, I had to do a lot of psychic work.

It took me a while to realize that Patrick could not see that I was nervous. It helped me to realize how patients, like me, often hide their panic. I also realized that I had hidden, not entirely but to a large extent, my own panic from my analyst. The thing that seemed most obvious to me, that I was sick with panic, was not visible to Patrick and the thing that was most obvious to him, a calm tranquil nonchalance, was quite hidden from me. I had much more sympathy with patients, usually categorized as borderline, who believe that I must see their distress or their suffering and yet it had been mostly hidden. This realization helped me a great deal with patients, especially one who in the consultation used a lot of jargon words. At the time I had interpreted this as his need to impress me with his knowledge of psychoanalysis but quite missed the reason for it: a panic fuelled by a mass of disconnected fragments inside.

Patrick was my main instructor but quite often I had another. There was one common denominator in them all: they all got angry with me. It took me time to realize that I was unconsciously provoking them—I think through a façade of nonchalance. It makes me think of times when I have reacted to the patient's defence and not realized the inner state of panic that generates it. That panic was not something that I could feel in patients, but had to deduce it. So, also, I had to deduce that this panic-stricken mouse in the cockpit was radiating provocation. In both cases it was a piece of deductive knowledge. It seemed, and still does seem, very important that the central experience for each person in the contractual partnership of an analysis is frequently not accessible through feelings but only through deductive reasoning. I think one of the greatest errors is the assumption that all knowledge of oneself can be arrived at through one's own feelings. I also realized that what appears as arrogance or contempt may be an outer manifestation of inner panic. I think this is one of the most important discoveries that I made and has led me to believe that what is often read or interpreted as an intention is in fact a manifestation of inner terror.

Although in that first test flight the instructor had told me to pull back the control column and so take the plane into the air, Patrick did not allow me to do this. He would take off and head for the training area and when we were established on our flight path he would hand over to me. In the first lesson I had to fly the plane "straight and level". It is not as easy as it sounds. The control column is a delicate instrument: a slight touch on it and the plane ascends or descends. If a violinist draws the bow half a centimetre above the right place a different tone will be sounded. So it is with the control column. It is a delicate instrument and a two-millimetre adjustment will lead the plane to climb or descend. It is easy to lose several hundred feet in a few seconds. "Just look to the horizon and keep two thirds sky and one third ground—that will keep you level", said Patrick. My problem, of course, was to keep my psyche level. Hardly had I finished that first lesson than I was on to the next and was learning to climb and descend. Then the whole next week I was going over it and just wishing that I could stay on "straight and level" a bit longer. I was always supposed to be ahead of where I actually was. Like when the day I got married I was supposed to be a husband, the day I qualified as an analyst I was supposed to be an analyst, but in reality I was always far behind, trying desperately to catch up.

I was always a stage behind. As soon as the "climbing and descending" lesson was over I was on to "turns" and then, most frightening of all, "stalls". A plane flies because, due to Bernoulli's principle, there is more air pressure under the wing than above it; so, as long as the wing does not exceed an angle of 16%, it will hold the plane in steady flight. If the pilot pulls back the control column so that the wing exceeds the 16% angle, the wings stall: in other words, the wing no longer exerts lift but instead plunges down.

Every pilot must know what to do in that eventuality so it is one of the early lessons.

"Now, pull the control column right back . . . No, further . . . right back . . . no, that's not far enough." I gave one last yank and the plane suddenly flipped earthwords. I thrust in the control column again and the wings unstalled, put on the power and climbed up, but I had lost about 500 feet. "Well, that's not bad for a first go," said Patrick, "we'll try again." The next time I lost 350 feet, but my inner world had lost all its contents. After that lesson I told myself that this was ridiculous, that I would give it up, I was just too anxious, it was clearly not for me, but then, as the days of the week crept past, I changed my mind.

All this had one beneficial effect in the analysis of my patients. When I first went into analysis I was very nervous but nothing like the nervousness that I felt when I was up in that bloody little plane. When I went into analysis I was cut off from a severe panic; it had never been analysed. I now had much more sympathy for panic in my patients. It was not just that: it was also that I could see panic through a piece of deductive reasoning, which I had not realized before. I now knew that panic is often hidden behind behaviour that is outwardly enormously provocative.

Slowly, very slowly, one hurdle after another was overcome. The plane was a very good object to carry projections from the emotional states of my inner world. It is difficult to stay straight and level in the midst of turbulence. Outwardly, people had believed that I was stable and to be trusted. I remember once when I was at the Tavistock, clumping down one of the corridors, a colleague said to me, "Your footsteps make me feel that you are absolutely reliable and that I would refer any patient to you and be sure that you could contain them." These were flattering words that I believed at the time, so out of touch was I with my inner turbulence. Even my analyst was deceived by this exterior. So here was this analyst, assured, trusted, and stable, but within was a trembling jelly. I came to realize that I would never be able to fly straight-and-level until I had overcome this psychological panic. I knew that the degree of my difficulty in flying straight-and-level was a perfect indicator of my own difficulties in remaining contained in the face of turbulence. It came home to me how often I had reacted to rather than contained turbulence. However, the day did come when I was able to fly straight-and-level, though I still did not have the inner confidence to match it. Also, on one occasion between flights I became aware of the inner turbulence within myself, and then on the next flight, as the plane started rocking about in the sky, I made contact with the inner see-saw and my fear of the wind buffeting the plane receded.

I had no trouble descending but climbing made me very nervous, although I knew logically that the opposite was the case. In a plane the higher you are the safer you are (I am talking of light aircraft, which usually keep under 10,000 feet). It is much safer to be up at 8,000 feet than at 1,000 feet. In the event of engine failure the plane at 8,000 feet has much more gliding power and so the pilot's choice of places to make a forced landing is much greater. He also has more chance of getting the engine started again, more time to transmit radio messages, and he has more time to check which way the wind is blowing and more time to think. So I *knew* that to climb to a decent height was the safest thing to do but I *felt* the opposite. What was so difficult about climbing? Some people have been ruined because climbing high has stimulated their omnipotence to fatal destruction. So I *knew* that I would not be able to climb with confidence until I had started to address this problem. So, omnipotence was one element in a narcissistic structure that I had to deal with. For a long time I was terrified when I had to put the plane into a climb. When, much later, on my second solo navigational flight I climbed up to 7,500 feet and loved it, I think I had made a start with this internal problem.

I had no trouble descending, but that was not true when it came to landing. Landing is the most difficult manoeuvre for a pilot. He has to judge the height, the speed of the plane, lower the flaps, speak to the control tower, watch for other planes, be ready to "go-round", obey instructions from the tower, be prepared to change runway and so on. My problem, however, was in the very last stage of the landing. A plane lands in three stages: descending down to the threshold, rounding out, and touching down. The first two I managed well enough, but the last presented a big problem. Paradoxically, when the plane is flying level to the runway the pilot must not point the nose down at the runway, but put the power off and bit by bit pull the control column back as if to fly off again and the plane slowly sinks on to the runway, back wheels first and the nosewheel last. I was in such a hurry to get back to ground that I would either point the nose at the runway or lower the nose of the plane too soon. Patrick would say: "Hold it, Neville, hold it", and "Hold off, hold off." In other words: "Wait, don't be in such a hurry".

I took Patrick's words "Hold it" and "Hold off" as interpretations. I had frequently noticed that I would come in too quickly when something became clear to me in a session with a patient. I also noticed that I did this in the conduct of my private emotional life. "Hold off", said Patrick. Another day I had a different instructor and he said to me even more severely, "You could kill yourself if you don't hold off." So it was now a matter of life and death—no longer a quiet option: that it would be better if I held off. No supervisor ever spoke to me as firmly as that second instructor. One supervisor had once said to me that when treating a patient in psychoanalysis I could afford to wait longer than in psychotherapy to see what developed, but he had not got through to me. It was as if he had said, "It would be *better* if you hold off", but that second instructor told me that I could kill myself if I did not hold off. I took what he said as real *and* as an interpretation. I was soon landing the plane beautifully and I observed that I was more contained emotionally.

The face of death is extremely sobering. These young men who were my instructors did not mince their words:

"You must look left right and centre before turning or you could hit another aircraft—no, do it properly."

"This is the third time I've told you that the first thing you do is to turn towards the field on downwind in the event of engine failure. I've told you three times and you'd think once would be enough."

"You were taxiing quite madly."

Flying a plane is terrific fun, but it is also dangerous. Conducting an analysis can be deeply satisfying, but a wrong interpretation, an unfortunate response, can also be dangerous. Why was I always so sensitive if a supervisor spoke to me from the shoulder but could accept it from these young flying instructors? There can be only one answer: that I placed a greater value upon bodily survival than emotional life. The high value of emotional life came through to me as a discovery. Bion's statement that we have not yet recovered from the Battle of Marathon rang often in my ears.

In learning to fly a plane I was challenging myself to overcome a fear of death but that was not all. I was a frightened child inside an adult's skin. This child had never been touched in analysis. Now the child began to grow up and as he grew up a catalogue of memories floated before him of self-destructive acts and foolhardly actions and also attitudes that I had taken up towards myself, others, and the world. I had warded off adulthood and self-knowledge by keeping a part of myself in childhood innocence, insulated from those sense impressions that would have brought me to adulthood. Again, the title of Bion's last talk to the British Society came back to me: "Making the best of a bad job". This is what I had to do with this uncensored film of my life that now unrolled before the eye of my mind. Until now I had not had the emotional resources to be able to roll out my past life in front of me. I had not ever, in fact, entered the depressive position, but I did now.

There was another way in which learning to fly was for me an analysis. When I started I thought that it was just a matter of learning to fly the plane, but my vision of what that involved was very restricted. Apart from the actual mechanical knowledge of how to fly the plane there was also enormous background knowledge that had to be acquired. Most students went for a year or two years to night school to learn aviation theory. I opted instead to do this on my own with the use of text-books. Unlike with learning to drive a car, a pilot has to have knowledge of the engine of the plane and also how the flight instruments and engine instruments work. Some of the former are activated through gyroscopes, some by the pitot-static system, and some of the latter are activated through the electrical system and some through a vacuum system. A pilot needs to know which is which and understand them. For instance, the altimeter works through measuring the changing air pressure, and as air pressure changes each day and in each location the altimeter needs to be set accordingly. Also, if the static vent ices over or gets blocked, then the altimeter becomes dysfunctional. There is a lot to learn in order to understand how each of the flight instruments works, and yet this is only a fraction of the knowledge required in order to be able to fly a plane. I will mention just one other area and must ask you to take it on faith that these are only two of many to be learned. If you are flying a distance of 150 miles from A to B, the pilot has to work out in advance the height he is going to fly at and then find out from the special daily aerial navigation forecast what the wind will be at the time when he is making the flight. He must work out the track that he will need to fly in order to arrive at B and then, in order to ascertain the actual heading into which he will need to point the plane, he has to adjust his heading according to the wind component. If he does not do this he can be miles wide of his destination. In other words, he will have to calculate the degrees of drift to allow for the wind at the particular height at which he intends to fly (wind rates varying at different heights from the ground). It is very easy to become lost up there in the sky and many pilots have perished because of it.

I had had no idea of all this learning that I needed to acquire. I had to pass the BAK—Basic Aeroplane Knowledge and then some months later the GFPT—General Flying Progress Test, in which I was tested in these two areas of knowledge and many others. I often thought of a patient who started treatment in October and wanted to be finished by Christmas, but her analysis took eight years to complete. What I had engaged upon in learning to fly was a much more extensive and deeper process of learning than I had consciously contemplated. It also took me deeper into my emotions than I had ever suspected it would—the journey I had started out on was a much more comprehensive affair than I had ever realized.

Internalization was another very important work that was achieved while learning to fly. I was instructed to give reports over the radio while in flight. After turning on to a new heading I was instructed to give a report thus: ALL STATIONS—TAMPICO, JULIET TANGO ECHO—BATHURST 12—TRACKING TO CROOKWELL ON 175—MAINTAINING 6,500. Now, it may amaze you, but at the start it was just a report that I had to send out. I had to do it. I had been told to do it. The superego was instructing me so therefore I must do it. I never asked myself "To whom am I addressing this message?" Then one day I realized that I was addressing other aircraft in the area so they would know where I was. I was speaking to other pilots and soon I was glad also to hear their position reports. If someone was coming the other way at the same height and on the same track I could inform him or her that I would change my height. I came to realize that in that first state of affairs when I was giving out a report according to an instruction, I was in a state of panic. Then, as the panic subsided, I found myself in relation to others. In panic

I was not in relation either to myself or others. I believe I had lived in panic until early adulthood, when a beam of light first began to penetrate it. In learning to fly I was now working through an encapsulated portion of myself that had remained untouched through all my previous years of introspection, formal analysis, and self-analysis. Only the challenge of learning to fly stimulated this change that enabled me to get in touch with deep fears within myself.

As I came out of this frozen state many realizations of past fool-hardy acts came home to me. Periods of my life began to be integrated as they came before the eye of my mind. I was appalled by some realizations and I began to wonder whether I was well equipped enough emotionally to be an analyst. I did, however, know that I must be better equipped now that I could see than when I had been blind. It also made me realize that I had blinded many others. Just as Patrick, my instuctor, was blind to my panic, so also I had blinded others. I had been quite respected and looked up to in the analytic world. Some of this was justified, but this blinding of others and myself was a provocative outer seduction. I believe that this particularly worked in the analytic school in which I had been trained and to which I belonged.

When at last I passed my Private Pilot's Licence I knew that a very important piece of analysis had been done, but I still did not have inner confidence. I had the piece of paper, the certificate, and could go to any flying school and hire a plane and take it out for a flight, but confidence I did not have. Then I found a new flying school run by a man and woman. The woman, an intuitive person who had had her own psychological problems and addressed them, immediately saw that I did not have the inner confidence to match the outer qualification. She set about putting me on the road to acquiring this. Her name was Aminta and her partner was Ray. I knew immediately that they both had true inner experience and the confidence born of years of experience of flying. Now, when I was high up in one of their planes, I knew I had two strong, firm parents down there on the ground. I grew in confidence extraordinarily quickly. I think these "air-parents" outside mirrored access to good parents inside.

The question I want now to address is: could this piece of self-analysis have been achieved without learning to fly? Could it have been achieved by having some more formal analysis? I cannot, of course, *know* the answer to that question, so what follows are my thoughts.

Formal analysis versus "analysis in flight"

In *The Long Week-End* (1982), Bion describes how he directed his tank towards the place where the bullets were showering with greatest intensity upon the armour plating. In learning to fly I directed myself at the place where my fear was greatest. For someone else this place might be to make a speech in public, to do a painting, write a poem, swim from the shore out to an island, play in an orchestra, attend a social function, eat a sheep's eye, go to the dentist, watch a surgeon in the operating theatre, speak to a frightening person. I do not think going into analysis again would have been that "frightening place" and I do not think anything less than confronting that panic would have catalysed this area for self-analysis.

There is another implication, however, in what I am saying: I could not envisage that an analysis would, by itself, have been able to confront me starkly enough at the place of my fear. I certainly know that neither of my two analyses did so. I also believe that no other analysis could have done so without the assistance provided by that little plane bumping me around in the sky. Is there a more general truth to be learned from this: that an analysis on its own does not confront the patient in the place of greatest fear; does not reach down to the panic-stricken infant; does not strip away the hypersensitivity born of narcissism? I have a suspicion that I should have found it extremely difficult to find an analyst who could have done what the process of learning to fly did for me.

I think the fruits of this analysis should be clear from what has been written, but I will just summarize them. An infantile part of the personality that had been encapsulated and undeveloped was brought into connection with other parts of the personality. There was a marked reduction in superego attitudes and greater ego-strength acquired. Also some symptoms were significantly reduced.

I want to challenge the idea that self-analysis needs to occur in an atmosphere of calm and tranquillity. I know this is the case for some, but my experience tells me that a turbulent activity may be the right medicine for others. It certainly was for me.

There is one advantage of having had an analysis in this strange way. I have learned to fly and I love it. It has broadened the scope of my life both practically and emotionally. I doubt whether an ordinary formal analysis would have done that for me quite so incisively or so fulfillingly.

CHAPTER TWENTY-THREE

The way forward

"A person makes his appearance by entering into relation with other persons"

(Buber, 1987, p. 85)

Experience and reflection upon experience are the two components that push forward emotional development. One role of the arts is to expand emotional experience, but there are some experiences that we shrink from. The very thought of them frightens us, but sometimes we are at the same time drawn to what frightens us. I believe that what draws us is an inchoate knowledge that our lives will develop and be enriched if we allow ourselves to face what we fear.

John Klauber stressed that the psychoanalytical procedure was itself traumatic, and it is probable that he may have believed that it encompassed our deepest panics. This may be so at some very deep level of sensitivity but, for rough souls, some outer assistance may be needed. I suspect it is omnipotent to believe that psychoanalysis alone can unveil our subterranean terrors. It may be necessary to shake up the personality through confronting these primordial fears. I have explained how this occurred for me when I was learning to fly a plane.

However, there is a supposition, written deep into our theory and practice, that our prime task is to repair the damage done to us in our infancy. I think now that my task is to create out of all the raw material, damaged and undamaged, a person. This is a different task, which begets a new perspective. Our job is not to repair what is there, but rather to create a new form from what is there. The person is, I believe, this creation. As it is a creation, those models of the mind based either on computational or anatomical analogies are misleading because they suggest a static state of affairs, whereas the person is the ongoing consequence of a subject *doing* something. There is a doing, not a being, at the heart of the matter. We are all called to *do* something—create ourselves into persons. Just as a painting is not a given but, rather, something created by the artist engaged in his or her raw materials, so also the person is an inner creation.

My emphasis upon the need for the stable elements to be shaken up is that the work of creating a person cannot occur until this has happened. The raw material is not there until after the shake-up.

I have come across many patients where the following kinds of statements are made. A woman who said that she was beginning to *feel* that she had neglected her daughter just after she was born. At the time she was living in Las Vegas, where her husband was out all day managing a casino. When people asked her had she enjoyed it there she would say, "Oh yes, it was terrific fun." A few sessions into her analysis she said, "In Las Vegas I was terribly bereft. I felt lonely and unsupported." She was beginning to be in touch with herself—a lonely bereft little one-year-old. The sign that she was becoming a person is that she was beginning to feel lonely and bereft. What I am saying here is that someone is a person when he starts to feel his own emotional state of being. The Las Vegas woman felt at one time that being in Las Vegas was terrific fun. Later she said that she felt terribly bereft and lonely. The former feeling is one generated by an image of what she ought to feel, whereas the latter is a true representation of her individual state of affairs. One feeling is the expression of someone who is isolated; the other feeling arises out of someone who is in communication with another person. This woman came to see me because she was seeking a more personal life. When she was not isolated, but in personal relation to myself, she began to feel that she had been lonely and unsupported when she had been in Las Vegas.

The isolated state is compatible with membership of a crowd. People in a crowd are not in personal relationship with each other. Ecstasy is generated when the individual is reduced to being a unit in a huge mob, which acts as an anaesthetic against loneliness.

Loneliness is, I believe, a pain at the heart of living. There are many ways of anaesthetizing this pain. Drink, drugs, and sex are common means of negating the self that is suffering. Another way is to become absorbed into an inflamed mob. The commotion that floods through the crowd drowns my own individual self.

In other words the capacity for thinking, which is personal creative activity, is smothered by group agitation.

There are two ways in which this loneliness can be mastered: through anaesthesia, which smothers the loneliness, or through a personal act that transfers it into a framework in which it is not blotted out but felt to be worth enduring for the sake of a greater good.

What is it that enables me to say that the latter feeling of the Las Vegas woman was genuine whereas the former is not? It must, I believe, be that in the second instance the woman was in conversation with a person, whereas in the first emotional state she was not. It seems to be that the person comes into being through relationship with a person: that a person generates personhood. What on earth do I mean by this?

It is that the potential for the birth of a person is there within the personality. The person is Janus, facing in two directions: towards the Other outside the personality, and also inwards, towards all that is. It is there at birth and probably before birth. It is generated into being through meeting the Other as Person.

John Macmurray puts it this way:

I can know another person *as a person* only by entering into personal relation with him. Without this I can know him only by observation and inference; only objectively. The knowledge which I can obtain in this way is valid knowledge; my conclusions from observations can be true or false, they can be verified or falsified by further observation or by experiment. But it is abstract knowledge, since it constructs its object by limitation of attention to what can be known about other persons without entering into personal relations with them. [1983, pp. 28–29]

There is another important point: that all human beings are able to distinguish between truth and falsity. People say things like, "I sensed that he was not telling the truth"; or "I felt he was uneasy when the subject of money came up"; or "I did not believe her when she said she had never been jealous." So, there is some faculty that connects us to the emotional truth.

It is *the person* who feels guilt, who feels shame, who feels grief, who feels regret, or who feels disappointment. Our reason for avoiding the personal relation with another is it is capable of bringing our own personhood to birth but this brings with it all these inner agonies.

So, the person can only come to birth through being present to the person of another. Therefore, a clinical technique can only be effective if the person of the psychoanalyst is available to the other. If the person of the psychoanalyst is concealed behind a façade, then the patient has no chance of developing his own personhood. There is within psychoanalytical practice a tradition that counsels anonymity. I believe that this praxis prevents the development of the person and protects the individual from inner distress and also the experience of joy, beauty, and love. And it impedes self-knowledge. The aim of psychoanalysis is to develop and increase our self-knowledge.

I believe, therefore, we need to develop a practice based on a different foundation. I think if we manage to achieve this psychoanalysis will flourish again. It may be necessary to give it a different name. Anonymity is so woven into our image of psychoanalysis that for a technique that precisely repudiates this it may be necessary to find a new name. It is the emotional reality of our practice that we need to conserve, not the name of the folder into which it is deposited.

Our goal is self-knowledge and we believe that it is through this that mental healing comes about. This, I believe, needs to be at the centre of all our future endeavours.

REFERENCES

Beiser, H. R. (1984). An example of self-analysis. *Journal of the American Psychoanalytic Association, 32*: 3–12.

Bennett, A. (1969). *Anna of the Five Towns*. Harmondsworth: Penguin Modern Classics.

Bergson, H. (1919). *Creative Evolution*. London: Macmillan.

Berlin, I. (1980). *Vico and Herder*. London: Chatto & Windus.

Bion, W. R. (1962). *Learning From Experience*. London: Heinemann [reprinted London: Karnac, 1988].

Bion, W. R. (1963). *Elements of Psychoanalysis*. London: Heinemann [reprinted London: Karnac, 1989].

Bion, W. R. (1967a). A theory of thinking. In: *Second Thoughts*. London: Heinemann [reprinted London: Karnac, 1993].

Bion, W. R. (1967b). On arrogance. In: *Second Thoughts*. London: Heinemann [reprinted London: Karnac, 1987].

Bion, W. R. (1970). *Attention and Interpretation*. London: Tavistock.

Bion, W. R. (1975). *Brazilian Lectures, Volume 2*. Rio de Janeiro: Imago Editora.

Bion, W. R. (1978). *Four Discussions with W. R. Bion*. Strath Tay, Perthshire: Clunie Press.

Bion, W. R. (1982). *The Long Week-End*. Abingdon: Fleetwood.

Bion, W. R. (1991). *Transformations*. London: Karnac.

Brontë, E. (1847). *Wuthering Heights*. London. Penguin.

Brontë, E. (1996). The night is darkening round me. In: *Bronte Poems*. London: Everyman Library Pocket Poets.

Buber, M. (1987). *I and Thou*. Edinburgh: T. & T. Clark.

Burney, C. (1962). *Descent from Ararat*. London: Macmillan.

Bryant, A. (1969). *The Lion and the Unicorn*. London: Collins.

Calder, K. T. (1980). An analyst's self-analysis. *Journal of the American Psychoanalytic Aassociation, 28*: 5–20.

Carroll, L. (1974). *Alice's Adventures in Wonderland & Through the Looking Glass*. London: The Bodley Head.

Church, R. (1953). *Over the Bridge*. London: Heinemann.

Clark, P. L. (1933). *The Nature and Treatment of Amentia*. London. Baillière, Tindall and Cox.

Collingwood, R. G. (1969). *Metaphysics*. Oxford: Clarendon.

Coltart, N. (1992). *Slouching Towards Bethlehem*. London: Free Association.

Cook, D. (1978). *Walter*. London: Secker and Warburg.

Damásio, A. (1994). *Descartes' Error*. New York: Grosset/Putnam.

Dilthey, W. (1989). The facts of consciousness (Breslau Draft). In: *Selected Works—Introduction to the Human Sciences*. Princeton, NJ: Princeton University Press.

Disraeli, B. (1845). *Sybil of The Two Nations*. London: Longmans, Green.

Doll, E. A. (1953). Counselling parents of severely mentally retarded children. In: C. L. Stacey & M. F. Demartino (Eds.), *Counselling and Psychotherapy with the Mentally Retarded*. New York: Free Press.

Dostoyevsky, F. (1966). *Crime and Punishment*. Harmondsworth: Penguin.

Durkheim, E. (1951). *Suicide: A Study in Sociology*. J. A. Spaulding & G. Simpson (Trans.). New York: Free Press of Glencoe.

Eliot, G. (1876). *Daniel Deronda*. Harmondsworth: Penguin, 1979.

Engel, G. L. (1975). The death of twin: mourning and anniversary reactions. Fragments of 10 years of self-analysis. *International Journal of Psycho-Analysis, 56*: 23–40.

Fairbairn, R. (1958). *Psychoanalytic Studies of the Personality*. London: Routledge and Kegan Paul, 1976.

Ferenczi, S. (1968). *Thalassa*. New York: W. W. Norton.

Ferro, A. (2005). *Seeds of Illness, Seeds of Recovery*. Hove: Brunner-Routledge.

Freud, S. (1893f). *Charcot. S.E., 3*. London: Hogarth.

Freud, S. (1900a). *The Interpretation of Dreams. S.E., 4, 5*. London: Hogarth.

Freud, S. (1901b). *The Psychopathology of Everyday Life. S.E., 6*. London: Hogarth.

Freud, S. (1913i). The disposition to obsessional neurosis. *S.E., 12*. London: Hogarth.

Freud, S. (1914d). *On the History of the Psycho-Analytic Movement. S.E., 14*. London: Hogarth.

Freud, S. (1915e). The unconscious. *S.E. 14*. London: Hogarth.

Freud, S. (1916). Some character-types met with in the course of psychoanalytic work: criminals from a sense of guilt. *S.E., 14*. London: Hogarth.

Freud, S. (1917e). Mourning and melancholia. *S.E., 14*. London: Hogarth.

Freud, S. (1920g). *Beyond the Pleasure Principle. S.E., 18*. London: Hogarth.

Freud, S. (1927c). *The Future of an Illusion. S.E., 21*: 3–56, London: Hogarth.

Fromm, E. (1950). *Psychoanalysis and Religion*. New Haven, CT: Yale University Press.

Glover, E. (1960). *The Roots of Crime*. London: Imago.

Gosling, R. (1980). Gosling on Bion. *The Tavistock Gazette*.

Greene, G. (1980). *Ways of Escape*. London: Bodley Head.

Gregory, R. (1966). *Eye and Brain*. London: Weidenfeld & Nicholson.

Hazzard, S. (1981). *The Transit of Venus*. Harmondsworth: Penguin.

Hume, B. (1979). *Searching for God*. London: Hodder & Stoughton.

Hutchinson, R. C. (1983). *A Child Possessed*. Feltham: Zenith.

Isaacs, S. (1952). The nature and function of phantasy. In: J. Riviere (Ed.), *Developments in Psychoanalysis* (pp. 67–121). London: Hogarth.

James, P. (1966). *Henry Moore on Sculpture*. London: Macdonald.

Jones, E. (1916). *Papers on Psychoanalysis*. London: Bailliere, Tindall & Cox.

Jones, P. (Ed.) (1966). *Henry Moore on Sculpture*. New York: Viking.

Jones, S. (2002). Lecture on evolution. Given at the Australia Museum in Sydney and broadcast on the *ABC Science Show* on 12 January 2002.

Jung, C. G. (1935). *Tavistock Lectures. (Lecture Five). The Symbolic Life, C.W., 18*: 135–182, R. F. C. Hull (Trans.). London: Routledge & Kegan Paul.

Jung, C. G. (1984). *Modern Man in Search of a Soul*. London: Ark Paperbacks.

Kant, I. (1781). *The Critique of Pure Reason*. London: Everyman.

Kierkegaard, S. (1972). *Either/Or*. Princeton, NJ: Princeton University Press.

King, P., & Steiner, R. (Eds.) (1991). *The Freud–Klein Controversies 1941–45*. London: Tavistock/Routledge.

Klauber, J. (1968). The psychoanalyst as person. In: *Difficulties in the Analytic Encounter* (pp. 123–139). New York: Jason Aronson, 1981.

Klauber, J. (1981). Elements of the psychoanalytic relationship and their therapeutic implications. In: *Difficulties in the Analytic Encounter*. New York & London: Jason Aronson.

Klein, M. (1934). On criminality. In: *Love, Guilt and Reparation and Other Works*. London. Hogarth Press. 1975.

Klein, M. (1957). *Envy and Gratitude*. In: *The Writings of Melanie Klein, Volume 3: Envy and Gratitude and Other Works 1946–1963*. London: Hogarth, 1975.

Koestler, A. (1975) *The Act of Creation*. Picador: Pan Books.

Kohon, G. (1986). *The British School of Psychoanalysis: The Independent Tradition*. London: Free Associations.

Kohut, H. (1979). The two analyses of Mr Z. *International Journal of Psycho-Analysis*, 60: 3–27.

Kramer, M. K. (1959). On the continuation of the analytic process after psycho-analysis (a self-observation). *International Journal of Psycho-Analysis*, 40: 17–25.

Macmurray, J. (1935). *Reason and Emotion*. London: Faber & Faber.

Macmurray, J. (1949). *Conditions of Freedom*. Toronto, Canada: Ryerson.

Macmurray, J. (1983). *Persons in Relation*. New Jersey, NJ: Humanities Press.

Mannoni, M. (1972). *The Backward Child and His Mother*. New York: Pantheon.

McLaughlin, J. T. (1993). Unpublished paper given at Amsterdam Congress.

Moloy, R. (Ed.) (2001). *The Mark of Cain*. Hillsdale, NJ: Analytic Press.

Muller, M. (1904). *The Vedanta Philosophy*. New Delhi: Cosmo Publications, 1985.

Ogden, T. (2004) On holding and containing, being and dreaming. *International Journal of Psycho-Analysis*, 85: 1352.

Parker, T. (1970). *The Frying Pan*. New York: Basic Books.

Parsons, T. (1952). The superego and the theory of social systems. In: *Social Structure and Personality*. New York: Free Press of Glencoe.

Pearson, G. H. (1942). The psychopathology of mental defect. In: C. L. Stacey & M. F. Demartino (Eds.), *Counselling and Psychotherapy with the Mentally Retarded*. New York: Free Press.

Petocz, A. (1999). *Freud, Psychoanalysis and Symbolism*. Cambridge: Cambridge University Press.

Rayner, E. (1990). *The Independent Mind in British Psychoanalysis*. London: Free Association.

Rosenfeld, H. (1952). Notes on the psychoanalysis fo the superego conflict in an acute schizophrenic patient. In: *Psychotic States* (pp. 63–103). London: Hogarth.

Ruskin, J. (1901) Of kings' treasuries. In: *Sesame and Lilies*. London: George Allen

Russell, B. (1985). *ABC of Relativity*. London: Unwin.

Scharff, D. (1996). *Object Relations Theory and Practice*. Northvale, NJ: Jason Aronson.

Searles, H. (1975). The patient as therapist to his analyst. In: R. Langs (Ed.), *Classics in Psychoanalytic Technique* (pp. 103–138). New York: Jason Aronson.

Segal, H. (1957). Notes on symbol formation. *International Journal of Psychoanalysis, 38*: 291–397. Reprinted in: *The Work of Hanna Segal*. New York: Jason Aronson, 1981.

Segal, H. (1981). Depression in the schizophrenic. In: *The Work of Hanna Segal*. London: Jason Aronson.

Sertillanges, A. D. (1945). *La Vie Intellectuelle*. Paris: Aubier.

Sonnenberg, S. M. (1991). The analyst's self-analysis and its impact on clinical work: a comment on the sources and importance of personal insights. *Journal of the American Psychoanalytic Aassociation*, 687–704.

St Augustine (1972). *The City of God*. Harmondsworth: Penguin Classics.

Steiner, J. (1982). Perverse relationship between parts of the self: a clinical interpretation. *International Journal of Psycho-Analysis, 63*: 241–251.

Symington, J. (2000). *Imprisoned Pain and its Transformation*. London: Karnac.

Symington, J., & Symington, N. (1996). *The Clinical Thinking of Wilfred Bion*. London: Routledge.

Symington, N. (1980). The response aroused by the psychopath. *International Review of Psychoanalysis, 7*: 291–298.

Symington, N. (1981). The psychotherapy of a subnornal patient. *British Journal of Medical Psychology, 54*: 187–199.

Symington, N. (1983). The analyst's act of freedom as agent of therapeutic change. *International Review of Psychoanalysis, 10*: 283–291.

Symington, N. (1986). *The Analytic Experience*. London: Free Association.

Symington, N. (1990). The possibility of human freedom and its transmission (with particular reference to the thought of Bion). *International Journal of Psycho-Analysis, 71*: 95–106.

354   REFERENCES

Symington, N. (1993). *Narcissism: A New Theory*. London: Karnac.

Symington, N. (1993b) O narcisismo—uma teoria reconstruída. *Revista Brasileira Psicanalise V, XXVII*(3): 481–488.

Symington, N. (1996a). The origins of rage and aggression. In: C. Cordess & M. Cox (Eds.) *Forensic Psychotherapy: Crime, Psychodynamics and the Offender Patient, Volume 1* (pp. 187–192). London: Jessica Kingsley.

Symington, N. (1996b). *The Making of a Psychotherapist*. London: Karnac.

Symington, N. (2002). *A Pattern of Madness*. London: Karnac.

Taylor, G. G. C. (1963). *The Sky Beyond*. Melbourne: Cassell.

Teilhard de Chardin, P. (1960). *Le Milieu Divin*. London: Collins.

Thompson, F. (1913). *The Works of Francis Thompson vol. I: Poems*. London: Burns & Oates.

Thompson, F. (1913). Shelley. In: *The Works of Francis Thompson: Vol. III—Prose*. London: Burns & Oates.

Thompson, M. G. (1994). *The Truth About Freud's Technique*. New York: New York University Press.

Ticho, G. R. (1967) On self-analysis. *International Journal of Psycho-Analysis, 48*: 309–318.

Tolstoy, L. N. (1986). *Anna Karenin*. Harmondsworth: Penguin.

Trollope, A. (1869). *He Knew He Was Right*. Harmondsworth: Penguin, 1994.

Turgenev, I. S. (1977). *On the Eve*. Harmondsworth: Penguin.

Vygotsky, L. (1962). *Thought and Language*. Cambridge, MA: MIT Press.

Whitehead, A. F. (1958). *An Introduction to Mathematics*. Oxford: Oxford University Press.

Winnicott, D. W. (1958). *Collected Papers—Through Paediatrics to Psychoanalysis*. In: *Primitive Emotional Development*. London: Tavistock.

Winnicott, D. W. (1965). *The Maturational Processes and Facilitating Environment*. London: Hogarth.

INDEX

aggression, 12, 88, 96, 115–116, 120,
  133–134, 299
alpha function, 14, 97, 175, 198, 277
analysand(s), 8, 10, 163–166, 186,
  196, 258, 274
analytic investigation, 191, 192, 210,
  276, 317, 319
analytic process, 4, 22, 34, 39, 61, 64,
  84, 260, 352 see also:
  psychoanalytic process
anxiety, 15, 20, 43, 68, 82, 84, 105,
  110, 125–127, 130–133, 135, 137,
  148, 176, 261, 269, 271, 316, 319,
  324–325, 333–334

Balint, M., xxi, 3, 18, 158, 162, 253
Beiser, H. R., 331–332, 349
Bennett, A., 232, 349
Bergson, H., 141, 349
Berlin, I., 18, 68, 349
beta elements, 14, 97, 272, 274
Bion, W. R., xiv, xxi, 5, 14, 16, 21–22,
  29, 31–32, 34, 36, 42, 44, 47, 53,
  97, 104, 158, 173, 175, 187, 192,
  196, 198, 205, 208–209, 217, 221,

227, 231, 234, 240, 242, 247,
  253–267, 270–272, 274–278, 290,
  292–293, 307, 309, 318, 321, 329,
  338–339, 342, 349
British Association of
  Psychotherapists, 159
British Association of
  Psychotherapy, 98
British Psychoanalytic Society, xviii,
  27, 160
British Psychoanalytical Society,
  xiii, xx, 67, 84, 157, 169,
  178–179, 185–187, 191, 197, 283
British Psychological Society, 149
British Society, 17–18, 161–162,
  165–167, 177, 188, 196, 339
Brontë, E., 96, 100, 102, 215, 278, 350
Bryant, A., 3, 350
Buber, M., xvii, 345, 350
Burney, C., 295, 350

Calder, K. T., 331–332, 350
Camden Psychotherapy Unit
  (formally The Personal
  Consultation Centre), 97

355

356   INDEX

Carroll, L., 27, 350
Cassel Hospital, 97
Child Guidance Training Centre, 98
Church, R., 253, 350
Clark, P. L., 138–140, 142, 154, 350
Collingwood, R. G., 21, 228, 350
Coltart, N., 67–68, 217, 350
conscious(ness), xvi, 6, 8, 32, 38, 40,
    42, 46, 58, 61–63, 66, 106,
    111–112, 118–120, 139–140, 148,
    153, 174, 232, 234, 236, 244, 246,
    255, 303, 332, 340 see also:
    unconscious(ness)
container/containment, 5–6, 15, 21,
    103, 111, 220–221, 233, 235,
    261–262, 264, 273–275, 277, 336,
    228
Contemporary Freudian Group,
    162, 185
Contemporary Kleinian Group, 185
Cook, D., 147, 150, 350
countertransference, 30, 59–61,
    148–149, 152–153, 274, see also:,
    transference
creative communication, 219–224,
    226

Damásio, A., 269, 350
death instinct, 102, 181, 195, 247,
    272, 276, 292–293, 314
definitory hypothesis, 257–259
Dilthey, W., 313, 350
disintegration, 34, 46–48, 152, 290,
    305, 320 see also: integration,
    unintegrated
Disraeli, B., 171, 250
Doll, E. A., 143, 350
Dostoyevsky, F., 120, 207, 350
Durkheim, E., 301, 350

ego, 6, 12, 16, 20–21, 54, 59, 62,
    64–66, 68, 72, 77, 81–84, 105,
    110, 120, 138–140, 151–152,
    163–164, 166, 185–186, 202,
    208–210, 228, 237, 295, 300, 302,
    305, 314, 320–322, 342

-libido, 81–82
-structure, 151–152
super-, 13–14, 16, 22, 59–60,
    64–66, 68, 71–72, 198, 310, 314,
    320, 340, 342
archaic, 118–120, 310
Eliot, G., 95, 350
embryo mind, 118–119
emotional activity, 174–175, 177,
    190, 193, 209, 238, 283, 287, 290,
    295
emotional contact, 8, 16–17, 20, 22,
    83, 152, 316
Engel, G. L., 331–332, 350
envy, 61, 66, 83, 88, 107, 164, 166,
    181–182, 195, 197, 205, 212, 231,
    237, 243–245, 263–264, 271–278,
    283–287, 289–295, 297, 299, 306,
    310

Fairbairn, R., xxi, 15, 21, 159, 162,
    181, 208, 240, 244, 320–321, 350
fanaticism, xviii, 72, 186, 196–197
Fells Institute, 138
Ferenczi, S., 18, 138, 350
Ferro, A., 97, 350
Freud, A., xviii, 159, 162–164,
    185–186, 192, 237
Freud, S., xix–xxi, 16–18, 20–21,
    60, 62, 68, 72, 78, 96, 100, 107,
    115, 138, 141, 158, 165, 174,
    180–181, 188, 192, 195, 203,
    208–210, 224, 247, 253, 256,
    270, 304–305, 307, 315–316,
    318, 320–322, 325, 329,
    350–351
Freudian, xviii, 4, 158, 162, 185–186,
    191–192, 198, 208, 237, 285
Friern Barnet, 133–134
Fromm, E., 238, 247, 351

Glover, E., 96, 99–100, 106, 351
glue-like attachment/dependency,
    243–247, 276
godhood, 290, 292–294 see also:
    omnipotence

Gosling, R., 172, 182–183, 258–259, 351

greed, 88, 101, 231, 244–245, 264, 271–274, 276–278, 289–294, 299, 310, 317

Greene, G., 219, 351

Gregory, R., 142–143, 351

Grendon Prison, xix, 7, 96–97, 116

Group of Independent Psychoanalysts (Independent Group), xviii, 18, 157–159, 162, 177, 179, 185–187, 191, 195–197, 202, 285

guilt, 20, 34, 39, 68, 90, 97, 102, 105–107, 115, 117–121, 153, 175, 177, 210, 212, 217, 230, 257, 263, 274, 315, 348

hallucination, 27–30, 33, 41–42, 44–45, 47–49, 54, 68, 72, 234

Hazzard, S., 161, 351

Hume, B., 19, 239, 351

Hutchinson, R. C., 123, 351

hypostasization, 288–289

id, 21, 62, 208–209, 314, 320–322

idealization, 11, 136, 164, 283, 286–288, 291, 295

inner act(s), 38, 54, 58–59, 61, 67, 73, 77, 87, 190–191, 247, 249, 289, 376

inner mentality, 173, 188–190

Institute of Psychoanalysis London, xx, 96–97, 179–180, 186, 254, 260, 263

Melbourne, 267

Sydney, xiii, 204

integration, 12, 15, 21, 39, 45, 48, 131, 152, 179–182, 289, 319, 322–323, 341 see also: disintegration, unintegrated

introject, 81, 109, 151–153, 164, 176–177, 191, 198, 244

-ive processes, 107, 164 see also: projection, projective identification

Isaacs, S., 72, 80, 192, 351

James, P., 351

jealousy, 231, 244–245, 271–274, 276–278, 289–294, 299, 310

Jones, E., 139, 158, 351

Jones, P., 87, 351

Jones, S., 304, 351

Jung, C. G., 17–18, 40, 76, 99, 174, 220, 238, 351

Kant, I., 29, 64, 118, 221, 230, 351

Kierkegaard, S., 21, 39, 204, 256, 352

King, P., 192, 352

Klauber, J., xvi, xviii, xx, 3–22, 25, 47, 77, 95, 202, 345, 352

Klein, M., xviii, xxi, 18, 96, 100, 105, 120, 162, 164, 177–178, 180–182, 185–187, 192–196, 208–209, 219, 237, 244, 253, 261, 272, 276, 279, 289–290, 293–295, 352

Kleinian, xviii, 21, 107, 157–159, 162–163, 177, 179–180, 182, 185–191, 193–198, 202, 208–209, 237, 246, 254, 260, 285, 322

Koestler, A., 293, 352

Kohon, G., 67, 186, 352

Kohut, H., 79, 237, 352

Kramer, M. K., 331–332, 352

lifegiver, 210–213, 239

liquifier(s), 231, 244–246

Macmurray, J., 21, 51, 201, 204, 347, 352

Mannoni, M., 138–139, 352

masochism, 13, 55, 214

maturity, 26, 87–88, 92, 95

McLaughlin, J. T., 331–332, 352

metapsychology, 17, 63, 192, 210

Moloy, R., 96, 352

mother-infant/child relationship, 9, 20, 79, 102–103, 106–107, 113, 139, 152, 176, 210, 217, 223, 246, 261, 270–271

Muller, M., 285, 295, 352

narcissism/narcissistic, xv, 9, 15, 32,
    42, 46, 69–71, 76, 84, 91, 138,
    159, 163–164, 166, 169, 177, 182,
    198, 201–205, 207–216, 219,
    223–228, 231, 233–240, 242–247,
    259, 337, 342

Object Relations School, 205
object(s), 29–30, 57, 62, 65, 74, 76,
    78–79, 81–82, 84, 102, 106–107,
    109–110, 140–142, 145, 152, 164,
    168, 172–173, 176, 180, 186,
    191–192, 208–211, 213, 218,
    225–226, 228, 233–234, 240–241,
    246–247, 287–291, 297, 300, 305,
    348
    bad, 81–83, 244, 272
    good, 81–84, 336
    images, 12
    internal, 81–82, 105–106, 166, 272
    love, 104, 107, 140, 209–211, 213
    part-, 11–12, 180, 208, 295
    relations, 208–209
    sexual/sex-, 69–71, 74–75, 115,
        210
objectivity, 73
Oedipus/oedipal, 158, 331
    pre-, 21, 25
Ogden, T., 45, 352
omnipotence, 12, 31, 151–153, 163,
    225, 263, 265–266, 288–291, 301,
    305, 309, 337, 345 see also:
    godhood

paranoia/paranoid, 6–7, 11–12, 39,
    89, 104, 107, 151, 162–163, 166,
    231–233, 246–247, 263, 265,
    283–284, 289, 297–299, 301–302,
    304–307, 309–311
Parker, T., 116, 352
Parsons, T., 60, 352
Pearson, G. H., 134, 352
Petocz, A., 305, 353
phantasy, 8, 14, 26, 31–32, 69–84, 95,
    177–178, 180–181, 186, 190,
    192–195, 197, 293 see also:
    transference phantasy

Portman Clinic, 97
projection, 5, 15, 30–31, 42, 45, 62,
    76, 81, 107, 119, 162–164, 166,
    179–180, 202, 225, 234, 236, 241,
    246, 287–289, 295, 299, 336 see
    also: introjective processes,
    projective identification
projective identification, 61–62, 177,
    219–223, 261 see also:
    introjective processes,
    projection
proximal zone, 118, 126
psyche, 34, 45, 73, 76, 81, 83, 172,
    211, 231, 241, 248, 257, 295, 335
psychoanalysis/psychoanalytic,
    xiii, xvi–xx, 3, 7, 9–12, 14,
    17–18, 20, 27, 34, 38, 47, 59, 61,
    63–67, 69, 73, 78, 83–84, 89,
    91–92, 96, 100, 115, 118–119,
    138, 144–145, 160, 165–168,
    171–175, 177, 182, 186–187,
    190–193, 195–197, 202, 204,
    208, 210, 219, 221, 228, 230,
    238, 244, 247, 254, 256,
    262–263, 266, 270, 275–276,
    283–286, 288, 293–295, 300, 308,
    310, 313–315, 317, 319, 322–323,
    329, 334, 338, 345, 348
    process, 9–10, 67, 83, 92, 262 see
    also: analytic process
psychoanalyst, xiii, xvi–xx, 6–7, 20,
    25, 77, 81, 83, 88, 95–96, 115,
    118, 138, 154, 159, 161, 165, 168,
    188, 202, 204, 241, 253, 274, 285,
    290, 299–300, 305, 310, 314, 317,
    319, 322, 329, 348
psychologist(s), 168, 178, 237–238,
    272, 319
psychology/psychological, xiii, xvi,
    xix, 9, 19–20, 57, 61, 63–64, 69,
    77–80, 83, 89, 96, 100, 103–104,
    111, 124, 140–141, 150, 154, 175,
    177–178, 181, 188, 193–195,
    211–212, 231, 238, 241, 257, 270,
    283, 285–288, 290–294, 300–301,
    311, 336, 341

psychopath/psychopathy, xvi, 96–97, 99–100, 102, 104–112, 140, 278
psychosis, xvii, 21–22, 28, 31, 49, 54, 158–159, 238, 254, 288
psychotherapist(s), xix, 17, 20, 85, 96–97, 116, 181, 244
psychotherapy, 28, 36–37, 89, 97, 123–124, 127, 142–144, 147–149, 152, 160, 181–182, 187, 248–249, 338
    psychodynamic, 78, 145
psychotic, xvi, 16, 21, 25, 30–34, 37–38, 41, 48, 55, 58–59, 65, 67, 95, 140, 158–159, 187, 197, 222, 234–236, 238, 278–279, 288, 290, 295

rage, 32–33, 55–56, 96, 108, 120, 162, 164, 190, 229, 249
Rayner, E., 186, 353
reverie, 16, 58, 78, 260–261, 270–272
Rosenfeld, H., 21–22, 28, 31, 38, 67, 158, 187, 196, 235, 254, 353
Ruskin, J., 302, 353
Russell, B., 159, 185, 293, 353

sadism, 34, 37, 39, 54–56, 72, 110–112, 214
St Augustine, 227, 353
Scharff, D., 67, 205, 353
schizophrenia, 107, 128, 139, 240, 271, 278
Searles, H., 89, 353
Segal, H., 22, 138–140, 196, 240, 300, 305, 353
self image, 12
self-analysis, 329–333, 342
Sertillanges, A. D., 203, 353
Sonnenberg, S. M., 331–332, 353
spontaneity, 16–17, 19, 21–22, 56, 89, 196
Steiner, J., 76, 353
Steiner, R., 192, 352
subject, 69, 71, 78, 81, 105–106, 190, 198, 202–203, 287–290, 297–298

subjectivity, 82, 113, 192, 235, 298, 311, 346
Symington, J., xiii, 254, 316, 353
Symington, N., xiii, 38, 41, 47, 67, 96, 164, 174, 177, 187, 219, 237, 239, 254, 288, 353–354

Tavistock Clinic/Group, xiii, xx, 15, 98, 146–147, 149, 152–153, 160, 165, 171–175, 177–183, 186–187, 201, 235, 253 –254, 336
Taylor, G. G. C., 331, 354
Teilhard de Chardin, P., xvii, 354
telegraphic bits, 29–32, 41, 54
Thompson, F., xv, 69, 298, 330, 354
Thompson, M. G., 188, 354
Ticho, G. R., 331–332, 354
Tolstoy, L. N., 203–204, 207, 297, 315, 354
transference, xvii, 4–7, 9, 12–13, 16, 30, 35, 37, 45, 55, 57, 59–61, 77, 88, 104, 118, 136, 138, 147, 164, 173, 175–176, 197, 230 see also: countertransference
    negative, 5, 173, 214
    non-, 6–7
    phantasy, 4, 6, 13, 190 see also: transference phantasy
Trollope, A., 283, 354
Turgenev, I. S., 157, 354

unconscious(ness), 17, 36, 38, 40, 46, 55, 57–59, 61–62, 66, 73–74, 76, 78, 81, 102, 106–107, 110–112, 119–120, 138–140, 166, 174–175, 192, 209–210, 212, 236–240, 260, 274, 288, 295, 330, 334 see also: conscious(ness)
unintegrated, 175, 178–181, 295 see also: disintegration, integration

violence, 14–15, 30, 33, 39, 104, 118, 120–121, 124, 133, 135, 139, 142, 154, 172, 186, 190, 212, 231, 244, 246, 258, 264, 274, 278, 291–292, 299
Vygotsky, L., 118, 126, 141, 354

Wandsworth Prison, 116
Whitehead, A. F., 256, 354
Winnicott, D. W., xxi, 3, 5, 18, 45, 66, 158, 162, 164, 253, 298, 354

Wuthering Heights, 96, 100–113, 278

x-phenomenon, 51–52, 54, 57–59, 61–62, 66